Fly Fishing
HOUSTON
& SOUTHEASTERN TEXAS

IMBRIFEX
BOOKS

THE LOCAL ANGLER

Fly Fishing
HOUSTON
& SOUTHEASTERN TEXAS

Robert H. McConnell

IMBRIFEX BOOKS
8275 S. Eastern Avenue, Suite 200
Las Vegas, NV 89123
Imbrifex.com

IMBRIFEX.
BOOKS

Fly Fishing Houston & Southeastern Texas

Editor: Aaron Reed
Cover and Book Designer: Sue Campbell Book Design
Maps: Chris Erichsen
All interior photos by the author except as noted on page 360.
Cover Photo: Nick Simonite

Library of Congress Cataloging-in-Publication Data
Names: McConnell, Robert H., 1988- author.
Title: Fly fishing Houston & Southeastern Texas / Robert H. McConnell.
Other titles: Fly fishing Houston and Southeastern Texas
Description: First edition. | Las Vegas, NV : Imbrifex Books, [2023] | Series: The local angler; vol 2 | Includes index. | Summary: "The fourth-largest city in the U.S. has a secret hiding in plain sight: All that water means it's a fabulous place for fly fishing. Travel no further than to the city's "concrete flats" to stalk carp with Houston's iconic skyline as a backdrop. With Fly Fishing Houston & Southeastern Texas as your guide, discover the rewards for anglers this unique region offers, from inside the city limits to the countryside beyond"-- Provided by publisher.
Identifiers: LCCN 2022035399 (print) | LCCN 2022035400 (ebook) | ISBN 9781945501609 (paperback) | ISBN 9781945501616 (epub)
Subjects: LCSH: Fly fishing--Texas--Houston--Guidebooks.
Classification: LCC SH456 .M355 2023 (print) | LCC SH456 (ebook) | DDC 799.1/2409764--dc23/eng/20220726
LC record available at https://lccn.loc.gov/2022035399
LC ebook record available at https://lccn.loc.gov/2022035400
First Edition: February 2023
Printed in Canada

IMBRIFEX® is a registered trademark of Flattop Productions, Inc.
FlyFishingHouston.thelocalangler.com | Imbrifex.com | TheLocalAngler.com

For Mom & Dad

CONTENTS

First Things

INTRODUCTION TO FLY FISHING HOUSTON AND THE SURROUNDING WATERWAYS

FOR MANY YEARS, ANGLERS HAVE BEEN LOBBING FLIES INTO Texas waters. The beautiful Texas Hill Country, in particular, has been a fly fishing destination for locals and tourists for several decades. Additionally, Texas has hundreds of miles of coastline for fly fishers to explore. In fact, the Third Coast is considered by many to be the crowning jewel of Texas fly fishing.

Much has been written about fly fishing in this big and wonderful state. Native Texan Phil Shook has written extensively about fly fishing the coast as well as covered many of the State's inland reservoirs and rivers. Danny Hicks also covered many of the state's major rivers in his book *Texas Blue-Ribbon Fly-Fishing*. Kevin Hutchinson's *Fly-Fishing the Texas Hill Country* is a deeper dive into a specific region within the state. Most recently, Aaron Reed published *Fly Fishing Austin & Central Texas*. Reed's work—the first in The Local Angler series—is one of the most comprehensive guidebooks to date about fly fishing in Texas.

This guidebook is different from the rest in that it focuses on the lesser-known freshwater fisheries in a part of the state that is often overlooked by fly anglers. One of the main goals of this book is to highlight the unique freshwater ecosystems that exist in Houston and southeastern Texas and to facilitate greater interest in our regional waterways.

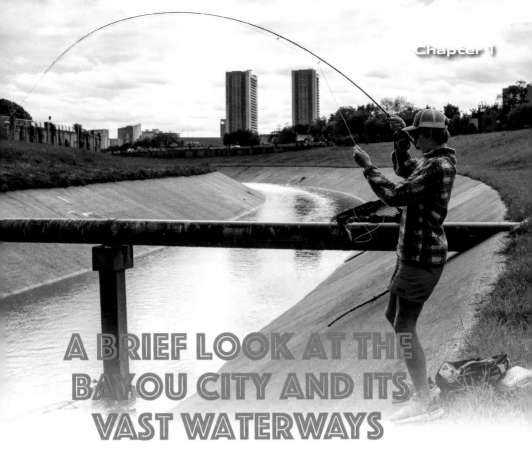

Chapter 1

A BRIEF LOOK AT THE BAYOU CITY AND ITS VAST WATERWAYS

THE STATE OF TEXAS HAS EXPERIENCED TREMENDOUS population growth in the last decade. The most recent stats rank the Lone Star State number two in population, just behind California, and third in the country for the highest growth rate. In 2014, my wife and I contributed to this surge in population when we added our names to the roster of folks who now call the city of Houston home.

Harris County, the county that contains the city of Houston and many of its suburbs, has experienced a doubling of population from 1990 to the present. More than 4.5 million people live in Harris County alone, making it the most populated county in Texas. If you take into account the Houston Metropolitan Statistical Area, which encompasses the adjacent counties of Fort Bend, Montgomery, Galveston, and others, you are looking at an area with a population of 6.7 million people, covering roughly 9,444 square miles. That is an area larger than several New England states, including New Hampshire, New Jersey, and Connecticut. Within the city itself, the population is roughly 2.3 million, which makes it the fourth-largest city in the United

Above: Jack Boyd hooks a nice common carp in Brays Bayou.

States, behind Chicago. Demographers project that by 2025, Houston will overtake the Windy City.

Houston was built on a flat coastal plain, and its urban development can truly be described as sprawling. There are approximately 55 miles of urban development from the Katy suburbs west of downtown to the industrial districts of Baytown to the east. The suburb known as The Woodlands acts as a metropolitan bookend to the north, and the Friendswood and League City areas act as the southern bookend, a stretch of about 48 miles.

The Houston area is massively urban, but interwoven among all the cement and steel exist lotic ecosystems teeming with life. It was the abundance of these streams and bayous that gave rise to the city of Houston in the first place. Heck, Houston's nickname is the Bayou City, after all.

White Oak Bayou is a prominent local waterway that flows towards downtown where it meets with the larger Buffalo Bayou at the historic Allen's Landing.

According to the Bayou Preservation Association, Houston has more than 2,500 miles of waterways. These creeks and bayous offer a much-needed escape from the daily grind of the urban lifestyle. These streams, along with the lands adjacent to them (known as riparian corridors), offer city-dwellers countless outdoor recreational opportunities. Every day, joggers, cyclists, picnickers, and fishermen can be found along the banks of Houston's bayous. Even in the shadows of the massive skyscrapers of downtown, kayak rentals can be found along Buffalo Bayou.

The waterways of southeastern Texas are immensely important to local anglers. Houston is uniquely positioned in that fly fishers can sample the gamut of warmwater environments. Many creeks north of the city convey a more traditional small-stream fly fishing experience. This area is known as the Pineywoods (the Texas portion of the great Southern Pine Forest, which contains as many trees as all of New England), and anglers have the pleasure of wading

Lotic and Lentic

Lotic and lentic refer to two types of water ecosystems. The term "lotic" comes from the Latin *lotus*, meaning "washing." Lotic is just a fancy way of saying that a body of water is flowing. Examples of lotic systems include creeks, rivers, and bayous. "Lentic" refers to the opposite—that is, bodies of standing water. Examples of lentic systems include ponds, lakes, swamps, and marshes.

Origin of the Word "Bayou" If you are unfamiliar with the term "bayou" (usually pronounced "buy-you"), it is a word for a slow-moving stream or river. The origin of the word is Cajun or French Creole. However, it's thought to be a mispronunciation of the Native American Choctaw word *bayuk*, which means "small river."

through flowing streams under a thick canopy of pines and hardwoods.

Within the city itself, there exist some of the most unique angling opportunities that can be found anywhere in the country. With the Houston skyline in the background, anglers can traverse miles of channelized concrete bayous in search of various native and invasive species of fish.

The Gulf Coast, where hundreds of miles of coastline and saltwater marshes can be explored, is a short drive from the city. Much has already been written about fly fishing the Texas coast around Houston, and this work won't attempt to recreate the excellent resources already available. Instead, this book will focus on the freshwater fisheries, with an emphasis on the flowing waterways that can be waded or paddled. This type of fishing is conducive to newcomers and to the do-it-yourself anglers.

"The ordinary traveler, who never goes off the beaten route and who on this beaten route is carried by others, without himself doing anything or risking anything, does not need to show much more initiative and intelligence than an express package."

—THEODORE ROOSEVELT IN *River of Doubt* BY CANDICE MILLARD

What's nice about fishing our local streams is that the capital investment to get started is minimal. You don't need a skiff or the latest rod and reel with state-of-the-art drag system. To have a memorable day on a local creek, you simply need a basic fly rod, a handful of flies, and a willingness to walk (or paddle). For some Houston-area fly rodders, the local freshwater fisheries are merely an afterthought to the larger saltwater scene. However, the heavy focus on saltwater fishing can be a blessing for the smaller freshwater fisheries. The local creeks are uncrowded and provide plenty of fishing opportunities.

In my opinion, the venerable act of fly fishing, in its truest form, is best coupled with hiking, wading, or paddling on moving waters. There is a raw connection to the environment when water is accessed through human power by sheer physical exertion. If sweat equity is involved in a successful day of fishing, then the sense of accomplishment is greater, the memory becomes lasting, and the cold beverage at the end of the day is that much sweeter.

Additionally, the sport of fly fishing was born on flowing waters, and it is the lotic environment in which it thrives. Not only that, but exploring

Peach Creek is a gorgeous waterway that flows under a thick canopy in the Pineywoods, north of the city of Houston.

the creeks in southeastern Texas is fascinating for those anglers who are intrigued by ecology and wildlife. Even if a day on the water is unsuccessful and the "fishing" experience merely becomes a hike with the fly rod, local streams are still best explored with a fly rod in hand.

Perspective Is Important

Before we go any further, some perspective is important. Please keep in mind that the waterways found in this book are vastly different from streams addressed in most fly fishing guidebooks. We aren't talking about the rocky, cold waters of the Yellowstone and the Madison. We aren't even talking about Texas's own crystalline rivers like the Llano or the Devils. We are talking about the streams of southeastern Texas: tannin-stained and slow flowing, but beautiful in their own unique

One of the more interesting creatures that lurks in the waters of southeastern Texas is the alligator snapping turtle. This specimen was a juvenile, no bigger than the palm of a hand, and was found on the East Fork San Jacinto River. However, these turtles can grow to massive proportions, sometimes weighing over 200 pounds. Creatures like this are what makes fly fishing in the Pineywoods a unique endeavor.

way. Some waterways are highly urbanized, and what's more, some are still on the mend from decades of pollution and neglect

In truth, many of the waterways addressed herein will never be seen on a postcard and will never make the list of *Fifty Places to Fly Fish Before You Die*. I make no claims about fish populations in the Houston-area waterways, nor do I know the specifics of how many fish reside in a given mile of a particular waterway. If anything is gleaned from this work, let it simply be that these waterways exist. They are here for our enjoyment. We can paddle them, go fishing, picnic on their sandbars, or just wade in their waters and turn over logs to ogle the aqueous world underneath. With that being said, I do have a sneaking suspicion that after you take your first steps into a local creek and land your first spotted bass, the hidden wonders of these streams will begin to unfurl in front of you.

Any misgivings one might have regarding local waters can be compensated for by the unique fly fishing opportunities that abound. Wild and crafty fish can be found throughout Southeast Texas. Fly anglers want to be challenged by their quarry, and luckily many wild fishes in this area rise to that challenge. In his fantastic book *The Sunfishes*, East Texas fly fisher Jack Ellis writes,

> *Some of us have compromised the current and accepted still water; others live without postcard scenery and will even fish murky water ... The one element that must be present for the art of fly fishing to be practiced in any sort of meaningful way, is embodied in the word wild. Without wild fish, our efforts constitute nothing more than an irrelevant exercise in futility—a vicarious sort of angling much like tying the leader to the cat's tail!*

Ellis's sentiments are certainly agreeable to the Houston fly fishing community. Whether casting for native panfish or invasive grass carp, there is no denying that these fish are as wild as they come and are completely at home in the local waters.

In recent years, there has been a new wave of outdoorsy fly anglers who are chasing all manner of wild fishes in waterways ranging from small creeks to concrete ditches. Many of these anglers show no prejudice toward fish species, their philosophy being that if the fish eats a fly, it's worthy of pursuit.

This is a great thing. It opens the sport of fly fishing to more people and expands the horizons of fly fishing into the realms of the unconventional and nontraditional. Anyone who experiences the joys of catching a fish, any fish, on the fly has the potential of becoming a lifelong advocate for the sport of fly fishing and for local waterways.

Gator Gar on the Trinity River

There are a handful of local fly anglers who have tested their mettle by heading to the tailwaters of Lake Livingston on the Trinity River. These exceptional anglers have proven that it is possible to fly fish for alligator gar on the Trinity River, but bear in mind that fishing for gator gar is a serious undertaking. These fish can grow to massive proportions (the All-Tackle Record for alligator gar on the Trinity River is 7 feet, 9 inches and 200 pounds) and can live for multiple decades. Some of the bigger gator gar are estimated to be about one hundred years old.

These fish were once feared and killed without discretion, but they have recently seen a surge in popularity as a worthy sport fish. However, before attempting to fish the Trinity, know that water levels, flow rates, and seasonal changes all dictate the success and the safety of the angler. Aside from gator gar, other species like black bass, big catfish, striped bass, and white bass can also be found. But again, because of the vastness of this large river, fishing this waterway is best accomplished with the use of a boat, with the help of an expert angler, or by hiring a local guide. Before attempting to fish the Trinity River, consider stopping at one of the local fly shops, like Bayou City Angler, to get the lowdown on this river and when the water levels are safe to fish. Catching an alligator gar on the fly is quite the achievement, but it's not worth drowning for.

This book is not intended to be the defining work on fly fishing locations in the Houston area. The truth is that there is just too much water to cover, and it would be nearly impossible to document every fishing location in the immediate area. Not only that, but such an endeavor wouldn't be prudent. So much of fishing is about exploration and discovery, and hopefully this book will kindle a fire for further escapades on local waters.

As you read these pages, you'll see that some of the area's major rivers have either been omitted or only briefly described. Specifically, I'm referring to the Brazos River, the San Jacinto River proper, and the Trinity River. While these waters do hold fish, I felt they were just too big for consideration in this guidebook. These prominent rivers offer exciting angling opportunities, but they require more than just a fly rod, a pair of creek shoes, or a paddlecraft. For example, the wide and daunting Trinity River can offer trophy-sized fish, but tackling this big water isn't for the faint of heart. If you are a beginner fly angler but still want to try fishing the Trinity, it is wise to hire a guide with intimate knowledge of this river.

Readers may also be curious as to why some urban or suburban

Angel Rodriguez holds a largemouth bass that was caught in a tributary to Greens Bayou. This fish is one of many that live in the vast urban waterways of Houston. Once you become familiar with the waterways within this book, it's doubtless you'll want to continue exploring. The waterways described herein are just the beginning.

waterways have been omitted from this work. While I would have liked to include more waterways, some of these streams didn't offer the enjoyable fishing experiences that were necessary to be included. This decision went beyond whether fish could be caught in these streams, because for the most part, they certainly can.

Bayous like Halls Bayou and Greens Bayou do hold decent populations of fish, and under the right circumstances can be a lot of fun, but on several trips to these bayous there were safety concerns to consider. In particular, Greens Bayou in the vicinity of I-45 was not a welcoming place for an urban fly rodder. I recommend that you avoid this area.

However, Greens Bayou deserves closer examination on the northeast side of the city, near Humble. At this location, you can also checkout Garners Bayou, which contains bass, carp, and even cichlids.

Clear Creek is another waterway that deserves recognition. At the invitation of a friend, Xavier Jaime, then a resident of Pearland, I made several excursions to this creek. Xavier showed me the potential Clear Creek has as another urban fishery.

While leafing through this book, you'll see that several local lakes make appearances. While an effort was made to focus on the flowing waters, some of these lakes deserved to be described in detail because of their recreational importance. These local impoundments can be a great place to visit when the streams are blown out from inclement weather. Additionally, certain notable fish species, like the native bowfin and non-native Florida largemouth bass, can be found in several local lakes.

A Plethora of Fishes

The waterways in southeastern Texas boast a diverse array of warmwater fish species. It can become a guessing game as to what kind of fish will turn up on the end of your line. Fly anglers in southeastern Texas are afforded the opportunity to hike into jungle-like streams and fling bow-and-arrow casts to native sunfish or creep along miles of urban ditches in an effort to land a skittish fifteen-pound carp. Anglers can also paddle through backwater sloughs and sight fish for bowfin while an alligator, basking in the sun, nonchalantly opens one lazy eye to watch the ensuing battle.

If you are a newcomer to the Bayou City, or to the sport of fly fishing, give the local freshwater scene a chance. It may come as a surprise how much fun can be had in the bayous and streams that are found right out the back door. It's been said many times before, and I recently heard it reiterated from Native Houstonian and Central Texas fly fishing guide Alvin Dedeaux, who said, "If a body of water [in Texas] doesn't dry up in the summer, it's got bass in it." This statement certainly holds true for Alvin's home city of Houston. In fact, it may be accurate to say that the majority of water in southeastern Texas holds at least some species of fish that's willing to take a fly. To illustrate this point, I will recall a quick story.

Nearly a decade ago, when I first moved to the Bayou City, the idea that fish could be almost anywhere was an unfamiliar concept to me. I would have never guessed that fish could be in ditches, detention ponds, and wastewater outflows. The concept seemed absurd. But this fact became clear one day while I was riding my bike through a city park.

There was a ditch, no wider than three or four feet, that ran beside the bike path. While I pedaled along, I noticed several cormorants (a semi-aquatic, fish-eating bird) that were hunting in the ditch beside the bike path. Intrigued, I hopped off my bicycle and quietly peered over the bank to see what the birds were doing.

The cormorants took turns diving under the surface of the water. Like black torpedoes, they swam up and down the length of the ditch. Each time they resurfaced, I could see a plump green sunfish helplessly wiggling in their hooked bills. The cormorants scarfed down more and more sunfish with each pass. I watched the slaughter continue, astounded at how many fish were being taken by the cormorants.

The birds became aware of my presence, and in the clumsy way that only a cormorant can muster, the bumbling group of birds furiously beat their wings, splashing down the ditch and eventually becoming airborne.

The next afternoon, I was back at the ditch. This time I had my 3-weight fly rod that I used on the freestone brook trout streams of my native state of Pennsylvania. I stopped along a section of the ditch where the water ran through a culvert. My hope was that some of the sunfish had found refuge from the avian onslaught by swimming into the culvert. I made a couple casts using one of my brook trout flies (a Royal Wulff, or something like that) and watched as a green sunfish casually swam out of the mouth of the pipe and sipped the fly from the surface.

That whole experience was eye opening. It taught me that even in an unassuming, cement-lined ditch, fish can still live. But not just merely exist, no. In fact, they thrive!

This is an important thing to know, especially for new residents to the Houston area. Opportunities for catching fish abound; you just need to keep your eyes open. Of course, catching a bass next to a busy freeway might not be an ideal fly fishing experience, but if you just want to fish for an hour or two after work and let the rest of the world go by, look no further than your local pond, or weed-choked ditch, or forgotten creek. There really are fish everywhere! Grab your fly rod and start exploring. If nothing else, it's great practice for your next trip to the mountains.

Xavier Jaime battles a bass in Clear Creek. Although this waterway didn't make it into the book, this is just another example of the many different streams, bayous, and ponds that await Houston-area fly rodders.

Seasonality and Water Clarity

No matter the time of year, anglers can still find fish to chase with the long rod. The fall (September to November) is a great time to explore the area's flowing waterways. The mild air temperatures, coupled with the pleasant water temperatures, allow anglers to enjoy comfortable conditions for all-day excursions. Black bass and sunfishes are still active due to warmer water temperatures, and they still readily chase topwater flies.

During the winter months, wet wading becomes harder due to declining water temperatures. Anglers may need to break out the waders in order to fish the local creeks. Fishing local lakes from a paddlecraft can be a lot of fun during this time of year. Most of the vegetation has died, and the water is free from these snags. Fishing streamers can be productive for lake-dwelling largemouth.

As the spring (mid-February to April) rolls in, many fly fishers shift their focus to the migration of temperate bass as they move from the lakes into the creeks. This can be an excellent time to hit the water. If the run of white and yellow basses is in full swing, it can yield nonstop fishing action. As the spring progresses, and water temperatures continue to climb, black bass begin pre-spawn feeding behaviors, and other fish like bowfin can be found cruising the shallows of local lakes. Additionally, carp fishing tends to heat up during this time as they begin their pre-spawn and spawning activities.

When the season transitions into summer (May to June), fishing continues to pick up as fish metabolisms go full throttle. However, the mid-summer months (July to August) can be punishingly hot. This can be a brutal time of year to be a local creek stomper. Not only does the heat take its toll on the anglers, but many larger waterways that are open to the harsh rays of the summer sun (Spring Creek, West Fork San Jacinto River, Brays Bayou, and White Oak Bayou) can get very hot. Water temperatures can climb into the mid-to-high-90s on the West Fork San Jac and Spring Creek.

You may want to try fishing in the early mornings or evenings when the temperatures are slightly lower, but even then, the fish can act lethargic and may reject any flies you put in front of them. If you do manage to catch a couple of fish during the dog days of summer, consider it an accomplishment, but return them to the water quickly. They may already be stressed from the soaring water temperatures.

Luckily, anglers and fish can find thermal refuge by heading north to the smaller creeks of the Pineywoods. Here, the thickly forested streams (East Fork San Jacinto River, Peach Creek, Caney Creek, and, farther east, Village Creek) can offer cooler water temperatures and can be fantastic places to pass the hottest days of the summer. Some fish even prefer to move out of the warm, large reservoirs and run into the cooler creeks.

On average, Houston gets a total of 53 inches of rain, per year, making it one of the rainiest cities in America. Houston's annual rainfall is about 18 inches more than Austin and about 12 inches more than Dallas. It should come as no surprise that much of our water appears cloudy or muddled at least some portion of the year. Local geology dictates water clarity, and because most of our streams flow through a landscape of fine-grain sediments, a muddy tinge is imparted to many of our waterways. Obviously, this is magnified after storms, but despite this, the fish still swim about, happy as ever.

Even though streams flow with a cloudy tint, there are several creeks outlined in this work that can be surprisingly clear, especially during Houston's "dry" season (December through March). Additionally, many of the smaller tributaries that flow into the major waterways can offer clear sight fishing opportunities.

In general, local waters often appear muddiest during Houston's wet season. This is usually during the late spring and early summer (May to July). This fluctuates from year to year, but for the most part, expect rain and high water during this part of the year. This is a good time to hit local ponds or lakes or focus on small tributaries. Minor creeks return to normal flows relatively quickly, even after heavy downpours.

Because of the low visibility of some of our waterways, it may be necessary to use different fishing techniques than some might be used to. Sometimes, simply fan casting an area, or blind casting repeatedly while covering water, is all it takes to find fish. Try fishing large streamer patterns that push more water and activate the lateral lines of predatory fish, or throw topwater poppers to create a commotion on the surface. Additionally, you may want to try fishing with sink-tip line or an intermediate line, but we will discuss this later. Most importantly, don't be afraid to experiment with different techniques. As you become more familiar with the local waters, you will develop techniques that work for you.

Joey Ramirez prepares to make another blind cast to a secluded cove in Lake Conroe.

Chapter 2

HOW TO USE
THIS BOOK

An effort was made to organize the waterways from north to south. The streams of the Pineywoods region will appear in the first half of the book, and the more urban waterways will be found in the second half of the book. A notable exception is Village Creek (chapter 24) which appears toward the end of the book. The wade descriptions for various streams will be presented in order, starting from the upstream-most reach and working downstream.

Each chapter focuses on a particular watershed, which may include some of the smaller tributaries that were deemed "fishy" enough to make the cut. For instance, the greater watershed of White Oak Bayou is covered in one chapter, which includes the minor tributary, Little White Oak Bayou. As another example, not only is the West Fork San Jacinto River covered in its respective chapter, but so is Lake Conroe. These waterbodies are part of the same watershed. If this is a bit confusing, I invite you to take a look at the maps provided within the pages of this book. This will help with visualizing particular watersheds.

The author attempts to stalk a koi in a local creek.

Road mileage and drive times are displayed prior to the wade descriptions. The driving distances shown will reference a starting point from downtown Houston, specifically the Heritage Society at Sam Houston Park, located at 1100 Bagby Street. Drive times to the stream access sites will be averages and are dependent on traffic conditions. Be sure to use a GPS device for more accurate drive time calculations.

Access points to particular waterbodies are identified with latitude and longitude coordinates. These coordinates take the reader to a parking area near the water. If it isn't obvious where to access the water from the parking area, then a brief description will also be provided. Be advised that some access points may require a hike to get to the water.

Be sure to read the route description before heading out the door. Where applicable, additional GPS coordinates are provided for general points of interest. I didn't go so far as to provide GPS coordinates for particular honey holes. I believe this detracts from one of the best characteristics of fly fishing, discovery and exploration. Instead, the wade descriptions of particular reaches should suffice to provide the reader with enough information to find productive water on his or her own.

The bulk of this guide will be the described routes within a waterway, known as "wades." A described wade will be accomplished either on foot, by using a human-powered watercraft (canoe, kayak, or stand-up paddleboard), or a combination of the two.

While reading through the description of a particular wade, you'll see references to two terms, "river right" and "river left." These terms are used to reference a particular side, or bank, of a flowing waterway from the perspective of someone facing downstream, as if they were floating in the direction of the downstream current. However, when given the option, fishermen generally prefer to wade upstream. Keep this in mind when you see references to particular sides of a creek. In general, I'll reiterate what side of the river is being addressed by referencing it to the "river right" or "river left" perspective.

USGS Stream Gauges. Prior to the wade descriptions, the reader will find USGS Stream Gauge numbers. It is suggested that readers check the respective stream gauge before hitting the water. The USGS Texas Water Dashboard can be found at the following URL: txpub.usgs.gov/txwaterdashboard/index.html.

Bookmark this page on your computer or phone. Prior to visiting a particular stream, search for the suggested stream gauge using the

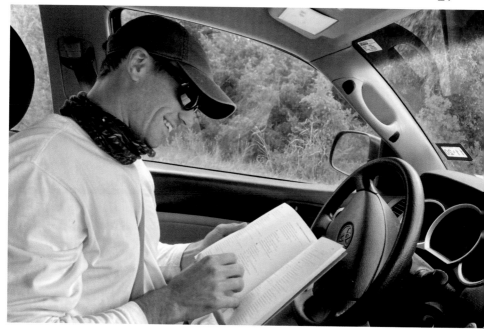

You will find GPS coordinates for stream access points in the back of the book and also before wade/paddle descriptions.

nine-digit number provided. The recommended gauge heights, flow rates, and occasional turbidity readings are meant to provide the reader with context as to what constitutes "low and clear" stream conditions. As a general rule, a low gauge reading and low flow rates (measured in cubic feet per second, or cfs) mean better water visibility. When turbidity readings are provided, the same rule applies. Turbidity is measured in Formazin Nephelometric Units, a standard unit of measurement that determines the concentration of suspended particles in the water. The higher the measurement, the hazier or more turbid the water is. The lower the number, the clearer the water.

QR Codes. In order to quickly find proposed parking areas associated with the wade descriptions, use your phone's camera and scan the QR codes provided. Latitude and longitude coordinates are also provided, and when access to certain waterways is not obvious, a description on how to access the particular wade will be given. Street addresses will also be provided in order to help reaffirm access locations when viewing the coordinates on your favorite GPS device. QR codes are designed to be a quick and easy way to pull up the GPS coordinates for the proposed parking area/access point.

For most newer mobile devices, the QR readers are built directly into the device's camera. This is true for iPhones using the operating system iOS 11 or newer. Most, but not all, Android devices can scan QR codes with the camera. If you are using an Android device that doesn't have a built-in QR reader, there are several QR code readers available from the app store. When you are ready to head to a particular fishing location outlined in this book, simply open your device's camera app or QR code app and hover the lens of your camera over the QR code. Make sure the camera can see all four corners of the QR code. Once the code is read, you'll often get a notification that will ask if you want to open the GPS coordinates in either the mapping app or web browser that's available on your phone. Allow the app or web map to open, and *voilà:* you have the GPS coordinates for the parking area/creek access point. It's as easy as that.

Icons. Before the description of each wade, you'll see one (or more) of the below icons. These icons identify the types of fishing scenarios that can be encountered at each of the locations. The order in which they appear is intended to be a suggestion for the most suitable means to access the described reach. If a particular reach is best kayaked for a particular portion and then waded for the remainder of the route, you'll see a kayak icon first, followed by a wading icon. The purpose of this is to quickly assess the equipment needed for a particular wade without having to read the detailed description.

Four icons identify the types of fishing available from each access point.

 Wade Bank Paddle Handicapped Access

Difficulty Ratings. The difficulty ratings of particular wades can be found before the detailed description. The difficulty of a wade may vary from "Easy" (the section of water is calm, there are paved sidewalks, and/or there is minimal vegetation surrounding the waterway to inhibit casting) to "Hard" (plenty of bushwhacking, scrambling, tripping, and the losing of flies to snags and overhanging vegetation is required). Of course, this is subjective and depends on many factors like water flows, seasonality, and the physical fitness of the angler.

Distances and Directions. Driving directions and distances are always provided in terms of "road miles." If a general statement is made about a particular town or brewery being "X" miles away, then this shouldn't be taken as a literal distance. It is merely a loose reference. All river distances associated with the wade descriptions are provided in yards or miles. A yard is a good unit of measurement because one yard roughly equates to one stride of a walking human. All of the "river miles" in the trip descriptions are provided as if the reader was walking (or paddling) with the meanders of a particular waterway.

Local Haunts. Lastly, at the end of each chapter on a particular waterway, a suggested watering hole will be provided. Enjoying a craft brew and discussing the day's fishing adventures is a great way to round out a day on the water. Toward the end of a chapter on a particular waterway, a brief description of an independent, angler-friendly brewery will be mentioned. Most of these local and independent haunts serve nonalcoholic beverages for minors. Many of these establishments have a food truck or a full-service kitchen for a bite to eat. Bear in mind, I'm no food critic, but I do recognize friendly staff, good service, and good beer. The description of these brew joints will mainly focus on the overall atmosphere and their friendliness towards soggy and muddy anglers.

After a day of stomping around local waters, it's my hope that you'll come away with a sense of joy and accomplishment. Remember to slow down and enjoy all the sights and sounds while you're out on the water. If you are new to fly fishing, it can sometimes be a frustrating learning curve. Don't get discouraged, take a deep breath, and have patience. Remember to relax; it's just fishing, after all.

Trey Alvarez presents a largemouth bass caught in the Buffalo Bayou.

Chapter 3

GEARING UP FOR SOUTHEASTERN TEXAS

THE FOLLOWING SECTION WILL PROVIDE A BROAD OVERVIEW OF what gear is best for fishing in the Houston area. By no means is this an exhaustive list. In fact, on the waterways of southeastern Texas you'll find that most folks care little for what kind of fly rod or sling pack you are sporting. Most of the time you'll see folks wandering the cement flats or local bayous wearing jeans or shorts and an old pair of tennis shoes or hiking boots. If you are new to fly fishing, this section may raise more questions than answers. If this is the case, do not hesitate to seek the advice of the men and women of your local fly shops. These folks will be happy to help with any tackle or equipment questions.

Rods and Reels

If fly fishing is a new hobby for you, choosing the right fly rod can feel overwhelming. However, if you think of fly rods in the same way you think of wrenches in a toolbox—that is, only one particular size of wrench can be used to loosen a bolt of the same size—then perhaps rod selection won't seem quite as nuanced.

C. Barclay Fly Rod Co. makes very fine lightweight fiberglass rods that are perfect for small stream scenarios.

If you are fond of hiking through the woods, wading in small streams, and catching native spotted bass and panfish, you will want to use a small ultralight rod, something in the 2-weight-to-3-weight range. Conversely, if you're interested in throwing meaty flies for largemouth and bowfin on big waters like Lake Conroe or Sheldon Lake, you'll want a heavier rod with a strong backbone, something like a 6-weight or 7-weight.

Some might consider the 4-weight and 5-weight rods to be a good choice for bridging the gap between small water and big. There is merit to this. In fact, I have heard the 5-weight rod called the Ford F-150 (or Toyota Tacoma, if you prefer) of the fly rod world. Either of these rods can be a fine choice when the angler believes they are just as likely to tangle with a 15-pound carp as they are a 2-pound bass. It never hurts to overcompensate with heavier gear if you think your day of fishing could result in a true Southeast Texas grab bag.

There are many value-conscious rod companies that are worth checking out, and it is somewhat hard to find poor quality gear these days.

Even big-box stores like Cabela's, Bass Pro Shops, and L.L. Bean all sell very capable entry-level rods. Fly rod manufacturing companies like Redington, ECHO, Orvis, and Texas-based TFO make a range of rods, from entry-level to high-end. These four companies are noted for their generous, no-fault warranties and terrific customer service.

One of the most important things anyone can do before purchasing a rod and reel is to stop in at a local fly shop and discuss your budget and options with the experts (for a list of fly shops in the Houston area, see the Appendices). The men and women that work at the local fly shops live and breathe fly fishing, and they will be more than happy to let you cast several rod and reel combinations before you decide to buy.

As time goes on and you continue your fly fishing journey, you'll absolutely want a combination of various rod sizes in order to maximize your fishing experience. As mentioned before, lightweight rods, in the 2-to-3-weight range, are excellent for chasing panfish and spotted bass on the smaller creeks of the Pineywoods. For my small-stream setup, I prefer a shorter rod, usually in the 6.5-to-7.5-foot range. Most of the creeks north of the city are surrounded by dense vegetation, and having a shorter rod allows for easier casting while fishing these brushy waterways.

As you become more accustomed to casting and the feel of a fly rod, you'll likely want to upgrade to a custom rod, especially one that is built to specialize in lightweight, small-water scenarios. Fiberglass rods (usually referred to as "glass" rods) make for wonderful small-stream rods. You can feel every vibration and pulsing run of even the smallest longear sunfish or bluegill when fishing with glass.

Texas-based Temple Fork Outfitters (TFO) and SAGE are two companies that offer excellent rods with fantastic warranties.

Originally from Kingwood, Chris Barclay, owner and craftsman of C. Barclay Fly Rod Co. out of North Carolina, builds beautiful small-stream fiberglass rods that were originally designed for the tiny freestone brook trout waters of the Appalachian Mountains. However, Barclay's rods are just as well suited for pursuing the multitude of panfish and small bass species lurking in the tight backwaters of southeastern Texas. Barclay's ultralight 2-weight rod is perfect when blue lining the small step-across waters of southeastern Texas.

Moonlit Fly Fishing is another fantastic company that builds fiberglass rods. Moonlit started by building furled leaders for delicate presentations on western streams. Since then, the owner, Brandon Moon, has expanded into manufacturing glass rods. My Moonlit rod (3-weight, 6 feet, 2 inches) has been great for small panfish and bass, but it also has subdued larger grass carp.

Having a top-of-the-line reel for a small-stream outfit is overkill. Seldom, if ever, will you need to use the drag system, and mostly the reel

The Sage Spectrum C is a large arbor reel that doesn't break the bank. This reel does well in both freshwater and saltwater scenarios.

is there to just hold your fly line. Cabela's, Okuma, Orvis, and Pfleuger all make inexpensive small reels. Keep in mind that you want your lightweight reel to balance with your lightweight rod. A fat and clunky reel hanging off the end of your feather-light creek rod creates imbalance and defeats the purpose of the ultralight setup. Author and Texas Hill Country fly fisher Aaron Reed likes to keep his lightweight reels smaller than 3 inches in diameter and weighing less than 3.5 ounces. This seems to be the sweet spot for a small creek combo.

On the other end of the spectrum, anglers who frequent large lakes and reservoirs will want a more heavy-duty rod. A 5-weight rod is fine for starters, but once you start throwing larger bass bugs, you'll want to upgrade to a stout rod that punches through gusty winds and turns over bigger flies. A 6- or 7-weight rod, 9 feet in length, is an excellent big bass rod for fishing local reservoirs and larger rivers.

When looking at reel options for heavier rods, it's best to consider large arbor reels. Large arbors have a bigger diameter than the standard trout-sized arbors and therefore can more quickly reel in significantly more line. This is hugely important for when a big bowfin takes your fly and runs into the weeds. You'll need to get the line back onto the reel in a timely manner in order to fight the fish using the drag system of the reel. The Sage Spectrum C is a great large arbor reel that isn't too pricey. Other budget-friendly options include Redington's reels and TFO's BVK SD reels.

Fly Lines, Leaders, and Tippet

For nearly all fly fishing scenarios in southeastern Texas, fly anglers can fish using a standard weight-forward floating line and be able to cover the majority of water described in this book. However, as you begin to experiment and grow as a fly angler, you'll want a variety of lines in your quiver. A sink-tip line, intermediate line, or both can allow anglers to access different depths and find fish that a floating line may miss. These types of lines are especially helpful when blind casting into deep pools and drop-offs in larger waterways.

Keep in mind that if you plan on doing most of your fishing from a canoe or kayak, it's okay if your sink-tip line has an extended head or a sinking running line. However, if you plan to wade fish with your sink-tip or intermediate line, considering buying a line with a shorter head and a floating running line. If you are wade fishing and your running line sinks, it will get caught around your feet or entangled in debris on the bottom of the river. A running line that floats won't get wrapped around debris on the streambed. Scientific Angler is at the forefront of fly line innovation. It makes a wide variety of sink-tip, full sink, and intermediate lines. Rio Products is another manufacturer than produces all kinds of lines that will suite your needs and budget.

If sinking fly lines don't interest you, that's no problem. Fishing various depths can still be accomplished with the use of weighted split shot and fluorocarbon leaders or tippet. Fluorocarbon is denser than monofilament and sinks about twice as fast. Also, if you keep a small pack of split shot in your sling pack, you can always pinch some extra weight onto your leader to get your flies down quick.

It is often helpful to have two fly rods with you when hitting the water. One should be rigged with a standard floating line and the other with a sink-tip or intermediate line. This way, you can easily switch rods depending on the different scenarios that you find. If you are in need of sink-tip or intermediate lines, stop in at one of the local fly shops and discuss your options with the experts.

For leaders, it is generally a good rule of thumb to keep the length of your leader close to the same length as your rod. For example, if you are fishing a 9-foot rod, you'll want your leader to be approximately 9 feet. For the majority of freshwater scenarios around Houston, tippet ranging in size from 3x to 2x will work just fine. However, when I'm throwing larger flies (hook sizes 2 to 4), it's easier to get these flies to roll over with tippet in the .012-to-.014-inch diameter range (this translates to tippet larger than 0x).

It's important to remember that when buying tapered leaders from your local fly shop, the tippet is already built into the leader. You don't need to tie an extra length of tippet onto the end of your store-bought tapered leader.

In fact, doing so will inhibit your casting. Only tie additional tippet onto your tapered leader after you have cut the built-in tippet back to the tapered leader section. Presumably, this would be after you have fished with your store-bought leader several times.

When fishing, keep in mind that once a fish is on the end of your line, it will be dragging the leader over concrete, rocks, sand, and logs. Simply put, leaders should be resistant to abrasion. Most of the water around Houston tends to be on the murky side, so don't hesitate to lean toward bulkier tippet and leaders. The lack of water clarity will usually hide the large-diameter leaders well enough.

Watercraft

While it's not a requirement for fly fishing many local waterbodies, having some sort of watercraft will improve your opportunities for exploring and fishing in southeastern Texas. *Joey Ramirez and Trey Alvarez prepare to launch* The scope of this book will only *their canoe into Lake Conroe for an early morning* address common watercraft that *fishing session.*

In the world of lightweight and portable inflatables, the Flycraft Stealth is a very versatile option.

can be transported to and from the water easily and can be propelled with a paddle, oars, and a little elbow grease.

Canoes and kayaks are probably the most popular and easily affordable watercraft in the nation. A brief search on Craigslist or any local classifieds will show dozens of results. It's not uncommon to find used, but still seaworthy, vessels ranging in prices from $1,000 (on the high end) down to $100. Check the local classifieds on websites like TexasKayakFisherman.com or the local Houston Canoe Club (thcc.clubexpress.com). On occasion, while browsing Craigslist or Offerup.com, you may even find perfectly good kayaks or canoes for the great low price of "free." Before purchasing a used canoe or kayak online, double-check the hull of the vessel to make sure there are no leaks. Also, don't forget the paddles or oars and the PFDs (personal floatation devices, a.k.a. life jackets). Texas does not require the registration of human-powered watercraft, but does require a PFD for each person, and an all-around white light if navigating after dark.

Of course, if you have the coin, purchasing a new kayak or canoe is never a bad idea. The fantastic folks over at Fishing Tackle Unlimited are a great resource and can answer questions regarding fishing out of paddlecraft. Outdoor-oriented companies like Academy, REI, Cabela's, and

Bass Pro Shops also have canoes and kayaks in stock.

These two types of watercraft each have their pros and cons. Canoes are bigger and bulkier than most kayaks, but they can hold many more pounds of gear, people, and dogs. Another added bonus for a canoe is that the person at the bow (front) can fish almost nonstop without having to worry about the trajectory of the watercraft. Canoes have a tendency to be tippy, but with practice, it's very possible to stand up in the bow to make longer casts. Also, outriggers can be purchased, or constructed at a nominal price, to make the canoe more stable.

Anglers have plenty of options when it comes to watercraft. Used canoes and kayaks are always great options for budget-conscious buyers.

Canoes

Canoes hold a special place in North American history. Much of the early trade between Native Americans and European explorers was established using the canoe. Native Americans and the French-Canadian *coureur des bois*, "runner of the woods," paddled thousands of miles in their canoes, trading furs and goods, throughout Canada and the Eastern seaboard. Writer, fly angler, and Texas native Nathaniel Riverhorse Nakadate writes in his poetic essay, "Paddling Past the Graveyard,"

There are few things more personal and intimate than being intertwined to the hips of a canoe. Far beyond the every-day hum and whir of a static existence, this is where life makes sense to me. I'm a believer in the restorative medicines of wanderlust and solitude. If anything has unraveled, nature stitches it together again. A simple kick of my boot from the shoreline and gravity is gone. The water holds everything aloft.

Bote's SUP, BugSlinger, is a great option for anglers who are short on space and can't store a larger paddlecraft like a canoe.

Pelican makes well priced and capable canoes that can often be found at the classified websites for very cheap prices. Old Town canoes are common and are a fantastic line of watercraft. Used Old Town canoes can be found online at reasonable prices. Buffalo Canoes, headquartered in Jasper, Arkansas, makes wonderful two-person canoes that are about 16 feet long. These canoes are made from a durable and lightweight material known as T-Formex. This new laminate has replaced the older Royalex material, which is no longer manufactured. On occasion, high-end canoes like Wenonah, Esquif, and Swift can be found online as well.

Over the last several decades, the sport of kayak fishing has exploded in popularity. Sit-on-top, polyethylene kayaks are some of the most versatile fishing vessels anywhere. Most fishing kayaks have plenty of room for storage, in the form of compartments on the deck or dry storage inside the hull. The modern fishing kayaks that are the most stable have tunnel hulls, also called pontoon hulls.

Again, with some practice, it's quite possible to stand up on these single-person vessels in order to make longer casts. Companies such as Wilderness Systems, Hobie, Native, and Jackson Kayak all make superb kayaks. Austin's own Diablo Paddlesports makes an incredibly stable and uniquely designed kayak that is part paddleboard and part kayak. Standing and casting from one of these is quite easy, and it builds confidence in an angler's ability to make long casts to unwary fish.

Stand-up paddleboards, or SUPs, are another form of paddlecraft that has made its way into the world of fly fishing. The company Bote makes an inflatable SUP called the Bug Slinger, which caters to fly anglers. SUPs are surprisingly stable and lightweight. This style of paddlecraft is a great option for anglers who don't have room to store a kayak or canoe or don't have the means to car top their watercraft.

Over the last five years, there have been some unique inflatable watercraft that have hit the market. These welcomed additions to the world of watercraft come from companies such as Flycraft and StealthCraft. Both of these companies have created small (98 pounds for the Flycraft and 150 pounds for the Hooligan) two-man inflatable driftboats that are incredibly stable and can be loaded and unloaded with relative ease. Both of these rafts can accommodate a small outboard motor, which increases their versatility. Speaking from experience, the Flycraft is a great vessel for exploring many of the smaller waterways of East Texas.

If you are interested in purchasing a watercraft, it may be best to buy an inexpensive used canoe. If possible, take it for a test paddle before purchasing, if the seller will let you. Most people are familiar with canoes, and being able to properly paddle and maneuver this type of watercraft is almost second nature to many folks. For even more control and ease of paddling, try using a kayak paddle with a canoe instead of the standard single blade paddles.

Other Gear to Consider

When fishing the rural waterways of Southeast Texas, wear lightweight long pants made of a fabric with a high percentage of nylon and spandex. Nylon is a strong and protective fabric that dries quickly. When exploring the urban cement flats, you'll usually be fine just wearing a pair of shorts. For sun protection, wear a long-sleeved shirt, hat, and bandana or buff. Of course, a good pair of sunglasses is also a necessity.

Footwear is another thing to consider. If you are just getting into fly fishing, an old pair of hiking boots or sturdy sneakers (preferably with ankle support) will do just fine for most scenarios. However, as you spend more time out in the water, you'll undoubtably want a specialized wading shoe. Simms, Patagonia, and Redington are just a few of the companies to choose from. North Carolina-based Astral Designs makes several varieties of excellent, lightweight wading shoes. Astral's Brewer 2.0 and Rassler 2.0 are two of my favorite wet-wading shoes. When looking to purchase a wading shoe, you'll want one with an aggressive rubber sole. Felt-soled wading shoes are pointless for exploring the sandy and muddy streams of southeastern Texas.

For the vast majority of the year, anglers can get away with wet-wading. However, during the months of January and February, you'll likely find the water to be a bit chilly. Wearing a pair of waders during this time of the year is prudent.

Some Safety Items

It's a good idea to carry with you a small first aid kit containing essential items. You can find first aid kits at outdoor stores like REI, but it is best to build your own. If you do, you can cater to your personal needs, and then you will know exactly what is in the kit and how to use everything. The following items are things I carry in my personal first aid kit: band-aids, antibiotic ointment, steri-strips, Tylenol, ibuprofen, syringe (for cleaning out wounds), Leukotape, Chapstick, whistle, water purification tablets, knife, and lighter. Other gear to consider having with you may include insect repellent and snake gaiters (if you plan on doing some hardcore blue lining). For more information on safety related items, check out the part titled "Legal, Safe, and Ethical."

Just Go Fishing

Getting wrapped up in the excitement of having the latest fly fishing tackle, apparel, and watercraft is something that will come with time, but if you are just getting started, remember that fly fishing is still just fishing. As time goes on, the desire to explore new waterways and seek different species of fish will grow; along with that, so will your need for additional equipment. If you are a newcomer to the sport of fly fishing, an entry-level rod, an old pair of tennis shoes, and a simple ALTOIDS box filled with half a dozen flies is all you'll need to have an exciting day of catching panfish and bass at the local pond or creek.

Chapter 4

A SOUTHEAST TEXAS FLY BOX

It is certainly true that the majority of water in southeastern Texas can be fished successfully by using many of the standard warmwater fly patterns. The tried-and-true Clouser Minnow, Muddler Minnow, Woolly Bugger, Gurgler, and BoogleBug all come to mind as patterns that work well for many predatory fish in the area. However, there are instances where specialized local patterns will outperform the classics. The following flies have a proven track record in the streams and lakes of southeastern Texas. These patterns have been developed by locals as well as fly tyers from outside of Texas.

Some of these flies are commercially available, like Danny Scarborough's famous Brasshawk carp fly, which can be found in many local fly shops. Other patterns can be purchased online or by contacting the fly tyer directly. In some cases, these patterns aren't available for sale; they are simply the creations of local fly tyers who are willing to share their recipes and expertise. Readers who are capable of tying their own flies may follow the recipes that are presented.

Contributing Fly Tyers

Mark Marmon has been using a fly rod to chase urban carp in the bayous of Houston since the early '80s. He is one of the first fly anglers in the country to do so. Marmon was a saltwater angler before he started fishing freshwater, and this shows in many of his favorite fly patterns. Marmon is a strong proponent of "guide flies" (that is, effective patterns that can be tied in just a couple of minutes). Mark Marmon can be contacted through his website: metroanglers.com.

Jason Martina is a resident of Wisconsin, but his handcrafted balsa wood poppers are absolutely killer on Houston-area bass. These poppers are true works of art. Martina creates a variety of top water flies including pencil poppers, damselflies, and frog poppers. Check out his work on his Instagram page, @basspopflyshop, or his Etsy page, etsy.com/shop/BassPopFlyShop.

Ron Mayfield is an FFI Certified Fly Casting Instructor as well as an Umpqua Signature Fly Designer. Ron's deer hair saltwater pattern, the Rattle Mullet, can be found through Umpqua Feather Merchants. With 50 years of fly tying experience under his belt, Ron's specialty is spinning deer hair, and he creates some ingenious baitfish and frog patterns for his home waters of southeastern Texas. Ron loves teaching fly tying, and he believes that anyone who learns to tie flies will garner a better understanding of the ecosystems in which they fish. Ron can be contacted via e-mail at southsideflycasting@gmail.com.

Don "Puck" Puckett is the current club president of Texas Flyfishers of Houston. When Puck was in the Army, he served for several years in Europe, where he pursued trout, grayling, and pike, all on the fly. After retiring, Puck returned home and fished much of the southern United States in pursuit of both freshwater and saltwater species. When it comes to fly tying, Puck uses the acronym SCE, which means simple, cheap, effective, to describe his flies. Puck wants to spend more time on the water and less time behind the tying vise. In his opinion, if he can't tie a fly in under five minutes, it's not worth the effort.

Joey Ramirez grew up in Houston, Texas. As a youth he enjoyed exploring local ponds and bayous. After a career in the Air Force, Ramirez retired in Minnesota, where he fishes for smallmouth bass, pike, and musky. When the Minnesota winters set in, Ramirez returns to his home city of Houston to visit family and chase largemouth bass, bowfin, and gar. Joey Ramirez can be contacted at proflyfish@hotmail.com.

Danny Scarborough is a native Houstonian who has made a living through the sport of fly fishing. He is a fly tyer and professional fly fishing guide, servicing both the Dallas and Houston areas. Danny is probably best known for his famous carp fly, the Brasshawk, although he ties many different patterns including saltwater flies and streamers for predatory freshwater fish. For special orders, contact Danny directly through Instagram at @flyinhand_tx or visit his website at houstonflyfishing.com.

Terry Wilson has been a prominent figure in the warmwater fly fishing community for several decades. Hailing from southern Missouri, Terry and his wife, Roxanne, have written many books and articles about fly fishing warmwater species. Wilson's fly patterns can be found in his books *The Bluegill Diaries* and *Largemouth Bass Beyond the Basics*. One of Wilson's most famous patterns is his Bully Bluegill Spider. You can order several of Wilson's fly patterns, along with his books, at thebluegillpond.com.

Bass Bugs and More

Bass Pop Fly

Jason Martina's balsa wood poppers are a blast to fish when the topwater bite is on. Chugging one of these flies across a pond or lake often results in a heart-pounding take.

Hook: Lightning Strike popper hooks (sizes 2 and 4)
Thread: 140 Denier (tyer's choice)
Body: Handcrafted balsa wood, hand painted, high strength two-ton epoxy
Legs: Sili legs (variety of colors)
Tail: Baitfish Emulator Flash and/or marabou

Weedless Baitfish

Danny Scarborough ties a variety of flies that he fishes specifically for bass and bowfin in heavy vegetation. His Weedless Baitfish is tied on a jig hook and rides hook-point up. The deer hair is trimmed in such a way that it acts as a weed guard when stripped through heavy clover.

Hook: Gamakatsu Jig-60 (size 2)
Thread: Olive or Black 210 Denier
Body: Deer Belly Hair (tyer's choice on colors)
Tail: Magnum Rabbit Zonker and marabou
Flash: Senyo's Laser Dub
Eyes: Medium or large dumbbell eyes

Lily Pad Jumping Frog

After years of trial and error, Ron Mayfield specially designed the forelegs of Lily Pad Jumping Frog so that it could be retrieved over the tops of lily pads without the fly turning onto its side and getting fouled on the edge of the pad. The forelegs of this fly push against the edge of the lily pad, which brings the hook point up and over the pad. There's no doubt that Ron's engineering background helped him conjure up this idea.

Hook: Mustad C52S BLN (size 1)
Thread: 210 Denier (tyer's choice)
Body: Deer Belly Hair (tyer's choice)
Legs: Buck tail
Tail: Yellow Grizzly Hackle
Flash: Pearl flashabou
Eyes: Googly doll eyes (6 mm)
Weed guard: 30lb mono

Mohawk Minnow Sunfish

Mayfield's Mohawk Minnow Sunfish is designed to mimic a small sunfish feeding near the surface. The fly is designed to rest with just the "mohawk" poking out of the water. When stripped, the large nose of the fly causes it to dive a few inches and then slowly resurface.

Hook: Mustad 3366 (size 2)
Thread: 210 Denier (tyer's choice)
Body: Deer Belly Hair (tyer's choice)
Tail: Yellow Grizzly Hackle
Flash: Pearl flashabou
Eyes: Googly doll eyes (10 mm)
Weed guard: 30lb mono

Panfish Vittles

San Jac Squirrel

Dave Whitlock was the first contemporary American fly tyer to popularize nymph patterns using squirrel hair. He first started tying his famous fox squirrel nymph in the 1960s. By borrowing many of Whitlock's teachings, this local squirrel hair pattern mimics both a dragonfly larva and a small baitfish. When stripped, swung, or dead drifted, this fly attracts the attention of panfish and spotted bass. Flies created from genuine Pineywoods squirrel hair can be found at flyfishingthesam.com.

Hook: Firehole 839 (size 10) or TMC 3761 (size 8)
Thread: Red UTC 70 Denier
Body: Mixture - grey squirrel hair and Orvis Ice Dubbing (UV black)
Ribbing: Red Ultra Wire (small)
Bead: 1/8"-5/32" Firehole tungsten bead
Tail: Grey squirrel tail
Flash: Olive/pearl Krystal Flash
Soft hackle collar: CDC feather in black (or similar soft hackle feather)

Squrat

Puck's Squrat is a quick and easy "guide fly" that only takes a couple of minutes to whip up. It uses two materials, a pine squirrel zonker strip and bead chain eyes. After you finish tying this pattern, it will probably look like an unorganized clump of fur. However, once the fly gets dunked, the fur compresses into a slim baitfish profile. Tying videos and tutorials for Puck's warmwater patterns can be found on the Texas Flyfishers of Houston website, texasflyfishers.org.

Hook: Mustad 94833 (size 12)
Thread: Black or Brown 6/0
Body: Pine squirrel zonker strip
Eyes: Small or medium bead chain

Bully Bluegill Spider

A staple for many panfish enthusiasts, the Bully Bluegill Spider was first invented by Terry Wilson in 1968. This fly is designed to be fished on the drop. Cast it and let it sink for a couple of seconds. It can also be used as a dropper on a hopper-dropper rig. It's important to note that this fly is intended to sink hook-bend (butt end) first. Therefore, when tying this pattern, be sure to make more wraps with the weighted wire near the bend of the hook before wrapping toward the hook eye. Not only does this pattern catch panfish, but it also entices local grass carp. If you plan on using this pattern for grassers, be sure to tie this fly with extra-stout hooks.

Hook: A wet-fly or dry fly hook (sizes 8, 10, or 12)
Thread: Black 6/0.
Body: Ultra chenille (tyer's choice)
Legs: small round-rubber legs (tyer's choice to match chenille)
Weight: .025 lead-free wire.

Small Flies for Big Carp

Brasshawk

Danny Scarborough invented the Brasshawk to mimic the damselfly nymph, which is a staple food of the local carp. The fly is designed to be a headstand-style and is readily eaten by both common carp and grass carp. Not only is this a great carp fly, but it is also an excellent general-purpose fly that dupes bass, panfish, and catfish when they are hugging the bottom of a waterway.

Hook: Tiemco TMC2457 (size 8)
Thread: Olive 6/0
Abdomen: Olive Ultra Wire (medium)
Thorax: Orvis Hare's Ice Dubbing (Peacock)
Wing case: Peacock hurl
Legs: Olive Hairline Barred Rubber Legs (medium)
Tail: Rabbit strip (olive)
Eyes: Black bead chain (medium)

Carp Booger

Another invention by Danny Scarborough, the aptly named Carp Booger may look like a mishmash of dubbing, but when it's plunked in front of a common carp's nose, be ready for a fight. Danny fishes Carp Boogers all over the state of Texas.

Hook: Orvis 62KC scud (size 8)
Thread: Rust/brown 6/0
Abdomen: Orvis Hare's Ice Dub (brown/orange)
Thorax: Cohen's Carp Dub (Cray-Zee Olive)
Bead: 1/8" gold cyclops bead
Tail: Rabbit strip (crawfish orange)

Bellaire Bonefish Fly

For this fly, Mark Marmon used the blueprint from the famous bonefish pattern known as the Crazy Charlie. This miniaturized version of this saltwater pattern is named in honor of Marmon's old Houston neighborhood. Over the decades, Marmon has caught many urban carp with this pattern.

Hook: Any strong, straight-eye hook (Mustad 3366) (sizes 14 to 10)
Thread: 400 denier (Big Fly)
Body: Thread, color choice is related to fly color
Wing: Pheasant tail, trimmed to length
Eyes: Black bead chain (small)

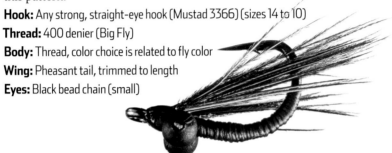

Gar Getter

Gar Funk (G Funk) Fly

Joey Ramirez created the G Funk Fly as a nylon rope streamer specifically for targeting gar. The G Funk can be tied in several varieties, incorporating different colors and a small rattle if the fly is fished in murky water. If you plan on chasing alligator gar with this pattern, use an ultraheavy hook and super strong braided line (maybe even heavy bite wire) to connect the trailing hook. Not only will this fly produce toothy dinosaurs, but it also gets smashed by catfish and big bass.

Front Hook: Gamakatsu B10S stinger (size 2/0)
Trailing Hook: Gamakatsu C13U keel style (size 2), attached to front hook with 50-pound braid
Thread: Uni-Thread 3/0 waxed

Body: Medium or Large Pearl E-Z Body tubing

Tail: 4-6 strands of nylon rope, 4-6 strands of S-Lon fiber, slinky fiber, and Baitfish Emulator Flash (SF Flash can also be used as a substitute)

Flash: Dyed-pearl lateral scale flashabou

Eyes: Fish Skull Living Eyes, 8.5mm or 7.0mm

Head: Epoxy over eyes and tubing for durability

Weight: (optional) .020 lead wire and/or glass rattle

Fish Don't Floss

After landing a gar with the G Funk Fly, it is crucial that you take your time and completely remove any residual strands of the nylon rope from the mouth of the gar. Failure to do this may result in the strands of nylon becoming hopelessly tangled around the fish's mouth, eventually leading to starvation. Carry a pair of leather gloves so you can hold the mouth of the gar open while a friend removes any remaining strands of nylon.

White bass are revered because of the fight they have when hooked. This white bass weighed in at over 2 pounds. It put up a great fight.

Part 2

Pineywoods Waters

BEHIND THE PINE CURTAIN

THE PINEYWOODS IS A MONIKER FOR THE REGION OF THE South containing a temperate coniferous forest. The ecoregion of the Pineywoods encompasses four states: southeastern Oklahoma, southern Arkansas, western Louisiana, and eastern Texas. The Pineywoods region of Texas is identified by dense forests of pines and lowlands containing a diverse array of hardwoods. Montgomery County, the county just north of Harris County, is the southwestern extent of this ecologic region. A section of the Pineywoods extends south into southeastern Harris County and is part of the Lake Houston Wilderness Park. The waters addressed in this section include the following: West Fork San Jacinto River (including Lake Conroe), East Fork San Jacinto River, Caney Creek, Peach Creek, and Spring Creek.

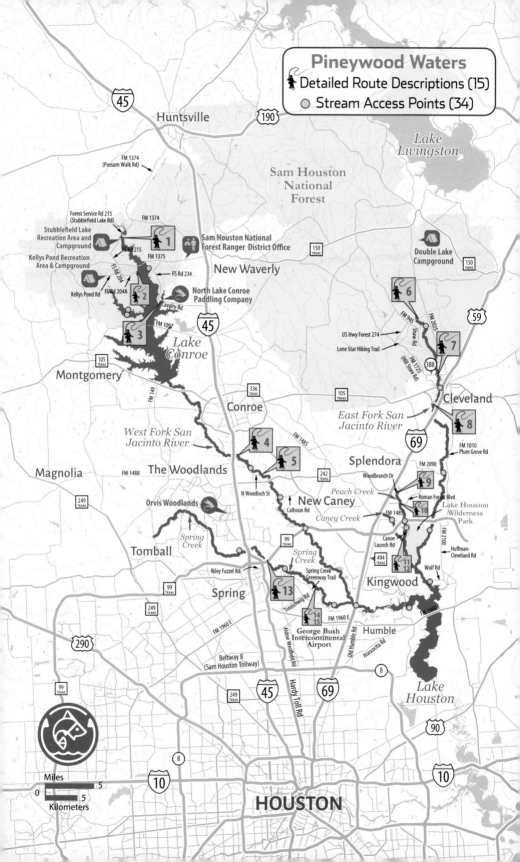

Riffles and pocket water on West Fork San Jacinto on the Woodloch Wade

Chapter 5

WEST FORK SAN JACINTO RIVER AND LAKE CONROE

Florida largemouth and bowfin in Lake Conroe, spring runs of temperate bass in the West Fork San Jac, spotted bass, crappie, drum, and channel cats.
Access Points: 13

THE WEST FORK OF THE SAN JACINTO RIVER (LOCALLY KNOWN as the "West Fork" or the "West Fork San Jac") is a major tributary in the Houston area. Its origin can be traced to western Walker County, west of Huntsville. Two impoundments exist along the West Fork's 90-mile journey south. The first is the 22,000-acre Lake Conroe, which lies northwest of the town bearing the same name. The second impoundment, Lake Houston, can be found downstream, south of the West Fork's confluence with its sister waterway, the East Fork of the San Jacinto River.

In addition to discussing the West Fork, this chapter will also focus on Lake Conroe. This lake is a popular destination for both anglers and pleasure boaters. Lake Conroe contains many of the usual piscatorial predators but also healthy populations of bowfin, Florida largemouth bass, and hybrid striped bass (palmetto bass). Bowfin, also called grinnel by folks in East Texas, can be found in the clear and shallow backwaters of Lake Conroe. This fierce predatory fish is very worthy of pursuit with the fly rod.

Shortly after the West Fork San Jacinto River exits the impoundment of Lake Conroe, the waters can appear murky and daunting. Sometimes, the West Fork churns into a muddy mass of chocolate milk because of a dam release from the San Jacinto River Authority or because of a rainstorm upstream along Lake Creek, a major tributary to the West Fork San Jac. Despite all this, there is hidden beauty to this waterway, not to mention hungry populations of black bass, catfish, panfish, and prolific runs of white bass during the early spring. The West Fork San Jacinto River can be a temperamental waterway for fly fishing, but some of the described waters in the following pages can be a lot of fun when the conditions are right.

USGS Stream Gauges along the West Fork San Jacinto and Lake Conroe

The levels of Lake Conroe tend to fluctuate throughout the year. This all depends on the amount of precipitation the area receives and how active the hurricane season is expected to be. Usually, water will be released from Lake Conroe in anticipation of hurricane season, and then the water level of the lake will be allowed to build during the winter. You can check the water levels of Lake Conroe at the San Jacinto River Authority dashboard, https://sanjacinto.onerain.com/dashboard/list/. For the last two years, Lake Conroe water levels have fluctuated from 198.5 feet to approximately 201 feet.

The water clarity along the West Fork San Jacinto, below Lake Conroe, is never so clear that sight fishing can be accomplished; however, the water can still be surprisingly clear during times of low flows. Check the stream gauge at I-45 (gauge number: 08068000) to get an understanding of water flows. This is an important gauge to check before hitting the water because this monitoring station is downstream of the confluence of Lake Creek and the West Fork San Jac. By checking this gauge, you can see whether Lake Creek has contributed higher volumes of water farther upstream. When the I-45 stream gauge reads 90 to 100 cubic feet per second or lower, and a gauge height of around 94.3 feet or lower, the water conditions will be easily waded and fished. This gauge also measures turbidity. Readings under 20 FNU means the water is clear enough to see the flash of a largemouth as it makes a swipe at your fly.

Lake Conroe

From 1949 to 1957, Texas experienced the worst drought in the history of the state. Farmers and ranchers were hit the hardest, and the number of farmers dropped 29 percent in just seven to eight years. As a result of the drought, Texas began constructing reservoirs along many of the major rivers. Lake Conroe is one of these reservoirs. The impoundment was completed in 1973, and the resulting 22,000-acre lake is now a playground for many pleasure boaters and fishermen in the Houston area.

Fly rodders can find the most action in sheltered backwater coves or at the mouths of feeder creeks. The shallow backwaters are mostly protected from wind and currents, and often contain a variety of plants that filter out the suspended sediment. This allows anglers to use sight fishing techniques. Bass, panfish, carp, gar, and bowfin can all be found in the backwaters and creek inlets of Lake Conroe.

Lake Conroe boasts a healthy population of bowfin. These prehistoric fish can be sight fished from a canoe or kayak, especially during the fall and spring, when the aquatic vegetation either has died or has not yet emerged. Springtime is the best time of the year to pursue bowfin. Spawning male bowfin exhibit gorgeous emerald green caudal and pectoral fins.

Houston-area fly fishing guide Danny Scarborough has perfected the art of angling for these dinosaur-fish in Lake Conroe. Danny paddles into the shallow backwaters and then slowly works the shoreline, watching the edges of the weeds and shallow banks. In order to get on the fast track and learn about fly fishing for bowfin, it is well worth your time to book a trip with Danny Scarborough. Visit his website at houstonflyfishing.com to connect with him and learn something about these amazing prehistoric fish.

What You Will Find

Generally, powerboats use the southern portion of Lake Conroe more frequently (especially on weekends) than the undeveloped northern portion. Much of the shoreline south of FM 1097 is dotted with lake houses, restaurants, and yacht clubs. The southern portion of the lake can be a hostile environment for kayakers and canoers. For this book, emphasis will be placed on the northern portion of the lake, especially in the sheltered coves and inlets of the various feeder creeks.

North of FM 1097, the majority of the land adjacent to the lake is part of Sam Houston National Forest. This area is undeveloped and has tall pines and hardwoods along the shoreline. The U.S. Forest Service manages this land, and it is open to the public for hunting, fishing, and camping.

Several free and fee-based public boat ramps are available along the northern portion of Lake Conroe. The fee-based boat ramps are where many of the bass boats launch from. If you are fishing from a canoe or kayak, feel free to launch from these locations, but the beauty of having a smaller watercraft is that you are not beholden to boat ramps. Therefore, some of the following launching locations are more primitive than a typical boat ramp. In the following descriptions, I'll attempt to mention which put-ins require more of a primitive, "guerrilla-style" launch.

Below: During the white bass run, the Stubblefield area can see plenty of pressure from conventional anglers looking to find schools of white bass. Left: A chunky white bass caught during the annual white bass run. Using a sink-tip line can help fly anglers get their flies down to the lake bottom.

Stubblefield Lake Recreational Area, Huntsville, TX
30.56391, -95.63570
Stubblefield Lake Rd., Huntsville, TX 77340
68 road miles, 1:20 drive time
Optimum gauge height: 200 ft.
Difficulty: Moderate

1 Stubblefield Lake Recreational Area

Stubblefield Lake Recreational Area is a popular campsite that lies adjacent to the northernmost section of Lake Conroe. The campsite lies on the west side of the West Fork San Jacinto River, just as the river empties into Lake Conroe. Stubblefield Bridge, which spans the water at this location, was severely damaged during Hurricane Harvey and was impassable for several years. At the end of 2021, the bridge finally reopened.

A gravel boat launch lies on the eastern shore of the lake (30.56391, -95.63570), in close proximity to the campsite. Launching a kayak or canoe is very convenient from this site.

During the summer, many of the backwater areas around Stubblefield are worthy of exploration. Sometimes they can be difficult to paddle

Didi Ooi landing a big white bass from her Hobie kayak

through because of the abundance of lily pads and other aquatic vegetation, but they are still worth exploring. In the spring, before the shallow backwaters fill with vegetation, you can paddle into these off-channel areas, where you may encounter grass carp, gar, or even bowfin.

In the early spring, white bass can be found in large numbers in the main channel. Paddle north of the Stubblefield bridge to the mouth of the West Fork San Jacinto (30.56870, -95.63618). Use a sink-tip line and a Clouser Minnow with some flash. If the white bass are running, there is a good chance that you will land a couple.

In the summer, there are plenty of gar, and you'll see them breaching on the surface. If you have a watercraft that holds two people, like a canoe, have your buddy at the bow of the boat ready and waiting to make a hasty cast to a breaching gar before it disappears into the murky depths.

Stubblefield Lake Recreational Area is adjacent to the waters of Lake Conroe and offers camping for a fee.

On occasion, alligators can be spotted in this area. It's nothing to be apprehensive about;

just be aware of your surroundings and don't harass them. Respect these ancient reptiles by giving them a wide berth.

Getting There

 From downtown, take I-45 North for approximately 55 miles until exit 102 for FM 1375. Drive around the traffic circle, heading north on East Feeder toward FM 1374 and TX 150. Make a left onto FM 1374. Head under I-45. You'll stay on FM 1374 for 8 miles. Turn left onto Stubblefield Lake Road. Continue down this road for 2.3 miles. You'll eventually come to the Stubblefield Bridge and the gravel boat launch on your right.

Forest Service Rd. 204A, Montgomery, TX 77356
30.51585, -95.61146
Forest Service Rd. 204A, Montgomery, TX 77356
70.3 road miles, 1:20 drive time
Optimum gauge height: 200 ft.
Difficulty: Moderate to Hard

2   The First Jungle

At the end of Forest Service Road 204A, there is a small dirt cul-de-sac. This area is often referred to as the First Jungle or the 204 Stump Flats. If the water level is low (around 199 feet), much of this area can be waded. However, even if the water is low, it is still a good idea to bring a kayak or canoe just in case you want to explore more of the area.

From the end of Forest Service Road 204A, there is a muddy path that leads through a shallow and weedy flat. This will take you to the open and shallow waters that are filled with submerged and decaying stumps. Throughout the year, duck hunters and fishermen use this trail to access the open water. If the water level is low, you may have to drag your kayak through the mud for 200 feet before reaching the water.

Once in the open water, work along the shoreline in either direction, being sure to cast to submerged stumps, points, coves, and weed lines. Make blind casts in a grid pattern to cover as much water as possible. Bulky flies that push a lot of water are often the best bet to prompt a strike from sizeable bucketmouths cruising the stump flats.

A bluebird day on Lake Conroe

Notice the vibrant green fins on this large male bowfin from Lake Conroe. Male bowfin display gorgeous coloring during their spawning season.

Be sure to fish this area in the spring (late February to April) when the bowfin and bass begin their spawning activities. During this time of the year, the absence of aquatic plants and algae will allow you to see fish moving along the weedy flats and possibly give you a chance at sight fishing for bowfin while they sit in the shallows.

When paddling around the backwater flats and marshes, it's important to remember to go slow. Seriously, really slow. Bowfin are masters at hiding in vegetation and mud. When they are in cover, it can be tough to spot them. You will need a keen eye and patience when hunting for these fish.

Cagle Recreation Area lies on the opposite side of the lake (along the eastern shore) from the First Jungle. This is a campsite/day-use area where two well maintained boat ramps can be found (30.51884, -95.59153). Entrance to this area costs $5.00. This is a popular launch for bass boats.

Getting There

Joey Ramirez presents a fat and healthy largemouth bass from Lake Conroe.

From downtown, head to I-45 North. You'll stay on I-45 North for approximately 51 miles until exit 102 for FM 1375. Drive around the traffic circle, heading west on FM 1375. After 5.8 miles, you will drive over Lake Conroe. In approximately 2.5 miles, you will see signs for Stubblefield Lake Recreation Area on your right and Kelly's Pond Campground on your left. Head to Kelly's Pond Campground, Forest Service Rd 204. Head down Forest Service Road 204 as if you were heading to Kelly's Pond Campground. Stay on Forest Service Road 204, passing Kelly's Pond Road on your right. Drive for another 0.8 miles until you see Forest Service Road 204A on your left. It is at the top of a knoll, so go slow, or you might miss it. Follow Forest Service Road 204A until the road splits. Stay to your left (the right-hand road is a private drive). Continue on for another 1.5 miles until you reach the end of the road.

Stow-A-Way Marina, Willis, TX 77318
30.47342, -95.56746
13988 Calvary Rd., Willis, TX 77318
55.6 road miles, 1:00 drive time
Optimum gauge height: 200 ft.
Difficulty: Moderate

3 Stow-A-Way Marina

Stow-A-Way Marina is a privately owned and fee-based boat launch that offers access to a sizable cove that connects to the main body of Lake Conroe. **North Lake Conroe Paddling Company** (northlakeconroepaddlingco.com) also operates out of Stow-A-Way Marina and offers fishing kayak rentals. When you pull into the marina, you'll need to run into the office and pay to launch your small watercraft

Nick Heaverlo and Tanya Xu fish along Hostetter Creek where it enters into Lake Conroe.

($5.00 for canoes and kayaks). Once you pay, there is a paved road that lies across from the office, on the far side of the boat ramp. There is a small sign that reads "Kayak Parking." This is where you'll find North Lake Conroe Paddling Company and where you can park to launch your kayak.

Roughly 0.7 miles north of the marina (on your right, standing at the launch looking toward the water), you'll find two creeks that flow into this large cove.

Gum Branch is a very small creek that flows in

A bowfin angled near the mouth of Hostetter Creek, north of Stow-a-way Marina.

on the northwestern side of the cove (30.48701, -95.56678). In the summer when the water levels on Lake Conroe are low, it's impossible to paddle into Gum Branch. However, around the mouth of this small tributary, there are some clear and shallow mud flats that offer the fly angler sight fishing opportunities for panfish and bass.

On the northeastern side of the cove, you'll find a much larger creek, Hostetter Creek (30.48555, -95.56562). By paddling into

Nick Heaverlo wrangles a bass that he hooked from under the dock behind him.

Hostetter Creek, you'll find backwater areas, coves, and canals, all of which can be fairly clear (assuming the creek is void of rainwater runoff). Paddle slowly and keep a sharp eye for bowfin. You'll find them laying low in weed beds and along the banks, usually adjacent to deeper water. Remember, even if you spook a bowfin from its lie, there's still a chance you can get it to eat. If you spook a bowfin from a weed bed, wait for the fish to stop swimming or slow down. Make a quick and accurate cast in front of the fish, and then strip the fly in front of its nose. In addition to bowfin, you'll also see bass swimming around in the deeper sections of the canals.

While paddling toward the northern end of the large cove, you'll likely notice the overgrown breakwater that was built along the northwestern side of the cove, in close proximity to Gum Branch. This is called Lake Paula (30.48457, -95.56830). Water from Lake Conroe flows freely in and out of Lake Paula through three gaps in the breakwater. If you paddle back into Lake Paula, be sure to make a couple of casts around the boat docks on the western shore. These are good places for bass to hangout.

Getting There

From downtown, head north on I-45. Stay on I-45 North for 46 miles until exit 97 for Calvary Road. Turn left onto Calvary Road. Stay on this road for 4.5 miles. You will see Stow-Away-Marina on the right as you approach the lake.

West Fork of the San Jacinto River (downstream of Lake Conroe) I-45 S, Conroe, TX

30.24518, -95.45663

Interstate 45 S, Conroe, TX 77304

41.4 road miles, 0:45 drive time

USGS Monitor Station: 08068000

Optimum flow: 90 to 100 cfs

Optimum gauge height: 94.3 ft.

Difficulty: Moderate

This is not a picturesque location to begin a fishing excursion. The ceaseless flow of traffic from I-45 will be roaring in your ears while you rig up your gear. However, once you get down to the river and start fishing, it won't take long before you forget the busy modern world buzzing along, high above the water's surface.

What You Will Find

The West Fork flows from the northwest to the southeast (from your right to left, looking at the water from the parking area). There's a chance that bank fishermen will be positioned along the banks angling for catfish, gar, and bass. In the summer, swimmers can also be found downstream of the railroad trestle, in the shallows. If you want to cast a line under the I-45 bridge, be extremely careful while making your way down to the

Just upstream from the confluence of Stewarts Creek, there lies a large pool. All sorts of fish swim in this deep water, including sizeable gar.

water. The concrete fill that is dumped here contains lots of rebar, which is protruding into the air. If you slip and fall on a piece of rebar, you could be in bad shape. To play it safe, start fishing around the railroad bridge, just downstream from I-45.

This section of water can feel big and wide. Gear up accordingly. I've seen some large gar boiling to the surface along this stretch. If you want to go dinosaur hunting, be sure to pack a stout rod, thick leaders, and flies with strong hooks.

4 I-45 Wade (Wading Downstream from I-45 Bridge)

Start fishing in the tailwaters of the long pool just upstream from the railroad bridge (30.24470, -95.45623). The gravel riffles are shallow enough to ford and make it possible to fish the opposite bank. Move downstream, staying on the right side of the river (river right). Walk along the gravel bar below the railroad bridge. The main chute that runs under this bridge should be easily identified. I've had success by standing below the bridge and casting a heavily weighted Woolly Bugger into the main chute and allowing the current to move the fly downstream. Bass will sometimes be hiding in the pockets next to the railroad trestles and debris.

A beastly creek-run bass from the West Fork San Jacinto. Nick Heaverlo used a Clouser Minnow to coax this specimen out from under a logjam.

Move downstream, below the tailout of this chute, before wading back to the bank, river left. Head downstream for roughly 150 yards, and you'll see where the bank along the opposite side of the river (river right) becomes steep and full of weeds, overhanging limbs, and submerged trees. River left is the shallowest side, but the middle of the waterway is only about waist high (at optimum flows). Chances are that you'll see gar moving to the surface to gulp air along this section. The deepest part of the river is adjacent to the far bank (river right) and contains plenty of woody debris.

As you make your way downstream around a large bend, you'll see a graveyard of sunken trees jutting up from the middle of the water. Look downstream, and you'll see where the river meanders back toward the east. Stay on the river left side and move downstream toward the cutbank on your left. You can wade out for several yards adjacent to this cutbank. This section of water is shaded from the afternoon and evening sun, and it can be a good location to catch a bass or two.

In order to move farther downstream, you'll need to cross the river, making your way to the sandy point bar on the right side. Before doing

Stewarts Run is a small creek that enters into the West Fork of the San Jacinto from the north. The confluence of these waterways lies about 0.4 miles downstream of I-45.

so, you must move back upstream to where the water is more easily forded. I've found that the water is shallowest just downstream from the gnarled limbs of the sunken trees. The water will likely be over your waist. Once you've made it across, you can see where Stewarts Creek comes in from the north (30.24872, -95.45343). The deep hole that is found on the upstream side of the confluence of Stewarts Creek and the West Fork has yielded white bass during the spring.

If you are fishless at this point in the wade, consider hiking up Stewarts Creek. There are several small pools just shy of half a mile upstream. Tie on something small (size 10 should be fine) and fish around the uprooted trees and sticks. Largemouth bass in the 8-to-10-inch range can be found in Stewarts Creek, as can longear sunfish.

The next productive section of water along the West Fork San Jac is roughly 500 yards downstream from Stewarts Creek. You'll see a tree leaning out over the water (assuming a flood hasn't washed it away) along the right side of the river. This is the start of a productive chute that lies under the cutbank along this side. Once you fish downstream, the water shallows, and the start of another productive deep chute is formed on the other side of the river, river left.

At this point, you'll almost be one mile away from the parking area. This is a good place to turn around and head back. There's a lot of water to cover and many deep holes and pockets can be worked over again on your way back upstream.

Sand Mining along the West Fork San Jacinto River

The banks of this river are mostly comprised of sandy substrate. These sand deposits are substantial and seen as an important natural resource for the construction industry in the Houston area, which in recent years has been going gangbusters. When viewing aerial images of this waterway, you can see sand mining operations dotting its length, especially from I-45 south to Lake Houston. Like all mining and drilling operations, there's a delicate balance between extracting mineral resources for use in our modern world and preserving the natural one. In the last ten years, there have been important steps taken to preserve the ecology along the West Fork San Jacinto River. House Bill 571, passed in the Texas legislature, sought to curb some of the unregulated sand mining and the illegal discharge of contaminated wastewater into the West Fork. In addition to that, several nonprofit conservation organizations have been involved in buying tracts of land to preserve sections of wilderness along the river. Although it may not be a stereotypical fly fishing river, the West Fork San Jac is important to the Houston area for many reasons, including recreational and industrial.

Getting There

 From downtown, head to I-45 North. You'll stay on I-45 north for approximately 31 miles. Take exit 82 toward River Plantation Drive. You'll cross the West Fork San Jacinto just after exiting the highway, but continue heading north on the service road for approximately one mile. Use the U-turn lane at the first intersection you come to (River Plantation Drive) and pass under the interstate, heading south on the service road. Continue south down this service road for a little more than 0.1 miles and take the first road on your right. Continue southbound for 0.5 miles until the road veers under the I-45 bridge. By driving under the bridge, you'll come to a roundabout on the eastern side of the bridge where you can park.

N. Woodloch Street, Conroe

30.21795, -95.41098

2644 N. Woodloch St., Conroe, TX 77385

36.9 road miles, 0:43 drive time

USGS Monitor Station: 08068000

Optimum flow: 90 to 100 cfs

Optimum gauge height: 94.3 ft.

Difficulty: Easy to Moderate

The small community of Woodloch is incorporated within the city of Conroe. The West Fork of the San Jacinto River can be found northeast of the community. At this location, the river is wide (roughly 50 to 90 feet) and flows over a sandy substrate with numerous sandbars, gravel riffles, and an occasional outcropping of sandstone, which is quite a novelty in this part of the country.

What You Will Find

When you arrive at the end of North Woodloch Street, you will see a large greenspace with a nicely mowed park. You can easily find streetside parking, as there are no houses this close to the floodplain. You can find the river by walking across the field, heading northeast, adjacent to the ditch for stormwater runoff. You will find a little trail that runs through the woods (30.21841, -95.41078) and then parallels

If you enjoy trout fishing, you'll likely feel a pang of nostalgia as you drift your flies through the pocket water along this section of the wade.

the edge of the water. Work your way down the bank to the water. It's easiest to follow the ditch that runs in from the street all the way to the water's edge.

 5 Woodloch Wade (Wading Upstream from the Community of Woodloch)

Once your feet are wet, look upstream. The first feature you'll see is a large sandbar that is roughly 100 yards long. The majority of the water flows down the chute on the river left side (your right, looking upstream). Follow the sandbar upstream to the first riffle that is formed from several large sandstone beds that protrude from the river bottom. These riffles form a knee-deep flat, just upstream. It is best to stay river right as you fish this large flat. A white Clouser Minnow with a little flash works well on the largemouth bass and channel catfish that can be found here during the summer months.

Upstream and downstream from the wing dam, anglers can find some very deep pools. This can be a productive section during the white bass run.

At the top of the flat, you'll see a section of riffles with intermittent pocket water that extends for about 100 yards. This interesting stream feature is present because of the erosion-resistant sandstone beds that exist along the bottom of the river.

For folks who are accustomed to tight-line nymphing for trout, this section of water can be a blast to fish. Deploy heavily weighted flies that mimic dragonfly larvae, especially ones tied on jig hooks, and use nymphing techniques to work through the deep holes, bouncing nymphs through this small section of pocket water. Some of the holes are surprisingly deep and should be fished thoroughly. Fish will have to expend more energy to stay in these riffles and small pools, but during the summer, the oxygen rich water holds plenty of baitfish and insects. Largemouth bass, panfish, and channel catfish have all been angled from this fast-moving pocket water.

At the top of the riffle section, you'll find a deep pool that is hemmed in on either side by more sandstone bedrock. Fish this deep water with

Petrified Wood

While you traverse the riffles along the West Fork, take notice of the pieces of gravel under your wading boots. Much of the material you are walking over is petrified wood, which is technically a fossil. The state of Texas has an abundance of petrified wood. This unique fossil is formed when a fallen tree is quickly buried by sediments that cause the decay of the wood to slow drastically. As the wood decays slowly underground, water percolates into the cell structure of the wood, bringing in minerals like silica. Over time, the silica minerals replace the cell structure of the wood, creating a copy. This copy is as hard as the mineral that replaced the woody cells, which is to say, "rock hard." The petrified wood in East Texas is anywhere from 2.58 to 55.8 millions of years old. Although it's technically a fossil, Texas designated petrified palmwood as the state "stone" in 1969. Feel free to pocket a few pieces as a keepsake. You are legally allowed to take petrified wood as long as it's for personal use. No commercial collecting is allowed.

baitfish patterns. Work your way along the sandstone shelf and gravel bar, river right (your left). Upstream from this pool, there are several fairly deep flats that should also be fished.

The next deep hole is about 500 yards upstream. A worn-out wing dam constructed from sandbags protrudes from the bank on your right (river left). You may see bank fishermen with catfish lines deployed in the deep holes around the wing dam. Fish the eddy that exists downstream by standing below it, on the same side of the river (river left). To fish the head of the pool, you'll need to wade across the thigh-deep water (during optimum flows) to the opposite side (river right) before moving upstream to fish the top of the pool. You'll see two large metal pipes protruding from the middle of the deepest area. This is a good place to lob a couple of casts, especially in the early spring, when white bass and crappie can be found.

Another 400 yards upstream along the bank, river right, you'll see the remnants of an old metal retaining wall. The pool that eddies out behind the retaining wall is worth spending time to fish thoroughly. The pool is deep, so make sure you cover the entire water column by changing the weight of your flies and the speed at which you retrieve them. This is another hot spot for white bass during the run, but it is also a great place to find largemouth or spotted bass too.

Continuing upstream another 230 yards, you'll come to an interesting section of water. The bank on your left (river right) is steep from where

A sounder of wild pigs crosses the West Fork San Jacinto River at Woodloch.

hard packed clay deposits and some sandstone layers have sloughed away into the water. These deposits of rock offer habitat for smaller baitfish. At normal flows, the simplest way upstream is by wading up the middle. Send a couple of casts toward the river right bank, and you may find a spotted bass hunting baitfish in the shallows.

Just upstream from the steep clay shelf (river right), you'll notice a wide gravel riffle section. Continue on farther upstream, and you'll find productive water along the outside edge of the large bend. Fish the deep water along this whole bend. There is a house high on the bank on your right (river left). You can see the house when standing in the water. As you move upstream toward the house, the pool gets deeper. Several different species of fish can be found throughout this section.

At this point, you are roughly 1 mile from Woodloch. This is a good place to turn around and begin fishing back downstream. However, if you proceed upstream another 0.7 miles, you can find another access location from West Essex Drive (30.23232, -95.42738). Please note that if you intend to park a shuttle vehicle at this location, you must approach West Essex Drive from the north (Ehlers Road to Harris Road). The reason is that West Essex Drive has been washed away due to erosion, preventing an approach from the south. Another fun option for further fishing and exploration is to go upstream from West Essex Drive.

Getting There

From downtown, take I-45 north for approximately 30 miles. Take exit 79A for North Freeway Service Road in Shenandoah. Continue on the service road until the intersection with TX 242. Make a right onto TX 242 East. Stay on TX 242 for just over 2.5 miles. Make a left onto Needham Road. Stay on this road for just over 0.5 miles. Make a right onto South Woodloch Street. Take South Woodloch Street through the neighborhood, all the way to the end, where the street veers to the left and joins with North Woodloch Street. You can park anywhere along the shoulder of the road.

Further Exploration

If you follow the flow of the West Fork San Jacinto River downstream, it begins to slow as it enters into the impoundment of Lake Houston, adjacent to the

Hurricane Harvey and the West Fork San Jac

On August 28, 2017, as Hurricane Harvey inundated the area with unprecedented amounts of rain, the water level in Lake Conroe began to rise drastically. According to Alex Stuckey, writing for the *Houston Chronicle*, the San Jacinto River Authority was faced with an ultimatum: keep the flood gates closed and risk the possibility of a catastrophic dam failure, or open the flood gates, allowing the waters of the West Fork to rush downstream at flow rates rivaling that of Niagara Falls. The San Jacinto River Authority opted for the latter. The West Fork gushed downstream at 79,100 cfs at its peak flow, causing major damage to residences along the river in the towns of Conroe, Kingwood, and many smaller communities along the river, like Woodloch. There are several places along this waterway where the infrastructure that once existed has succumbed to the unpredictable whims of Mother Nature. When driving along the banks of the West Fork, it's possible you'll see a "Road Closed" sign and watch the road disappear over an eroded bank. These areas are testaments to the power of flowing water.

community of Kings River Village, which lies on the southern shore of the West Fork. A little park known as Lake View Park can be found in this neighborhood (30.02245, -95.16823). This location can be used as a site to guerrilla-launch your paddlecraft. From here, you can explore the islands of the impounded waters of the West Fork San Jacinto. Carp, gar, and the occasional largemouth bass can be found in the secluded waters. From Lake View Park, simply paddle across the open water to the islands and backwater channels. Look for breaching gar or make blind casts to structure to find bass. Keep an eye out for gators.

 B52 Brewing

b52brewing.com

B52 Brewing is located in Conroe, Texas, on the south side of Lake Conroe (12470 Milroy Ln., Conroe, TX 77304). This is a perfect place to grab a beer after a day of fishing for bass or bowfin on Lake Conroe. The taproom is open Wednesday to Sunday. B52 Brewing specializes in unique styles and flavors of beer. It creates everything from hazy milkshake brews to more "generic" pilsners and lagers. There is a huge outdoor seating area, so you can still enjoy a beer even if you smell like fish and lake water. Dogs and kids are welcome. There is plenty of room for little ones to run around. One or two food trucks are usually set up to provide some solid table fare. This is definitely a place you'll want to check out after getting off the water.

B52 has a large taproom where you can purchase drafts or cans to take home with you.

Chapter 6

EAST FORK SAN JACINTO RIVER

*Ecologically Significant River and Stream Segment,
wild and secluded wades, potential for backcountry-
style excursions in Sam Houston National Forest,
diverse populations of panfish, black bass, wildlife
viewing. Access Points: 8*

THE EAST FORK OF THE SAN JACINTO RIVER BEGINS ITS
southern journey 66 miles north of downtown Houston. The waters
of the East Fork San Jac sprout from various springs around the small
community of Dodge, located in eastern Walker County. For many
miles, the upper reaches of the East Fork twist through the Sam Houston
National Forest. Just before its confluence with the West Fork San Jacinto
at Lake Houston, the river traverses the eastern border of Lake Houston
Wilderness Park.

Referring to the East Fork San Jacinto as a "river"
might be a bit too gracious. For much of its length, the
water is usually too skinny to float any watercraft much

*Longear sunfish are some
of the most beautiful
panfish in North America.*

bigger than a canoe without needing to portage frequently. With that being said, this small waterway is great for wade fishing and can still be floated in shortened intervals.

Just like most Pineywoods streams, the water clarity is poor compared to the gin-clear Texas Hill Country streams, but the volume of fish and the unique junglelike ecosystem adjacent to the water more than make up for this potential shortfall. The entire length of the East Fork San Jacinto is designated an Ecologically Significant River and Stream Segment (ESRSS) by the state. At least six different species of sporting panfish call the East Fork home, along with spotted bass, largemouth bass, and crappie. Channel catfish also inhabit the deep pools and cutbanks and can often be angled from among the submerged logs. Closer to Lake Houston, schools of yellow and white bass can be found during their annual run upstream.

USGS Stream Gauges along the East Fork San Jacinto River

Check the stream gauge along the East Fork San Jacinto near Cleveland (gauge number: 08070000). Optimum flows for this section will be around 29 to 35 cubic feet per second and a gauge height of 4 to 5 feet. A low gauge reading and less flow means better water visibility. For additional data, there is a second gauge further downstream at FM 1485 (08070200), north of Lake Houston. When looking at this gauge, low flows are around 30 cfs and a gauge height of 46 feet. There is also a turbidity gauge at this monitor site. Low turbidity readings equate to higher visibility. A turbidity rating of less than 30 should be considered clear, at least by East Texas standards.

Sam Houston National Forest, Intersection of Shaw Rd and FM 945

30.422650, -95.136753

Intersection of Shaw Rd. and FM 945, Cleveland, TX 77328

53 road miles, 1:00 drive time

USGS Monitor Station: 08070000

Optimum flow: 29 to 35 cfs

Optimum gauge height: 4.3 to 5 ft.

Difficulty: Hard

The early morning sun pokes through the Pineywoods foliage as Jose Mata casts into the East Fork San Jacinto River.

A coyote peers through the underbrush along the East Fork San Jacinto River. Below:
Whitetail deer are a common sight along many of the waterways in the Pineywoods.

If you are looking for a truly remote section of water that has all the characteristics of a wilderness fishing adventure, then this section of the East Fork San Jacinto River is it. The East Fork flows for miles through the densely forested bottomlands of Sam Houston National Forest. This land is open to the public for many outdoor recreational activities, including camping and hunting (during certain months).

While fishing this section of water, it's entirely possible to spend days (and nights) without seeing another person. Because this wade is very secluded, remember to use your best judgement when fishing here. This is a genuine wilderness and should be treated as such. You likely will not have cell phone services while fishing this reach. If this is your first time wading this section of water, it's probably best to have a friend accompany you. With that being said, the unbridled seclusion that is felt while exploring the East Fork within Sam Houston National Forest is worth every bit of effort it takes to fish it.

Be sure to keep an eye out for the multitude of wild animals that live in the national forest. There are several species of snakes, whitetail deer, wild pigs, river otters, coyotes, and wood ducks. Also, there's a good chance you'll hear the telltale hooting of a barred owl: *"Who cooks for you? Who cooks for you-all?!"*

What You Will Find

After parking along the gravel pull-off at Shaw Road, you'll want to cross FM 945 and walk along the grass shoulder of the road. This is a blind curve for motorists, so be very careful and stay well off the road. The Lone Star Hiking Trail crosses FM 945 approximately 200 yards west of this parking area. Walk along the shoulder of the road until you come to the Lone Star Hiking Trail. Take the hiking trail on the right side of the road. It will head in a northeastward direction. Enjoy the 0.6-mile hike through the Pineywoods until you come to a footbridge that spans the East Fork San Jacinto River (30.42960, -95.13481).

 Lone Star Hiking Trail (LSHT) **Wade** (Wading Upstream from the LSHT Footbridge)

Carefully scramble down the steep bank under the footbridge to the edge of the water. Before entering the water from the left bank (river right), take a look upstream. There are several logjams that give way to deeper pools or chutes. A cast or two in the vicinity of these logjams often yields a longear sunfish or channel catfish.

Jose Mata makes a backhand cast into the East Fork San Jacinto River, upstream from Lone Star Hiking Trail bridge.

While moving upstream, stay to your right (river left) as you approach the first large pool. Move upstream slowly—you don't want to alert the resident fish to your approach. Deploy roll casts or bow-and-arrow casts to get the fly to the steep bank opposite your position.

The first pool that is found along the bend in the stream is quite deep, so be sure to thoroughly fish the head- and tailwaters. Swinging wet flies through the swift current at the head of the pool will often elicit a strike from a spotted bass. If you aren't having any luck while fishing this pool, try adding some weight to your flies and fishing them along the bottom of the streambed.

In order to head upstream from this large pool, it is easiest to backtrack slightly and cut overland across the bank on your right (river left). Once you make it over the bank, you will see what appears to be a tributary flowing in on the right (river left). This is actually an outflow from a backwater pool that peels away from the main channel farther upstream. Fish the deeper pockets that exist where these two swift tailwaters converge.

Jose Mata proudly displays a gorgeous spotted bass from the waters of the East Fork San Jacinto River. In the upper reaches of the East Fork, the fish tend to be smaller, but they are full of fight. Bring your 2-weight or 3-weight to get the most out of this stretch of water.

Stick to the channel on your left, river right. Take note of the ram-rod-straight loblolly pine trees that are adjacent to the banks. Make a couple of casts to the gnarled roots of the large loblolly a little farther upstream.

You'll arrive at the location where the previously mentioned backwater channel diverts away from the main riverbed. Scramble over the logs and blowdown in order to make a couple of casts into this backwater. By using a small flashy wet-fly, you'll likely entice a couple of bluegills or longears in this off-channel area. In another couple of decades, this backwater area will likely become an oxbow, while most of the waterflow will pass by, unabated, down the main channel. Sediments will build at the head of the backwater inlet and seal it off from the main current.

The next section of water (approximately 200 yards from the trail) contains a lot of structure in the form of logs and woody debris. This is usually a fishy section, so take your time. As you work upstream, you'll see another large pool along the next bend. This pool is too deep to wade, so exit the water on your left, river right, and head up the steep

embankment. As you walk along the high bank upstream, you'll see where two tailwaters converge into another large pool. Once again, this is where the waters of the East Fork have split, farther upstream, and reconvene at the head of this pool.

There is a lot of interesting water to cover in this short interval. If this is your first time here, consider calling it a day. However, it is worth noting that the East Fork can be fished for many more miles upstream. This waterway is often bordered, or entirely

Channel catfish can be a lively consolation prize when fishing the East Fork San Jacinto River.

Hmm ... Am I Lost?

Navigating the thickly forested landscape of the Pineywoods can be tricky. The area is devoid of topographic features like mountains or ravines, and on top of that, the incredibly dense foliage can easily become disorienting. Just remember that as long as you keep the flowing waters of the East Fork in your sights, you can orient your direction. The East Fork flows from the north to the south. If you're facing downstream, you're looking toward the Gulf. If you wander off the Lone Star Hiking Trail and can't find it again, don't panic. Just remember to walk downstream, *with* the flow of the East Fork, and you'll eventually come back to the footbridge. If you become disoriented while exploring downstream from the Lone Star Hiking Trail, keep moving *with* the flow of the water, and you'll eventually reach FM 945.

Before hitting the water, it may be prudent to stop in at the Sam Houston National Forest Ranger Station (394 FM 1375, New Waverly, TX 77358). Here you can purchase a map of the national forest that shows the forest service roads, hiking trails, and most importantly the creeks. Having this map can open up vast opportunities to strike out and explore safely.

surrounded, by the Sam Houston National Forest, which offers many more miles of opportunities for creek exploration.

If you are done fishing for the day, you can cut overland back to the Lone Star Hiking Trail. Walk up the steep bank (river right) and follow the flow of the East Fork downstream to where it meets the Lone Star Hiking Trail again. When you come to the trail, head to the right (southwest) back to FM 945.

Getting There

 From downtown, take I-69/US 59 north toward Cleveland, TX. As you approach Cleveland, stay on the interstate heading toward North Cleveland. Take the exit toward FM 2025/Coldspring. Make a left onto FM 2025 North, also known as Old Cold Spring Road. Continue on for 5.4 miles until the junction of FM 945 North. Make a left onto FM 945. There will be a small Valero gas station on your left. Continue on FM 945 North; you will drive over the East Fork San Jacinto, but continue on for 1.3 miles. Shaw Road will be on your left, and you'll see a small gravel pull-off. Park here.

Low Water Bridge Road, Cleveland
30.35538, -95.10852
Low Water Bridge Rd., Cleveland, TX 77328
49 road miles, 0:55 drive time
USGS Monitor Station: 08070000
Optimum flow: 26 to 35 cfs
Optimum gauge height: 4.3 to 5 ft.
Difficulty: Hard

On any hot summer day, you'll find locals swimming here. There could also be a couple of bank fishermen soaking bait for catfish under the Low Water Bridge. That's okay; there's plenty to explore, and it's easy to find undisturbed water. Many gravel bars are present at this location. They form pools, meanders, and chutes that offer plenty of fish habitat. There are many deep pools upstream. Be sure your cell phone and wallet are out of your pockets and stored in a high and dry compartment in your backpack or sling pack.

A view from Low Water Bridge Road, looking upstream along the East Fork San Jacinto River

What You Will Find

There is plenty of parking on either side of the Low Water Bridge Road (County Road 388). If there are other vehicles parked along the road, it's a good bet you'll find folks swimming or picnicking along the gravel bar just upstream from the parking area. Watch your step as you head down the bank toward the water. The county has dumped concrete, fill and the chunks of rubble can be very slick if the bottom of your shoes are wet.

7 Low Water Bridge (Wading Upstream from the Low Water Bridge)
"Hey buddy! That's where I caught the biggest bass of my life!" a local youngster hollered to me while he splashed in the waters of the East Fork. He was referring to the deep hole upstream of the Low Water Bridge. This pool sees plenty of fishing pressure, but it is still worth lobbing a couple of casts into. If the big bass eludes you, like it has me, you'll still likely find a longear sunfish or bluegill that's willing to chase your fly.

After fishing under the bridge, retrace your steps and head back up the sandy bank, walking along the shoulder of the road. It is easier to move upstream along the road than it is tripping through the concrete fill and numerous sunken logs upstream of the bridge. Take one of the

Travis Richards admires a native spotted bass. These fish can be found in chutes, logjams, and undercut banks.

Travis Richards fishes along an undercut bank.

well-defined trails from the parking area down to the gravel bars. Fish the first cutbank thoroughly before heading upstream to the large pool. Stand on the gravel bar next to the tailwaters of the pool. The opposite bank is tall and sheer. Make several reaching casts to the steep bank. Be ready for a channel cat to eat your fly on the drop.

Stay to your right, river left, as you move upstream. The high cutbank, river right, is a good place to target with several casts, although casting may be difficult due to the overhanding tree limbs. This pool will eventually shallow as you come to its head. Fish around the headwaters of this pool and the tailwaters of the next before moving upstream. Once you wade through the next pool, you'll need to cross to the right side (river left), where you'll find a gravel point bar.

Once you are standing on the gravel bar, you should see a metal staircase, bench, and fence along the top of the high cutbank opposite of you. This is private land. Do not trespass. The pool that is directly in front of you is 4 to 5 feet deep. Fish along the many submerged logs that lie in this section of water.

In order to continue upstream, you'll need to find the shallow spit of sand that runs parallel with the opposite cutbank. This sandbar can be accessed by crossing just downstream of the metal staircase. The water will be about waist deep at low flows, so if you're up to your chest in water, you missed the crossing. Try again. Once you make it to the shallow sandbar, stay river right and move upstream along the river bend.

Once around the bend, you'll see a wide and flat gravel bar on your left (river right). It is highly recommended that you do not walk on this gravel bar. It is best to stay within the waters of the East Fork and not climb out of the water and onto either bank while working through this stretch of water. Landowners through this section do not take kindly to trespassers. Although not openly hostile to wading fishermen (they recognize that we have a right to the water), past conversations have revealed, in no uncertain terms, that anglers had better stay in the waters of the East Fork and not even think about stepping onto the dry ground along the left-hand gravel bar (river right.)

With that being said, the next 100 yards of water is a fun section to fish. A swift current flows along the outside edge of the gravel bar, creating a sinuous channel. Slowly creep to the edge of the water so you don't alert the fish to your approach. Use weighted beadhead nymphs on jig hooks, casting them upstream into the current and letting them bounce along the gravel bottom. When you see your fly line stop its downstream

drift, set the hook. The water seems a bit too skinny to hold monster bass, but there are usually a few smaller spotted bass along this section.

This young alligator snapping turtle was discovered by Travis Richards while fishing the East Fork San Jacinto. This species of snapping turtle is the largest freshwater turtle in North America, sometimes exceeding 200 pounds.

Upstream another 200 yards, you'll find a large, slow-moving, and muddy pool. This section of water is what gives this wade it's "Hard" rating. The shallowest route appears to be on your left (river right), but it's messy and full of muck. As you move

This type of turtle spends most of its time on the bottom of lakes or rivers, where it remains motionless with its mouth wide open. A small, pink, worm-like tip on the snapper's tongue lures fish within striking distance of the turtle's powerful jaws. East Texas is about the extent of its western range.

along the pool, be careful of the logs and sticks half-buried in the mud. These can snag on your pant legs or boots and send you sprawling. As you make your way through this pool, you'll eventually see a gravel bar on your left. You're in the homestretch.

At the time of this writing, a massive fallen tree spanned the length of the East Fork at this gravel bar. By standing atop the fallen tree, it is possible to get a good view upstream of the chutes and pools that form numerous gravel bars.

Another 120 yards upstream lies a second large pool. This pool is over 5 feet deep. At the tailwaters of this large pool, you'll be a little over half a mile from the parking area at the Low Water Bridge.

At optimum flows, the East Fork meanders around gravel bars and cut banks.

In addition to wading upstream from the Low Water Bridge, there are opportunities to explore more downstream. If you do, you'll need a paddlecraft. If you decide to head downstream, just know that you'll be doing a lot of dragging and portaging. It is roughly 2 miles south to the West Southline Street bridge (TX 105 Business) (30.33636 -95.10370). This might not seem like a long way, but remember to factor in the amount of time and effort portaging through this reach. Rest assured that it will be a full day's adventure. For the first 600 yards downstream, the water flows in a riffle/pool sequence, after which it becomes a more sluggish and meandering stretch of water. I have not paddled this entire 2-mile stretch, but I've ventured downstream for about 0.6 miles and paddled back up. I saw some sizeable longnose gar and managed to hook a channel catfish on a streamer pattern.

Getting There

From downtown, head north on I-69/US 59 toward Cleveland. After 43.5 miles, take the exit for FM 2025/Coldspring. Take the exit ramp up to the stop sign. Make a left onto Belcher Street/Old Cold

Spring Road, driving over I-69/US 59. Continue on Old Cold Spring Road. You'll see a Love's Truck Stop on your left. Just past the truck stop, make the next left. This is Low Water Bridge Road, also called CR 388. Take Low Water Bridge Road for one mile. Just after you cross the East Fork San Jacinto, you'll see parking areas on either side of the road.

TX 105, Cleveland

30.31420, -95.11342

State Highway TX 105, Cleveland, TX 77327

46 road miles, 0:50 drive time

USGS Monitor Station: 08070000

Optimum flow: 26 to 35 cfs

Optimum gauge height: 4.3 to 5 ft.

Difficulty: Moderate to Hard

This is a quick wade downstream from the State Highway TX 105 bypass bridge. Along this 0.5 mile stretch, you can find bass, channel catfish, panfish, and crappie. Most of the water downstream from the bridge is easily waded, although there are some deep holes, so watch your step.

Upstream from the bridge you will see a long, slow-moving pool full of great structure in the form of submerged timber. It is definitely worth making a couple of casts into this large pool, upstream of the bridge. If you wish to continue farther upstream, you'll likely need a paddlecraft.

What You Will Find

On the northern side of the State Highway TX 105 bypass bridge, there is room to park on the grassy shoulder, well off the road. In addition to that, there is an expanded paved shoulder on the opposite side of the river (west side). Once you park, walk under the bridge. Mind your footing, as there is plenty of slick mud.

 One-Oh-Five Wade (Wading Downstream from the TX 105 bypass bridge)

Downstream from the bridge, for about 300 yards, the East Fork San Jacinto creates eddies and side pools that usually hold panfish and the occasional crappie. These eddies are usually fringed by vegetation that house lots of terrestrial insects like grasshoppers and katydid leaf bugs.

Riggs Cemetery

As you head north on I-69/US 59, about 3 miles south of Cleveland, you'll cross the East Fork of the San Jacinto River. After crossing the river, look for a small grove of trees in the median strip of the highway. This is Riggs Cemetery. Yes, a cemetery, smack-dab in the middle of the interstate. When the Texas Highway

Department wanted to expand the original US 59 from two lanes to four, it approached the Riggs family, who live in Cleveland, to see whether they would be open to the idea of moving the graves. The Riggs family was not interested. So there the cemetery remains, resting peacefully under a small grove of trees while the highway traffic buzzes back and forth ceaselessly. In 2012, the cemetery was designated a Historic Texas Cemetery by the Texas Historic Commission. One of the oldest graves appears to be that of Sergeant Thomas Riggs (1837–1915), a Civil War veteran who served the Union Army in the 2nd Maryland Infantry, Potomac Home Brigade.

With that in mind, lob your flies (size 10 works well) as close to the bank as possible to simulate a bug dropping into the water.

As you move downstream, you'll see a small unnamed tributary entering into the East Fork from the west, river right. The next meander downstream from this confluence should produce a longear or two.

Next you will come to a tranquil flat hemmed in on either side by low muddy banks covered in aquatic vegetation. This section can be a little tricky to fish. If you wade into the water, you'll likely spook many of the resident fish, but fishing from the bank offers its own set of challenges due to the overhanging trees that interfere with your backcast. With that in mind, it's recommended that you climb out of the water on your right and fish from the bank. Use roll casts to avoid the overhanging trees.

At the end of this flat, the water flows into a deep pool. Stick close to the river right bank because the water on the opposite side is well over 4 feet deep. Take your time fishing this pool all the way down to the next bend. Move slowly to minimize your chances of spooking the fish. Pay special attention to the logs that are stacked up against the outside bend of the far cutbank. This is a good place to catch a bass. In addition to the

Nick Heaverlo fishes near submerged logs, downstream from the TX 105 bridge.

bass, there are fat-slab longear sunfish that reside in this pool.

Around the next bend, there are two surprisingly deep pockets that lie under a sycamore tree on the left bank. If you're fishing this in the summer, you may see longear beds in the shallows. Lob a wet fly into both of these small but deep holes and see what you get.

A little over 100 yards downstream, you will come to a very deep and wide pool. The water is hemmed in on either side by steep and overgrown banks. The land adjacent to the water is privately owned. The wade ends here, but before turning around, be sure to fish the head of the pool and the backwater area that exists adjacent to the left bank. It's approximately 0.5 miles back to the State Highway TX 105 bypass bridge.

Getting There

From downtown, head north on I-69/US 59 toward Cleveland. After 41 miles, look for the exit TX 573/Washington Avenue. After exiting the highway, take your first right onto South Travis Avenue, crossing the railroad tracks. The road will bear to the left, heading north. Make

Panfish are prevalent through this stretch of river.

the next right onto CR 319/Wells Road. Stay on Wells Road for 0.7 miles until a T-intersection. Make a right onto FM 1010/ Plum Grove Road. Stay on FM 1010/Plum Grove Road for 0.8 miles until State Highway TX 105. This is a newly built bypass highway. Turn right onto State Highway TX 105 West. Stay on TX 105 West, crossing over I-69/US 59. Exit TX 105 immediately after crossing the interstate. Drive down the exit ramp, passing the intersection for US 59 southbound, and head back up the ramp as if to merge back onto TX 105. Before getting back on the highway, pull off on the right-side shoulder. You can access the water from here by walking down under the bridge. As mentioned before, there is additional parking on the opposite side of the river, along the expanded shoulder (30.31668, -95.11803).

Further Exploration

Some local anglers hit the East Fork San Jacinto farther downstream, where FM 1485 crosses the East Fork, east of the Lake Houston Wilderness Park (30.14497, -95.12508). This area is easy to access and sees fishing pressure during the white bass run. However, I can't say that I fully endorse this area as an access point. Numerous stray dogs mill around here, and some sketchy activities have been observed. If you'd like to access the lower reaches of the East Fork, I recommend doing so within the Lake Houston Wilderness Park. Take the hiking trails through the park for 2 miles in order to reach the East Fork via the Forest Trail to the North River Trail (30.13278, -95.12969).

Lastly, there is a section of the East Fork San Jacinto River that is really more akin to paddling a lake than a river, which makes sense because this area is just north of Lake Houston. BJ's Marina (27907 Calvin Rd., Huffman, TX 77336) sits on the eastern shore of the East Fork San Jac (30.05918, -95.13176) and charges a $5.00 fee to launch a watercraft. Fishing can be pretty tough along this stretch of the East Fork, but there are many weedy backwater pools that are shallow and have the potential of holding sport fish. Be aware of the powerboats that run up and down the main river channel. There's also a chance of seeing an alligator while you paddle around this section of water.

Channel catfish offer an exciting fight on lightweight fly rods.

The taproom at DECA Beer Company is family friendly.

DECA Beer Company

decabeer.com

DECA Beer Company (25428 TX 494 Loop Suite G, Porter, TX 77365) is conveniently located near I-69/US 59. This location makes it a great place to stop if you have finished exploring the East Fork and are driving back to Houston on Eastex Freeway. This owner/operator brewery was started by four friends, all of whom were homebrewers. Each one specialized in their own unique style of beer. When they all decided to put their homebrewing skills together, DECA was born. The taproom has nice big windows allowing in lots of light. There is outdoor seating at the front of the building under the shade of tents. Dogs and kids are welcome.

The Old Three Hundred

In the early nineteenth century, American immigrants from various Southern states began settling in the regions adjacent to the East Fork. Moses Austin, the father of Texas founder Stephen F. Austin, began orchestrating a mass migration of Americans to East Texas in 1820, after obtaining a grant from the Spanish government in San Antonio. This migration consisted of 300 families of farmers, now referred to as the Old Three Hundred. The lands between the Colorado River to the west and the East Fork San Jacinto to the east were the boundaries for the grant.

Chapter 7

PEACH CREEK AND CANEY CREEK

Picturesque wades, spotted and largemouth bass, spring runs of temperate bass, solitude in lower and upper reaches, camping opportunities in Lake Houston Wilderness Park. Access Points: 6

TWO CREEKS WILL BE ADDRESSED IN THIS CHAPTER, PEACH Creek and Caney Creek. Peach Creek is a scenic stream that is wadeable for its entire length, while Caney Creek is a slightly larger, more muddled stream. Peach Creek eventually flows into the larger Caney Creek, the confluence occurring along the western edge of the Lake Houston Wilderness Park, a heavily wooded preserve of 4,787 acres. For the purposes of this chapter, Peach Creek will receive most of the attention, although Caney Creek will also be described briefly.

Adventurous anglers who want to explore more of Caney Creek can start with the access points listed in the back of the book, but I opted not to delve into Caney Creek because its fishing opportunities can

A beautiful white bass from below the confluence of Peach Creek and Caney Creek

sometimes be unpredictable. On top of that, the lower reaches of Caney Creek pass through unconsolidated loamy soils, which decrease visibility considerably. Overall, this creek does hold fish, but anglers will find more scenic fishing opportunities in its major tributary, Peach Creek.

Peach Creek is one of the most highly prized waterways for small-stream-loving Houston fly fishers. The spring-fed waters of Peach Creek begin in San Jacinto County, just outside of the small Texas community of Old Waverly. This creek runs south for about 33 miles through sections of pine timber and farmlands. It acts as the boundary between the counties of Montgomery and San Jacinto.

All along its southward run, it picks up contributing flows from tributaries like Gum Branch, Jayhawker Creek, and Lawrence Creek. It's not until the lower reaches of Peach Creek where the waters eventually flow adjacent to land that's accessible by the general public. Peach Creek forms part of the western boundary of Lake Houston Wilderness Park.

The streambed of Peach Creek is mostly composed of sandy soils. The white sands pile up along the point bars and islands, offering great places to stop and admire nature. During optimum conditions, the waters of Peach Creek are surprisingly clear for a southeastern Texas waterway. The water usually carries a slight tannic tinge, but that's expected for a stream flowing through the Pineywoods.

When fishing this creek, remember your small-stream strategies. These fish can easily spot you, so stay hidden as much as possible. Be mindful of your shadow and minimize your movements, especially during times of low flows, when the water is the clearest.

USGS Stream Gauges along Peach Creek and Caney Creek

Because the substrate of Peach Creek is mostly sand, the water clarity can be quite good. However, clarity is poor during times of high flows, and it's best to wait for flows to subside before wetting a line. Check the stream gauge on Peach Creek just west of the town of Splendora (gauge number: 08071000). Flows around 30 cubic feet per second or lower and a gauge height of around 5 feet are often good indicators that the water is low and clear. With that being said, I've still had great days on Peach just after a rain when the flows were around 45 cfs and gauge height was 5.5 feet. As with most things related to fishing, performance of a waterway is subject to many different factors.

If you are checking out Caney Creek, look at the stream gauge near Splendora, Texas (08070500). An optimum discharge rate for Caney Creek is around 20 to 30 cfs and a gauge height of 3 feet. If you plan on fishing the lower reaches of Caney Creek, near its confluence with Peach Creek, it's prudent to check the gauge height of Lake Houston (08072000) as well.

Woodbranch Drive, New Caney

30.18245, -95.18428

86 Woodbranch Dr., New Caney TX 77357

35.2 road miles, 0:42 drive time

USGS Monitor Station: 08071000

Optimum flow: 20 to 30 cfs

Optimum gauge height: 4.5 to 5 ft.

Difficulty: Moderate

There isn't much development happening along the banks here, which offers a feeling of tranquility. The decommissioned Woodbranch Bridge, a.k.a. "Bridge to Nowhere," which spans Peach Creek, was originally built to provide access to a planned neighborhood. However, due to the unruly flooding that Peach Creek is subject to, the neighborhood never came to fruition. Now the lonely Bridge to Nowhere stands as a gateway to this gorgeous, undeveloped reach.

What You Will Find

Take a walk onto the abandoned bridge and watch as the waters of Peach Creek flow under you. You may see folks swimming in the summer. The mixture of hardwoods and pines make a thick canopy of foliage that keeps the waters of Peach Creek cool, even during the dog days of summer. There are plenty of sandbars, riffles, flats, and calm pools upstream from the bridge. Numerous downed trees and logjams create great habitat for spotted bass and longear sunfish. Most of the fish along this section of Peach Creek are small, so consider sizing down your rod

The Peach Creek swimming hole is a popular spot during the summer months.

(1-to-3-weight rods) and fishing with smaller flies (sizes 10 to 12).

 9 **The Bridge to Nowhere**
(Wading Upstream from the Bridge)

Let's start on the upstream side of the bridge. There is a nice chute that runs along the steep bank (river right) beginning upstream of the bridge. Dead drift a small bead head Woolly Bugger or crawfish pattern through this section.

Approximately 400 yards upstream, you'll come to a riffle. Just upstream of this riffle, you'll find a deep section. Spend some time casting to both banks and any woody debris that is in the pool. As you move upstream, it's best to stay closer to the bank on your left (river right). The pool is deeper along the opposite bank.

Another 130 yards upstream (0.3 river miles), the creek makes a slight bend to the east. Along the outside cutbank, you will find a deep hole that is usually full of sunken logs. This is great habitat for spotted bass. Make sure you fish the whole water column. In the summer months, try poppers and mouse patterns on the surface or use a heavy fly and allow it

Tanya Xu fishes along Peach Creek with the abandoned Bridge to Nowhere looming in the background. Inset: Tanya Xu presents a nice spotted bass.

to sink to the bottom. Decent-sized Peach Creek bass have been hooked (and some missed) along this reach, so be sure to fish it well.

Around 0.5 river miles, you'll come to a wide, deep hole. The banks on either side are steep. Its easiest to wade right up the middle, but do so slowly so as not to alert the fish to your presence. The bank on your left (river right) will have numerous sunken logs jutting out of the depths.

Nick Heaverlo works a popper around a submerged tree.

Make targeted casts to the root balls of the sunken trees and allow your fly to sink. Remember to keep a little tension on the line while the fly is sinking; that way, if a fish eats the hook on the drop, you can feel the take.

In the next hole upstream, there's a good chance that you'll find people swimming or swinging off a large rope swing. If there are no sounds of laughter, splashing, or happy screams, you likely have the hole all to yourself. This is another deep pool that should be fished thoroughly. If you don't have any luck in this lower pool, move upstream, around the large steel retaining wall (river right), and fish the log-filled chute. You

may have to scramble around some blowdown by crossing through the current and walking along the gravel bar on your right (river left).

Work upstream, around the next bend, for about 180 yards. Eventually, you'll come to another deep hole. Stay close to the bank on your right (river left) as you cast toward the opposite bank. This hole is fairly deep, and the water could be up to your waist. There are a couple of deep eddies that swirl around adjacent to the hard clay banks and logjams.

While you fish these eddies, watch the surface of the water and take notes of where the main current carries most of the leaves, bubbles, and debris. These "bubble trails" are great places to cast either a dry fly or wet fly and allow the current to carry your fly downstream. Fish will often wait under these bubble trails for a tasty morsel to come drifting by.

Another 100 yards upstream, you'll notice a small pipe on your right (river left) that intermittently discharges water into Peach Creek. This is a treated wastewater outlet from the community of Patton Village, east of Peach Creek.

From this point, it is another 0.6 miles until the I-69/US 59 overpass. This is a beautiful stretch of water that can yield some great fishing opportunities. The next big hole you'll encounter is adjacent to a hard-packed clay bank on your left (river right). Tackle this from either side of the creek. Sometimes, I prefer to stand on the clay ledge and cast parallel with the bank, but be sure to move back downstream, away from the deepest hole, before jumping in the water and heading to the head of the pool.

As you move upstream, there are some great areas of slack water on either side of the creek that should be fished, but the next really productive section is another 320 yards upstream. Tackling these pools and deep cutbanks is entirely up to you. The clay shelves that exist adjacent to the holes are great places to cast from, and they can offer the best natural drift for your fly. However, you'll eventually need to be on the opposite side of the creek, river left, if you wish to continue on. This fantastic reach stretches for about 230 yards until the muddy waters of a small tributary, Mare Branch, join with Peach Creek on your left (river right).

It's another 377 yards upstream to where Peach Creek flows under I-69/US 59. You are approximately 1.6 miles from your vehicle. That's a solid day of creek stompin'.

Getting There

From downtown, head north on I-69/US 59 toward New Caney. Exit the interstate at the TX 242 and head north on the feeder road for 1.5 miles. Make a right onto Woodbranch Drive. You'll enter into the small community of Woodbranch Village. Stay right at the "Y" and continue on Woodbranch Drive for 0.7 miles. Woodbranch Drive turns into a skinny paved road at the Magnolia Road intersection, but continue straight along Woodbranch. You'll see a large water tower on your right, and you'll eventually come to several roadblocks and a gravel turnabout. Park somewhere along the turnabout. The Bridge to Nowhere can be found just down the road. Access the water by following the faint trails on either side of the bridge.

Roman Forest Boulevard, New Caney
30.17288, -95.17702
1715 Roman Forest Blvd., New Caney, TX 77357
35 road miles, 0:40 drive time
USGS Monitor Station: 08071000
Optimum flow: 20 to 30 cfs
Optimum gauge height: 4.5 to 5 ft.
Difficulty: Moderate

The Roman Forest Park offers easy access to Peach Creek. The creek flows behind private residences on the western side of the stream and large swaths of privately held timberland on the eastern side. Remember to respect all private property and stay within the bounds of Peach Creek's streambed. In this area, there are portions of the creek that are too shallow to fish, especially during low flows, but there are some deep holes that can yield fish. During the summer months, it's likely that you'll run into people splashing around in the cool waters. To avoid the crowds, try fishing this section in the mornings, or when the kids have returned to school.

What You Will Find

The Roman Forest Park has a community park and swimming pool. It also has public restrooms attached to the rear of Burke Pavilion. Access to the water can be found under the Roman Forest Boulevard bridge. Another access point, which requires less scrambling, can be found by cutting across the large field northwest of the park.

 10 Roman Forest Wade (Wading Upstream from Roman Forest Boulevard)

Start working your way upstream from the bridge, staying close to the western bank (river right). A little over 200 feet upstream, you'll see where a small pipe discharges water from a wastewater facility on the western bank. There is a knee- to thigh-deep hole just in front of this discharge area. Small minnows and baitfish can be seen

This sandbar is a popular spot for swimmers and picnickers during the summer. It can also produce spotted bass and longear sunfish.

swimming around in the oxygen rich waters. This is a good place to make several casts. In the summer, small bass can be found in the deeper section of this pool.

After fishing in front of the discharge area, wade across the creek to your right (river left). The stream is shallower along this bank, and it's easier to move upstream and fish the next deep hole. Roughly 25 yards upstream, you'll see where floodwaters have eroded the opposite bank (river right) and formed an eddy. There are usually logs or debris at the tailing end of this eddy. Cast as close to the eroded bank as you can. Longears, bluegill, and spotted bass will often be hiding next to the bank.

About 130 yards upstream, you'll come to a lovely sand point bar and two deep pools. With any luck, there won't be any swimmers, and you'll have the productive pools to yourself. Start on the sandbar and cast into the tailing section of the deep hole on the opposite bank (river right). After fishing this hole, cross to the other bank (river right), just below the second deep hole. Now you can easily fish the pool upstream. Take your time fishing this section; there's a lot of structure, including root systems from the trees aligning the banks. You may need to use a weighted fly, like a Brasshawk, to get deeper in the water column.

Head upstream for another 230 yards. Again, you'll find another deep pool. You'll see where the eastern bank has given way to flooding and many logs and stumps have tumbled down into the water. Drift a crawfish pattern or nymph pattern around these logs.

For the next 0.3 miles, the stream contains several off-channel areas and deep pools that deserve some attention, but much of the stream

Peach Creek, looking upstream along a deep chute

channel is relatively straight and shallow. Although this section of water may not produce many fish, it is still a lovely wade. The trees form a high canopy above the creek. I often throw my fly rod over my shoulder and simply enjoy the scenery and cool water as I head upstream.

Eventually, you'll come to a large pool that is full of structure in the form of downed trees. It can be difficult to navigate and cast while moving through this section, but it is definitely worth fishing. You may have to scramble along the western bank (river right) to get around the deeper holes and tree trunks. Remember to stay within the streambed so as not to trespass onto the private property.

Another 400 yards upstream, you'll see a large bridge. This is the abandoned Woodbranch Drive bridge, or as the local residents refer to

Some sections of Peach Creek may be too shallow to hold any spotted bass. You can either try to find smaller longear sunfish in the pocket water along the banks, or just bypass these shallow areas.

it, the "Bridge to Nowhere." This is a great place to park another vehicle as a shuttle (30.18245, -95.18428). Once you reach the bridge, you'll be approximately 0.8 river miles from Roman Forest Boulevard.

Getting There

 From downtown, head north on I-69/US 59 toward New Caney. Exit the interstate at the TX 494 Loop/Roman Forest Boulevard. Head north on the feeder road for 1.1 miles. Make a right onto Roman Forest Boulevard. Continue on Roman Forest Boulevard for 1.5 miles. You'll drive right over Peach Creek. Just across the creek, on your left, you'll see the Roman Forest Park. Park in this city-owned parking lot.

Lake Houston Wilderness Park, New Caney
30.11978, -95.17304
Canoe Launch Rd., New Caney, TX 77357
38.5 road miles, 0:47 drive time
USGS Monitor Station: 08071000 (Peach Creek)
08070500 (Caney Creek), 08072000 (Lake Houston)
Optimum flow: 20 to 30 cfs (Peach Creek),
20 to 25 cfs (Caney Creek),
Optimum gauge height: 4.5 to 5 ft. (Peach Creek),
3 ft. (Caney Creek), 41. ft. (Lake Houston)
Difficulty: Moderate

This area serves as a starting point for two separate wade descriptions. This is the farthest downstream reach of Peach Creek before it empties into Caney Creek. Access to this section of water is achieved through the Lake Houston Wilderness Park. The entrance fee to the park is $3.00 for a single day or $25.00 for a whole year. The park is closed on Tuesdays.

From the Canoe Launch Road parking lot, it is just a couple of yards to the bank of Peach Creek. If you walk downstream, approximately 120 yards from the parking lot, Peach Creek meets with Caney Creek (see the following wade description, Confluence Float).

From the parking area, a highly trafficked trail leads to a sandy beach with two picnic tables. This area is a popular swimming hole in the summer.

A Brief History of Lake Houston Wilderness Park

Lake Houston Wilderness Park was not always owned and operated by the Houston Parks and Recreation Department. In fact, it used to be owned by the state and was operated by the Texas Parks & Wildlife Department (TPWD). In 2006, all 4,787 acres of densely wooded land was transferred to the city of Houston. This is now the only park operated by the City of Houston that allows overnight camping. There are several different camping options to choose from, including rental cabins and primitive campsites along the hiking trail adjacent to Peach Creek. If you get off the water in the evening and have a hankering to look for wildlife, take a drive along Five Mile Road, which runs northeast/southwest. In the waning evening light, you may see whitetail deer or wild pigs foraging along the powerline right-of-way that runs next to Five Mile Road.

What You Will Find

Next to the parking area, there's a good chance that you'll find people picnicking, swimming, or fishing. The water can sometimes appear muddled, especially if it's a summer weekend and there are people swimming. No matter; fishing upstream or downstream from this section can be a great time. If it's late winter or early spring, during the white

*Peach Creek, upstream from Canoe Launch Road
Inset: Ameri-Trail hiking path*

Think outside the box and try casting to some sections of water that appear too shallow to hold fish. Inset: Longear sunfish can be found in surprising places.

bass run, you could have a day filled with lots of action.

For this entire wade, the land adjacent to the eastern bank of Peach Creek is part of the City of Houston Parks and Recreation Department and open to the public. There is a nice hiking trail (Ameri-Trail) that runs parallel to Peach Creek, starting from Canoe Launch Road and heading north to the Nature Center and Peach Creek Lane. The total distance is roughly 1.5 miles. If at any point you want to get out of the water and head back to your vehicle via the hiking trail, just scramble up the eastern bank, bushwhack for several yards, and find the hiking trail. You can then take the Ameri-Trail back to Canoe Launch Road.

 11 Canoe Launch Wade (Wading Upstream from the Canoe Launch Road Parking Lot)

This reach is a popular fishing location for fly anglers and conventional anglers alike. If you see another angler, remember your courtesies and don't go splashing through the area they are fishing. A simple wave and greeting could result in a friendly conversation and a new fishing partner—you never know.

While fishing Peach Creek, keep an eye open for wildlife. Green herons can often be found hunting frogs and minnows along the banks of Peach Creek.

As mentioned before, during the summer months, there is a good chance that people are swimming in the large wide pool that is adjacent to the picnic area. But if not, this is a productive bend, especially when the white and yellow bass are spawning. Panfish, crappie, and black bass can also be caught here.

Once you wade around the first bend in the river, upstream from the picnic area, you'll come to a slow-moving section of water. It is best to wade along the left-hand side (river right) and lob casts to the opposite steep bank. You'll want to move slowly so as not to send a wave upstream.

Walk onto the first exposed sandbar on your left (river right). Once you're out of the water and standing on the sandbar, face the opposite bank. The water here is deep and full of structure. If you are confident in your balance, try standing on one of the partially submerged logs to present flies to the backwater eddies. These can be difficult to reach otherwise due to the overhanging vegetation. As you move upstream, stick to the river right bank and thoroughly fish the deeper holes along the opposite cutbanks. This is another great hole for white bass.

A little over 100 feet upstream, the waters of Peach Creek are necked-down and more easily forded. You'll see a gravel bar on the right side of the channel (river left). Use the "knees" of the cypress trees protruding from the bank, river right, as a marker for where to ford the creek. Head for the gravel bar on the opposite bank.

Another 450 yards upstream, you'll come to another wide and deep pool. It is best to slowly wade through the middle of this pool while casting to the submerged logs. For the next 600 yards, you'll find many intriguing pools and deep channels adjacent to the cutbanks. As you round the wide bend in the creek, you'll see a high bank that is eroding into the stream. The water just downstream of this tall cutbank forms a fairly deep chute.

Around the next wide bend in the creek, another 700 yards upstream, you'll find a fairly deep flat that is usually full of logs and woody debris. The logjams in this section often form off-channel eddies and deep pools. Fishing this pocket water can be a chore, but it can also yield longear sunfish. To fish some of the backwater pools, it's often easiest to scramble on top of the logjams and cast parallel to the submerged logs. Allow your fly to sink low in the water column, but be prepared to set the hook. Longear sunfish often dart out from under the logs and make a swipe at your sinking fly. Due to the logjams in this section, there is an

Paddling downstream on Peach Creek, towards the picnic area

Typical spotted bass from Peach Creek

unfortunate amount of trash that gets stuck here. Consider packing some out when you're done fishing for the day.

There are several more productive chutes as you move upstream, but in approximately 450 yards you'll come to another popular swimming area. This area is adjacent to the Nature Center and the Peach Creek Lane bridge. This swimming hole offers a nice beach and picnic area for people who want to beat the summer heat. This is a good place to either park a shuttle vehicle (30.13739, -95.16873), or turn around and wade back downstream. From Canoe Launch Road to Peach Creek Lane, it is approximately 1.5 river miles.

There is still more water to explore upstream from Peach Creek Lane; however, most of the productive holes are several hundred yards upstream from the Peach Creek Lane bridge. There is additional access to Peach Creek, outside of Lake Houston Wilderness Park, where the FM 1485 bridge spans the creek (30.14688, -95.17150). At the time of this writing, there is major construction happening where TX 99 is being extended eastward, running parallel to FM 1485. It is roughly 2 river miles from the bridge at FM 1485 North (upstream) to the access point at Roman Forest Boulevard (30.17287, -95.17694). This section of water is another area that's worth exploring.

 Confluence Float (Paddling Caney Creek, Upstream from the Confluence of Peach and Caney Creeks)

This route description shares the same starting point as the previous route, but instead of heading upstream along Peach Creek, you will head downstream to the confluence of Peach Creek and Caney Creek. The confluence of these two watercourses receives heavy fishing pressure during the temperate bass spawning season (February to April), but is still a great place to wet a line.

Before you fish this section, check the USGS Monitor Station for Caney Creek (gauge number: 08070500) and also Lake Houston (08072000). Doing this will give you a better understanding of what the water will be like when you arrive. The higher the gauge height on the

The confluence of Peach Creek (right) and Caney Creek (left)

lake, the deeper the water will be around the confluence of Peach Creek and Caney Creek. If the Lake Houston gauge height is showing a height of 42 feet or higher, this often means the holes around the confluence could be over 6 feet deep.

The Canoe Launch Road parking lot (30.11968, -95.17311) is adjacent to the banks of Peach Creek, which flows into Caney Creek just a short distance downstream. Launch a paddlecraft into the waters of Peach Creek and float downstream until reaching the confluence (30.11843, -95.17210). As mentioned before, this area gets crowded during the white bass run, but anglers can escape the crowds by paddling upstream along Caney Creek.

Begin fishing along the sandbar spit that runs along the inside seam of Peach and Caney. This is a very deep hole, and it can be fished by standing on the sandbar between the adjoining watercourses, or by beaching your paddlecraft on the river right bank.

Nick Heaverlo shows off a fine white bass (left), while Didi Ooi holds a slab white crappie (right).

Fish along the logjams and deep holes on your left (river right) as you paddle upstream. Both temperate bass and black bass can be found along this side of the creek.

Another 300 yards upstream, there is a deep run on your right, river left. This section can be easily fished by standing on the white sandbar (only exposed at low flows) along the opposite bank. Make sure to cast as close to the overhanging bank as possible.

Another 250 yards upstream, the river makes a slight bend to the west. This productive hole and cutbank is flanked by a large bald cypress tree that towers over the water. Make targeted casts to the steep bank and the cypress knees. Allow your fly time to sink in the water column. Panfish, catfish, spotted gar, white bass, and yellow bass can all be found adjacent to the cutbank. Plenty of woody structure exists along this section, so be prepared to lose several flies to the many snags. Just think of it as penance to the river gods.

Another 200 hundred yards upstream, the water begins to shallow and may require you to hop out of your watercraft. It may be best to beach your kayak or canoe on a sandbar and continue on foot. There are several nice riffles that give way to deeper pools.

While fishing this section of water, it is important to remember that both sides of the creek are privately owned. Respect the property owners and do not trespass on their land. Unfortunately, some people do not respect the rights of these property owners, and in past years this has led to some conflicts between anglers and landowners. Make sure to stick within the bounds of the creek channel while fishing Caney Creek.

It is another 2.25 river miles upstream to the FM 1485 bridge, which spans Caney Creek. This is another access point (30.14886, -95.19249). Anglers who want to try exploring more of Caney Creek can fish upstream of this bridge. Unfortunately, you'll likely see a lot of trash from illegal dumping. It's approximately 260 yards upstream to a cutbank that can produce black bass and catfish. Be advised: as you go farther upstream through this section of water, the wade can be difficult in some places. There are large sandbars that appear solid and stable but are actually unconsolidated, and an unwary angler could sink down a foot or more into the soft sand. This is nothing to be overly alarmed about, but it can add to the difficulty of wading this section of water.

A Note on Finding Temperate Bass in the Late Winter or Early Spring

Prior to their actual spawning, white bass males will run upstream into the creeks of Caney and Peach in preparation for the females, who may take another month to join them. By using a kayak to paddle up and down the length of Caney Creek, you can find the staging areas of white bass and yellow bass. If the temperate bass aren't found in the shallower and easily waded sections of Caney and Peach creeks, then simply paddle downstream, below the confluence of Peach and Caney. Fish around eddies or slack water to find where they are preparing for their run upstream. Depending on the timing of the annual spawn, it may be necessary to paddle half a mile or more downstream before finding the sand bass.

Getting There

From downtown, start by heading north on I-69/US 59 toward New Caney. After 27.4 miles, take the exit for FM 1485 to New Caney. Continue to head north on the Eastex Freeway Service Road for 0.7 miles. Turn right onto FM 1485. Continue on FM 1485 for 0.2 miles, and then make a right onto TX 494 South. Turn left back onto FM 1485 East and continue on for 2.7 miles. Make a right on Wilderness Road, at the entrance of Lake Houston Wilderness Park. Continue through the park gate and make a right on Highland Loop Road at the T-intersection. Continue on Highland Loop Road for 1.2 miles until you find Canoe Launch Road on your right. Continue down Canoe Launch Road until you reach the roundabout and parking lot.

 Back Pew Brewing
Company
backpewbrewing.com
Back Pew Brewing Company is
located in Porter, Texas, just off of
I-69/US 59. The brewery is open
weekends only, starting Friday
afternoon until Sunday at 5:00
pm. The taproom itself is unique
in that it is an old church. The
folks who work here are wonderful, smiling people, and their beer
is darn good too. Try the Tanuki
IPA if you're into ales.

Back Pew's taproom is in an old church building. There are plenty of wonderful beers on tap in the "sanctuary."

If you are wet and muddy from a day of creek stompin', there's plenty of seating outside, under towering loblolly pines. There is usually at least one food truck serving up hot meals. Back Pew is kid- and dog-friendly, so feel free to bring the whole family. This is a great place to stop and grab a beer and quick bite to eat before heading back to the city.

Chapter 3

SPRING CREEK

Runs of spawning temperate bass, decent populations of black bass, large catfish, downstream reaches offer open streambeds for longer casts, canoe launch areas available. Access Points: 5.

THE HEADWATERS OF SPRING CREEK BEGIN IN WALLER COUNTY and flow southeast for 64 miles. For much of its length, Spring Creek delineates the border between Harris County to the south and Montgomery County to the north. Large metropolitan areas, such as The Woodlands, Spring, and Humble, are all in close proximity to this waterway. Spring Creek eventually converges with the West Fork of the San Jacinto River, west of I-69/US 59 and the community of Kingwood. The lower half of Spring Creek boasts the longest contiguous urban greenspace in the country. Harris County's Spring Creek Greenway spans an impressive 33 miles and covers over 12,000 acres. The Spring Creek Greenway Trails run along the length of this waterway and offers many miles of trails for hiking, biking, and horseback riding.

The streambed of the lower half of Spring Creek is comprised of loose white sand. These sand deposits form picturesque point bars and fine beaches. Due to flooding events and constantly shifting sands, the streambed of this creek is continuously changing. A deep hole that produced bass one year may be silted in by the next. Despite this fact, one thing remains constant: the fish can be found around structure. So look for sunken trees, clay shelves, undercut cutbanks, and deep channels. When you find such structure, take your time and fish these areas meticulously.

As winter turns to spring, this creek shines as a hot spot for spawning temperate bass. Finding schools of fish often requires sloshing through the creek for several miles, but when you find the pools that hold fish, it can be well worth the effort. By the time late summer rolls around, the water temperatures of Spring Creek can climb as high as 96 degrees Fahrenheit during the day. Fishing Spring Creek during the dog days of summer tends to be less productive. However, if you can manage a couple of Spring Creek largemouth during these hot days, you should consider it an accomplishment. Just be sure to return the fish to the water quickly; they may already be stressed from the soaring water temperatures.

USGS Stream Gauges along Spring Creek

The stream gauge at I-45 (gauge number: 08068500) is a good gauge to check before hitting the lower half of Spring Creek. This gauge has turbidity readings in addition to flow rates and gauge height. A discharge

A calm summer evening on Spring Creek

rate around 40 cubic feet per second and a gauge height of less than 74 feet is considered low and clear. By checking the turbidity graph, you'll get an idea of clarity. The closer the graph is to the baseline of zero, the clearer the water will be. Readings of around 20 to 25 FNU are fairly clear.

Riley Fuzzel Road Preserve, Spring
30.09333, -95.40567
Old Riley Fuzzel Rd., Spring, TX 77386
27.2 road miles, 0:30 drive time
USGS Monitor Station: 08068500
Optimum flow: 40 cfs
Optimum gauge height: 73 to 74 ft.
Difficulty: Easy to Moderate

This access site lies in Montgomery County, on the northern bank of Spring Creek. This location is within a nature preserve that is associated with Montgomery County's Spring Creek Greenway Nature Center. The Spring Creek Greenway Nature Center can be found just on the other side of Riley Fuzzel Road. At the Nature Center, you can find bathrooms, along with all sorts of interesting information about animals and plants of Southeast Texas.

Deep pools like this one, which can be found downstream from TX 99 bridge, offer plenty of cover for all manner of fish species.

Largemouth bass can be found near cut banks, chutes, holes, and any woody debris.

On the opposite bank of Spring Creek, the south side of the waterway, is Harris County's Dennis Johnston Park, one of the farthest upstream parks along the Spring Creek Greenway. Dennis Johnston Park also offers bathrooms and access to the Spring Creek Greenway Trail.

What You Will Find

When you turn down the Old Riley Fuzzel Road, you'll see a set of construction barricades just before the road dead-ends. A gravel parking lot can be found on the right side of the road. Spring Creek is just a few yards past the barricades.

13 Riley Fuzz Wade (Wading Upstream from the Bridge)

When you crest the bank and peer down onto Spring Creek, you'll see the Riley Fuzzel Road bridge spanning the water, along with two culverts protruding from the bank you are standing on. There is a nice pocket just under these culverts that warrants several casts.

From there, ford across Spring Creek to the opposite bank and march upstream to the sandbar. Fish the swift-flowing chute opposite the sandbar (river left). After drifting a couple of flies through this chute and tickling the tongues of any bass or catfish that lurk there, turn your attention upstream. Work your way back across the water to your right (river left). You're going to stick to this side of the creek for the next 230 yards. As you move upstream, be sure to make casts to the steep bank on the opposite side of the creek (river right).

Just before the next bend, you'll see a rather large hole flanked on the left side (river right) by steep clay banks. This can be a good hole for white bass during the run, but it's also a good spot to catch a freshwater drum. After thoroughly fishing this section, move upstream toward the monstrous TX 99 (Grand Parkway) bridge (30.09350, -95.41018). There is a deep section along the right side of the creek, so stay to your left (river right) while you work upstream. At the top of this deep section, you'll find a nice cutbank that can produce white bass during the spring.

As you emerge from under the TX 99 overpass, make your way to the opposite bank (river left) and head upstream along the large sandbar. There is a deeper chute (3 to 4 feet deep) that lies along the opposite cutbank, about 200 to 250 yards upstream from the bridge.

Zach Wallace fishes the wide pool of the cichlid ditch before it joins with Spring Creek.

Rio grande cichlids can be angled from the man-made ditch that enters into Spring Creek, river left.

As you continue to work upstream around the large bend in the creek, you'll see two black culverts protruding from the opposite bank (river right). A mishmash of concrete fill and rocks have been dumped in front of the outflow of these culverts to prevent erosion of the streambed. Lob a long-distance cast to the front of these rocks.

Spring Creek flows in a straight path for the next 400 yards. Most of the deep water lies adjacent to the bank on your right (river left). An erosion-resistant clay layer creates a nice shelf with a deep chute adjacent to it. Drift or strip a Clouser Minnow along the bottom of this chute, and there's a good chance you'll feel the tug of a largemouth.

When you begin hiking upstream again, take note of the large pool that flows into Spring Creek, river left (30.09842, -95.41015). This is an interesting man-made concrete feature and is formed from the large spillway that can be seen from the streambed. This will be our turnaround point, but before you go anywhere, you absolutely must fish the pool at the base of the concrete diffusers and hike up to the top of the dam to fish the deep ditch on the other side. Bluegill, green sunfish, longears, and of course the ubiquitous largemouth can all be found in this pool and in the ditch above the dam. As an added treat, a substantial population of Rio Grande cichlids also calls this ditch home.

Up to this point, hiking in Spring Creek has been great fun, but this ecologically diverse, man-made trench is the icing on the cake. The water is fairly clear, and the banks of the "cichlid ditch" are high, which makes a stealthy approach crucial. Some portions of the ditch appear very deep, so be sure to fish the entire water column. Don't forget to cast toward the pile of rocks at the outflow of the ditch.

Getting There

 From downtown, take I-45 North for approximately 21 miles. Take exit 70A toward FM 2920/Tomball. Turn right onto East Louetta Road after traveling about 0.4 miles on the frontage road. Stay on East Louetta Road for 1.5 miles, and then make a left onto Aldine Westfield Road. Make a right onto Riley Fuzzel Road after 1 mile. After taking Riley Fuzzel Road for about 1 mile, you will drive over Spring Creek. Just after crossing Spring Creek, get in the left lane, and then use the left turning lane to turn onto Old Riley Fuzzel Road. Take this road all the way to the end, where you'll find a gravel parking lot.

Carter Park, Spring
30.05281, -95.32654
7221 Treaschwig Rd., Spring, TX 77373
www.hcp4.net/parks/carter/
27.4 road miles, 0:35 drive time
USGS Monitor Station: 08068500
Optimum flow: 40 cfs
Optimum gauge height: 73 to 74 ft
Difficulty: Easy to Moderate

Carter Park is one of many parks that can be found along the Spring Creek Greenway Trail. Pundt Park (30.08242, -95.37847) is another popular park that is found approximately 4.4 miles upstream of Carter Park, and Jesse H. Jones Park (30.02370, -95.29400) lies about 3.6 miles downstream. All three of these parks offer areas to launch a canoe or kayak, as well as other amenities like bathrooms. If you plan on launching a watercraft at Carter Park, be sure to register online by filling out a form at the following website (https://apps.hcp4.net/pct4forms/canoekayak.aspx).

Despite its close proximity to the city of Houston, Spring Creek can offer anglers a feeling of seclusion.

You need to give the Precinct 4 Parks Department a full 24-hour notice if you are planning a canoe trip during the weekdays. For weekend trips, the registration form must be submitted before 3:00 pm on Friday.

Prior to arriving at Carter Park, it may be prudent to call the park office at (281) 353-8100 and let the staff know that you are on your way. They can open the gate and allow you to drive your vehicle to the launch site. However, sometimes the gate is still locked upon arrival; therefore, bring a wheeled kayak cart in your vehicle just in case. It's approximately one-third of a mile from the parking lot to the canoe launch. That makes for a long portage if you forgot your kayak cart.

During times of optimum flows, Spring Creek can be waded easily. There are lovely white sandbars and deep chutes that can offer opportunities to catch black bass, temperate bass, gar, and catfish.

It is worth noting that all parks along the Spring Creek Greenway Trail close at dusk. If you are not off the water by the time the park closes, your vehicle will be towed. Before you head out on the water for a paddle trip or a wade trip, be sure you have enough time to get back to your car. If you want a specific time for when the park will close, just call the office at (281) 353-8100 and they will let you know. You can also check the signage at the parking lot.

What You Will Find

From the parking area (30.05281, -95.32654), it is 0.3 miles to the canoe launch and the water. In order to find the canoe launch, head past the first gate just beyond the parking area. You'll pass the bathrooms on your left. Hang a left at the first intersection, and then stay to the right at the next intersection (30.05292, -95.32401). You should see a blue sign that reads, "Canoe launch use by reservation only." Watch out for cyclists

This collapsed bridge is a great place to stop and fish thoroughly. There are deep holes above and below the remnants of this structure.

while you make your way through this intersection. This is a blind curve, and if you are carrying a canoe or kayak, you won't be able to see cyclists coming around the bend. Once you take the second right, you'll continue down a road for 211 yards. The road veers sharply to the right. Stay to the right, and you'll see a large sandbar and the waters of Spring Creek.

 Carter Park Wade (Wading Upstream from Carter Park Canoe Launch)

As you wade through this section of Spring Creek, you'll see areas where sand deposits form a shelf that usually drops away into deeper pools. Anytime you see this, make a cast to the edge of the sandy shelf and let your fly drift over the edge. Bass can be waiting downstream of these features and will take a swipe at anything that goes drifting by.

As you move upstream from the canoe launch, pay close attention to the bank on your left (river right). At first it will appear shallow and lacking in structure, but as you move upstream, you'll find overhanging trees and weedy banks that offer plenty of bass habitat. For about 410 yards, the bank on your left (river right) offers good fishing opportunity.

Once the cutbank peters out, you'll have about 450 yards of shallow riffles until you come to another cutbank that is worthwhile. It will be on your right (river left). The farther upstream you go, the deeper the water will be. This whole outside bend (river left) is worth fishing. As you move upstream, you'll find a little chute on the opposite bank (river right) that will need fished, but for the most part, keep moving upstream.

Once you work around this large bend (about 690 yards in length) you'll come to a collapsed structure (I think it's an old bridge) on your left (river right). A large pool is formed on the downstream side of this bridge. If you take a couple of minutes and watch the surface of the water, you'll likely see gar breaching to gulp air. You may even see minnows jumping and a boil on the surface from a predatory fish attempting to catch a meal. You can fish along the left side (river right), but you will eventually want to move upstream by working your way along the opposite bank (river left). Fish the entire cutbank, moving upstream from the collapsed bridge. Dark-colored baitfish patterns work well. Don't be afraid to switch flies and cover as much water as you can.

Once you fish your way to the top of the bend, you'll be about 1.2 miles away from the Carter Park canoe launch. Feel free to turn around and head back downstream. It's roughly 3.2 river miles farther upstream to Pundt Park.

15 Bald Eagle Wade (Wading or Paddling Downstream from Carter Park)

As mentioned before, in order to paddle any section of the Spring Creek Greenway, you must register online with the Precinct 4 Parks Department by filing an online form that states your plans for the canoe trip (locations of put-in and take-out and launch time).

During optimum flows, Spring Creek can be waded from the Carter Park Canoe Launch down to the confluence of Spring Creek and Cypress Creek (30.03239, -95.31076). After the confluence, a watercraft will be necessary if you intend on going any farther downstream. If you simply wish to make your fishing excursion an out-and-back trip, wading

Nick Heaverlo arrives at the kayak launch at Jesse H. Jones Park. This is a popular location for bank fishermen.

downstream from Carter Park to the confluence can be accomplished with ease.

Before deciding to float downstream from Carter Park to Jesse H. Jones Park (30.02961, -95.29436), please know that the optimum water levels for Spring Creek, outlined previously, might be a bit skinny for paddling. However, if you are willing to jump out a handful of times in order to drag your kayak or canoe over sandbars, then you will find this paddle to be very enjoyable even during low and clear conditions. Most of the time, the deepest channels can be found closer to the banks. If you find these deeper channels, you can often float along without having to do much dragging. Spend a little time reading the water, and you'll eventually get the hang of finding the channels that can easily float your watercraft.

From the wide sandbar at Carter Park Canoe Launch, you will find a chute that's about 4 feet deep along the first cutbank, downstream from the put-in. This deep section gets hammered pretty hard during the white bass run because of its close proximity to the canoe launch and trail. Nevertheless, be sure to fish this reach as you work downstream.

After moving downstream for nearly half a mile, you'll come to a decent cutbank on your left. Fish the channel that runs along the outside bend. The tail end of this cutbank has a deep hole that often contains fish. If you're not having any luck, try the deeper chutes at the base of the cypress trees that are found on either bank, about 100 to 150 yards downstream.

In another 600 yards downstream, you'll find an interesting riffle section. As you float (or wade) by, you'll see what appear to be the roots of old, long gone cypress trees that act like an anchor system and hold the streambed in place, creating this small riffle. As you continue downstream, you'll work around a large meander in the creek that will offer several more cutbanks and deeper chutes that are worth making a couple of casts to.

Tanya Xu with a white bass from Spring Creek, caught during the annual white bass run

Nick Heaverlo and Tanya Xu fish for white bass in a deep hole along Spring Creek.

Hiro Yamamoto battles a white bass as it makes a run back to deeper water. Inset: Hiro Yamamoto with a white bass from Spring Creek

For the next 0.6 miles, you will float along a wide bend in the creek. You may hear the sound of golfcarts or hear golfers chatting along the high bank on your right. After you move around this bend, there are several deep holes that are positioned along the steep cutbank, river right. These holes often hold white bass during the annual spawn. Another 100 yards farther downstream, there is another productive hole close to the left bank.

Eventually, the creek flows relatively straight. This section of water is about 600 yards in length and doesn't offer much in the way of angling opportunities. Sit back and enjoy the float. If you are wading, simply continue sloshing through the knee-deep waters. Keep an eye out for the bald eagles along this stretch. They may be perched in the tops of the trees or soaring high above.

Next, you will come to the confluence of Cypress Creek and Spring Creek (30.03239, -95.31076). At this point, if you are in a watercraft, you will have another 1.2 miles left in your float once you see the waters of Cypress Creek flowing in from the west (river right). Cypress Creek contributes substantial amounts of water to the Spring Creek system, and once you reach this confluence, you will no longer need to drag your watercraft, even during times of low flows. This makes for a more enjoyable float.

Immediately downstream from the confluence of Spring Creek and Cypress Creek, there is a large hole against the bank, river right. This area can be an excellent place to find white bass during the spawn. The Spring Creek Greenway Trail overlooks the water at this location, so it can be a popular spot for anglers. Paddle downstream about 300 yards to the first cutbank on your left. This area can yield fish as well. Make casts to the overhanging grasses and shrubs.

The final mile of the float is wide and fairly deep. It can be difficult to fish this section with fly gear. This is another popular fishing area for bank fishermen who are on the hunt for catfish or white bass. In the summer, as you paddle downstream, you may see nice-sized gar gulping air on the surface. The Jesse H. Jones Park canoe launch, the take-out site, is on the right side of Spring Creek (30.02961, -95.29436). You'll see a large concrete wall as you approach.

Once you are safely off the water, you'll need to walk 0.3 miles along Canoe Launch Trail back to the parking lot at Jesse H. Jones Park to pick up your shuttle vehicle. Stop in at the park office by the front gate and let the staff know that you have arrived and need the gate opened. Once the gate is unlocked for you, you can drive down the paved trail and pick up your watercraft.

Getting There

From downtown, head north on I-45. Take I-45 for about 18 miles. Take exit 66A toward Humble/Addicks/FM 1960. Continue on the feeder road and make a right onto FM 1960 East. Take FM 1960 for approximately 2.5 miles. Use the left two lanes and turn left onto Treaschwig Road. Continue on Treaschwig Road for 4.3 miles. You'll see the entrance to Carter Park on your left. Use caution when making this left-hand turn into the park. This is a blind curve, and oncoming traffic may not see you when they come around the bend.

 Prohibition Texas

prohibitiontexas.com

If you have never visited Old Town Spring, you need to check it out. This nineteenth-century, historic area was once a hub for a bustling railroad industry. The town is still preserved in its old-timey state. There are plenty of boutiques, ice cream parlors, restaurants, and bars. Prohibition Texas (26420 Preston Ave., Spring, TX 77373) is one of the local watering holes in Old Town Spring. You can grab a specialized cocktail or craft beer and enjoy the evening breeze on the front porch.

The Akokisa Indians

The lush wooded landscape adjacent to Spring Creek has a deep history. A population of Native Americans known as the Akokisa inhabited the shores of Spring Creek until the nineteenth century. At least two Akokisa settlements were documented by early Spanish explorers. One settlement existed at the confluence of Spring Creek and Cypress Creek. The other was in close proximity to Jesse H. Jones Park, near the confluence of Spring Creek and the West Fork San Jacinto River. According to the Harris County Precinct 4 Parks Department, the Akokisa were skilled fishermen, canoe makers, and excellent tanners of bear hide. The Akokisa used cypress logs to build dugout canoes for transportation along Spring Creek and other waterways in the Houston area. If you are interested in learning more about the Akokisa people, you can find more information at Jesse H. Jones Park.

Part 3

Legal, Safe, and
Ethical

KNOW YOUR RIGHTS, BE SAFE, RESPECT THE RESOURCE

DUE TO THE NOVELTY OF FLY FISHING IN THIS PART OF THE country, it's worthwhile to touch on three topics that seem mundane but are important nonetheless. In the following chapter, we'll take a look at the legality of exploring the Houston-area waterways. Then we will consider several matters of safety. Lastly, we will focus on how we can all be ethical anglers.

Chapter 9

TEXAS LAWS REGARDING ACCESS TO OUR SHARED WATERWAYS

UNDERSTANDING TEXAS RIVER LAW IS VITAL FOR EDUCATING newcomers to the sport of fly fishing, and for educating seasoned fly anglers who are Texas transplants. Knowing your rights as a Texas angler will help diffuse any sticky situations that could arise with landowners or government officials.

The history of Texas is unique, and so are the laws regarding its waterways. Certain creeks, rivers, and bayous have an inherent public importance, and utility, that the state of Texas recognizes. Texas claims ownership of particular waterways and grants its citizens the right to use these common resources. The state also reserves the right to public access of some streambeds it does not own. It can sometimes be tricky to sort out whether a stream or creek is owned by the state (or the public's right to use it is guaranteed).

In short, there are two ways that a waterway can be considered open to public access.

1. It is deemed perennial and was recorded in historical
   Spanish or Mexican law.
2. Under the current Texas law, the waterway is considered
   "navigable."

Historic Perennial Waterways

Prior to Texas becoming a state, the land was first claimed by the
Crown of Spain. Under Spanish civil law, certain "perennial" waterways
(waterways that maintain flow throughout the year with normal rainfall)
were deemed open to the public for use in transportation and trade.
Throughout the centuries, as the landmass of Texas changed hands from

Spain to Mexico, to the Republic of Texas, to the state of Texas, the rights of Texans remained the same with regard to accessing particular perennial waterways. Without having access to historical documents, fishermen can still make accurate assumptions as to what creeks are likely "perennial" and had been claimed under Spanish jurisdiction. These are usually larger waterways (although there are some exceptions) with inherent historical significance. Examples include the San Antonio River, Colorado River, Trinity River, Brazos River, Neches River, and San Jacinto River.

   In addition to the waterways originally granted under Spanish and Mexican civil law, the Texas Constitution grants the public the right to

Nick Heaverlo, Tanya Xu, and their dog, Nile, paddle along Cypress Creek, downstream from the bridge at Aldine Westfield Road.

access waterways that are deemed to be "navigable." The State of Texas determines a waterway's navigability if it meets the criteria of at least one of the following two terms: "Navigable in Fact" and "Navigable by Statute." These two terms are defined below.

Navigable in Fact

If a waterway is able to transport a boat, kayak, canoe, or even timbered logs, it is deemed to be navigable "by fact," and therefore open to the public. In a court case in 1863 (*Selman v. Wolfe, 27 Tex. 68, 71*), it was determined that if a waterway is considered useful for travel and trade, then the public's use of that waterway may not be impeded. You might be saying to yourself, "Sure, but that was probably with regards to big steamboats and ferries," and yes, you would be correct in this case. However, in 1917, another court case, *Welder v. State* (196 S.W. 868 (Tex. Civ. App.)) determined that navigability "in fact" is not solely determined by the commercial use of a waterway. It is determined by the public utility.

What's more, the court actually took the time to address some of the nuances of this ruling in its statement: "... hunting and fishing, and even pleasure boating, has been held to be proper public uses."

So, there you have it: if you can float a watercraft down a particular stream, you have the legal right to fish those waters.

Navigable by Statute

Before Texas gained its statehood and became part of the United States of America, the Republic of Texas passed a law claiming that all streambeds with an average width of 30 feet or more are regarded as navigable and therefore owned by the state. These waterways were deemed navigable "by statute" or navigable "by law," as it was sometimes written. When Texas was accepted into the Union in 1845, this law came with it.

In the book, *Fly Fishing Austin & Central Texas*, Aaron Reed uses the following example to illustrate this law:

Little Creek is 45 feet wide where it joins Big River. It maintains a width of 45 feet for five miles above the confluence. For the next 10 miles, above that, Little Creek maintains a width of 30 feet. For the next five miles above that, 15 feet. Little Creek is navigable by statute to mile 20 above Big River. That is what the letter of the law says.

It is important to note that a stream is considered navigable by statute, regardless of whether the stream has flowing water within its channel. Intermittently flowing waterways are fairly common throughout central and western Texas, especially during the dry summers and periods of drought. So just because a 30-foot-wide river channel is dry in the summer doesn't necessarily mean it isn't still navigable by statute.

For the purposes of defining navigability by

Downstream from the FM 2090 bridge, massive bald cypress trees line deep pools along the East Fork San Jac. A kayak is necessary to access most of this water.

statute, it is prudent to understand how the state determines the width of a streambed. To measure a streambed, the entire width of the channel is measured from one "fast land bank" to the other. The Texas Parks & Wildlife Department (TPWD) defines the "fast land banks" this way: "These are the banks which separate the stream bed from the adjacent upland (whether valley or hill) and confine the waters to a definite channel." Again, a streambed does not necessarily need to be covered in flowing water to be considered navigable; it merely must maintain a channel width of 30 feet on average.

For further reading, check out TPWD's "Texas River Guide" (https://tpwd.texas.gov/landwater/water/habitats/rivers/index.phtml). Also, Texas Streams Coalition (tx-streams.org) is a nonprofit that aims to protect the waterways of Texas and the citizen's right to use them. There are some great write-ups on Texas river law on its website. Lastly, as previously mentioned, Aaron Reed's, *Fly Fishing Austin & Central Texas* provides an excellent chapter on this subject. At one point, Reed was an employee of TPWD, and through his research into Texas river law, he has crafted a concise and illuminating look into this subject that is well worth reading.

Public Access in Sam Houston National Forest and Wildlife Management Areas within the Pineywoods

The state of Texas contains four national forests: Sabine National Forest, Angelina National Forest, Davy Crockett National Forest, and Sam Houston National Forest. All of these national forests are positioned on the eastern side of the state. Houstonians are lucky in that we live so close to these public lands that offer hunting, fishing, hiking, and camping opportunities.

The Sam Houston National Forest, or the Sam, is located roughly 60 miles (1 to 1.5 hours) north of downtown Houston. The banks of Lake Conroe and the East Fork of the San Jacinto River share borders with the Sam Houston National Forest. This important recreational resource has special rules and regulations that need to be followed in order to fully enjoy this area.

The Sam Houston National Forest's 161,500 acres of forested terrain all falls within the management practices of the United States Forest Service. These lands are operated under a multiuse philosophy that allows not only outdoor recreation but also natural resource extraction such as logging and oil-production. Sam Houston National Forest is

The Lone Star Hiking Trail weaves its way through the Sam Houston National Forest. Here the trail spans the East Fork of the San Jacinto River.

unique from other national forests in Texas because the entire boundary of the Sam is also designated as a Wildlife Management Area (WMA) by TPWD. Because of this designation, the rules regarding camping are stricter in the Sam than other Texas national forests.

Camping in the Sam. Imagine hiking along the Lone Star Hiking Trail to the East Fork San Jacinto River with your camping backpack and fly rod or paddling along the northern section of Lake Conroe, in a canoe laden with cook pots and tents in preparation for an overnight fishing trip. This experience can be had in certain areas of Sam Houston National Forest; just be sure to follow some basic rules.

During the hunting season, usually September 1 to February 1, camping is only allowed in designated hunter camps or in developed recreational areas. An example of a developed recreational area would be the Stubblefield Lake Recreation Area on the northern end of Lake Conroe (see the chapter on fishing Lake Conroe). Outside of the designated

A beaver peers out of its bank hole along a Houston-area river. Beavers that live in flood prone rivers often dig holes into mud banks instead of building lodges. Beavers are a fairly common animal in Sam Houston National Forest, but because they are nocturnal, sightings occur infrequently. Inset: Most of the time, anglers see signs of beaver more often than the animal itself.

hunting season, anglers may make primitive camps along the Lone Star Hiking Trail within the national forest except where it's specifically prohibited (Big Creek Scenic Area).

While exploring Sam Houston National Forest, you'll likely come across "inholdings," or parcels of private property. Always respect private property and never trespass on someone's land. While you have a right to explore the navigable waterways in the Houston area, as well as the lands of Sam Houston National Forest, you do not have a right to traipse onto someone else's land without permission. Private land holdings are prevalent throughout the Sam Houston National Forest, and landowners usually post their property with "No Trespassing" signs or denote their property with purple paint. If you see tree trunks that have been painted with purple paint, Texas law states that this is the same as displaying a "No Trespassing" sign.

Exploring the secluded Pineywoods area of Sam Houston National Forest can yield some great fishing adventures. For more information on the Sam, pick up a copy of *Fly Fishing the Sam: A Guidebook to Exploring the Creeks, Rivers, and Bayous of the Sam Houston National Forest*. To find maps of the area, go to the Sam Houston National Forest Ranger Station, located at 394 FM 1375 West New Waverly, Texas 77358 (30.53019, -95.53642). At the ranger station, you can find waterproof maps and other information about the area. Using smart phones, readers can access a variety of digital maps showing the area.

River Access Laws in the City of Houston

While conducting research on river access laws in the city of Houston, I came across Houston's Parks and Recreation Department's website. As I read the laws regarding the city parks, I was dismayed to see the following:

Rule 211.26 FISHING PROHIBITED - EXCEPTION:

No person shall fish within the parks except in the designated areas of Lake Houston. This provision shall not apply to Hermann Park Lake provided such person is twelve (12) years of age or less or sixty-five (65) years of age or older, or where fishing is authorized by special permit of the Director.

I called the Houston Parks and Rec. Department to confirm my reading of the law. Once again, I was disappointed to hear the woman on the end of the line confirm my fears: "No, you may not fish in the city parks run by the Houston Parks and Rec. Department, with the exception of Lake Houston and Hermann Park, as long as you are within the age range."

While I listened on the other end of the line, I thought back to all the times I had seen people fishing from the banks of various city parks. When she was done talking, I followed up with another question: "On a regular basis, I see people fishing along the banks of the city parks in the downtown area. So just to confirm, those anglers are breaking the law?"

Her answer was definitive, "Yes, they are."

After I hung up the phone, I shook my head. I felt defeated. How could this be? Not only did Houston have a robust urban angling scene, but TPWD has also published tackle records for several urban bayous in Houston, including Brays Bayou and Buffalo Bayou. Something was amiss.

I began to think back to popular fishing locations in the Houston area. One such area, Terry Hershey Park along the Buffalo Bayou, popped into my head. I jumped on the website for Terry Hershey Park and found the telephone number. After a brief introduction, I began describing my conundrum to the employee of the Harris County Parks Department. She replied that while the city has rules against fishing in its parks, Terry Hershey Park is part of the *Harris County Parks Department*. It's not a city park. "You can fish as much as you want in a Harris County park!" she said.

This was great news! Many of the greenspaces, trails, and parks inside and outside of the I-610 loop are managed by Harris County, not the city. In other words, these areas are open to fishing, unless specifically stated otherwise.

To clarify further, parks such as Memorial Park (south of I-10) and Moody Park (East of I-45) are city parks, therefore (officially and legally) no fishing. Parks like Terry Hershey (south of Memorial Drive) and George Bush Park (within Barker Reservoir, west of South TX 6) are Harris County parks, so fishing is allowed. To make matters extra confusing, some of the bayou greenway trails are under the jurisdiction of both city and county (more on this in the coming paragraphs). Harris County has an online interactive map where you can scroll around and find various parks throughout the greater Houston area. Just go to harriscountytx.gov.

Ellen Dortenzo enjoys a leisurely float along the Buffalo Bayou through Terry Hershey Park, a park run by Harris County.

In my quest to better understand the laws related to fishing in Houston, I decided to check one last place for additional information, this time TPWD. Once again, I was on the phone. This time, I spoke with a biologist for TPWD. During our conversation, the biologist admitted that understanding the laws for urban angling can be confusing, but as long as anglers are in the stream channel of a navigable waterway (even within a park managed by the city) anglers have a right to fish it.

While we talked, the biologist wanted to be very clear. Signs reading "No Fishing" in city parks are not for mere show. "No Fishing" means *no fishing*. But most of these signs can be found on city property along riverfront walkways, city-owned ponds, or more popular urban areas. However, if an angler is in a watercraft, and is fishing in navigable waters from a canoe or kayak, then the angler is well within his or her rights. Fish on!

As our conversation continued, we discussed the many hike and bike trails along the Houston-area bayous. Some sections of the trail system along Brays Bayou, White Oak Bayou, and Buffalo Bayou are under the jurisdiction of both the city and the county. How would anglers know if they were inadvertently fishing on city property? Luckily, the answer from the biologist was simple. In short, as long as anglers are fishing within the banks of the stream channel, then that is considered to be within a navigable waterway. Another win for urban anglers!

Understanding the fishing laws within the city can be about as clear as the Buffalo Bayou after a heavy rain. I hope that this chapter helped distill some of the unclear rules by which anglers must abide. If this chapter raised more questions than answers, I recommend contacting TPWD or a local game warden. For a list of game wardens by county, go to https://tpwd.texas.gov/warden/game-warden-list.phtml and find your county in the list. The more we know about the laws regarding our shared waterways, the better angling we all can have.

Chapter 10

STAYING SAFE IN THE WOODS AND URBAN FISHERIES

BECAUSE OF THE AREA'S DISTINCTIVE FISHERIES AND environment, it's prudent to briefly review some safety protocols. If you are new to the Houston area, there is a learning curve for understanding the waterways and how to approach them in a safe manner. Before hitting the water, read over the following safety items to better prepare yourself.

Weather and "Quicksand"

It will come as no surprise that Texas can get blisteringly hot in the summer months. If you are heading out for a summertime creek stomp, remember to bring lots of water (keep some water purification tablets or a filter in your pack for emergencies) and be sure to wear sunscreen or a lightweight, long-sleeved shirt. Heat exhaustion can be deadly if the body is unable to cool itself. If you begin to feel nauseous while fishing during the summer months, stop immediately and call it a day.

Conversely, winter months can seem deceptively mild, but winter weather in Texas shouldn't be scoffed at. Overnight, temperatures can drop below freezing, and most years, Houstonians will wake up to a layer of frost covering the grass. Water temps can drop and be unpleasant for wet wading (sub-50-degrees). Some anglers don't seem to mind the cold water, and they still attempt to wet wade for the majority of the year. Nevertheless, having a pair of waders for winter fishing is a good idea for most people. If you plan on hitting the white bass run in the late winter to early spring, definitely consider purchasing a pair of waders. While fishing in the winter, it's generally a wise decision to have a pair of warm clothes in your vehicle in case you need to change into something dry to ward off the winter chill.

Early summer often brings wet weather to the Houston area. Most of the time, fishing in the rain isn't a big deal (excluding a thunderstorm, of course), but there are some instances where a deluge of rain could bring an end to the day's fishing excursion. Flash flooding events aren't uncommon in this region. Keep an eye on the water levels and be prepared to call it quits if you are on the water during a heavy rain.

Additionally, it is worth mentioning that some of the regional waterways have streambeds comprised of unconsolidated sand. In some of these streams, anglers can inadvertently sink down a foot or two. Some folks refer to this as "quicksand," although I tend to shy away from this term because it usually conjures images of Hollywood movies where someone slowly gets sucked into a pit of sand or mud, never to be seen again. My experience with "quicksand" in our local streams is much less insidious and usually means sinking up to a knee or thigh and having to wiggle free. It is hardly ever life-threatening; it is just uncomfortable. With that being said, it is something to be aware of while trudging through our local streams. Some of the waterways where you might encounter this hazard include Caney Creek, Spring Creek, the West Fork San Jacinto River, and Village Creek.

Animals

One of the greatest joys of fishing in Southeast Texas is the abundance and diversity of wildlife. You'll encounter local wildlife not only in the rural Pineywoods but also in the urban environments. Most of the wildlife encountered will bring a smile to your face, but it's important to remember that wild creatures aren't meant to be cuddled, no matter how cute they appear.

The word "quicksand" often brings to mind harrowing scenes in Hollywood adventure movies. However, the quicksand that is encountered in many Houston-area waterways is hardly ever life-threatening. Most of the time, stepping into "quicksand" is merely an inconvenience and you may have to spend some time wiggling your feet or legs free.

Through conversation with other Houston-area fly rodders, I find a common source of apprehension stems from snakes and alligators. While these critters can be intimidating at first, the more you are outside sloshing through creeks or paddling through the bayous, the more comfortable you will become with the local wildlife. Never feed the local wildlife. Doing so will cause them to lose their fear of humans and increase the risks of unwanted close encounters. In fact, feeding local fauna is illegal in many cases (feeding alligators can result in a $500.00 fine). Below are a list of animals encountered in both urban and rural settings and some helpful tips for staying safe while observing them

Snakes. Southeast Texas is home to a wide variety of snakes. Most of these snakes are nonvenomous and harmless, but there are four types of snakes that are venomous, and all of them are found in the area covered by this book. The rattlesnake, coral snake, cottonmouth (water moccasin), and copperhead are all local reptiles that can send an angler to the ER. The cottonmouth and copperhead are two species in particular that are seen regularly. An unpleasant encounter with a venomous serpent can almost always be avoided just by simply being aware of your surroundings and keeping a watchful eye on the ground when approaching or leaving a creek. Being self-aware will offer the best protection to most anglers. For added peace of mind, try wearing a pair

The copperhead and cottonmouth are the two most commonly seen venomous snakes in southeastern Texas. The timber rattlesnake and coral snake are two other venomous serpents in the area, but they are often more secretive, or, in the case of the coral snake, fairly docile.

of snake gaiters. A durable yet flexible brand is made by Scentblocker. On days of exploration and bushwhacking, especially in the Pineywoods, it's generally a good idea to wear a pair of snake gaiters.

Alligators. Alligators are another common reptile in the greater Houston area. Not all waterways contain resident populations of gators, but there are several waterways that tend to have a substantial number of them. Throughout the book, an attempt has been made to mention the bodies of water where alligators have been spotted. Obviously, there could be areas where they have been overlooked. Alligators should be respected and a healthy berth given to them when they are encountered. The Texas Parks & Wildlife Department (TPWD) suggests keeping a distance of at least thirty feet at all times. Harassing or feeding alligators is against Texas law and is a Class C misdemeanor. During the spring months (March to May), alligators are the orneriest because this is their breeding and nesting season. Female gators will build nests of sticks and vegetation along the water's banks, and they will guard these nests from egg scavengers. If an alligator hisses and/or approaches you, back away. You are likely too close to a nesting female. Alligator attacks in Texas are incredibly rare, but they have happened. Be aware of your surroundings and never tempt fate by approaching alligators.

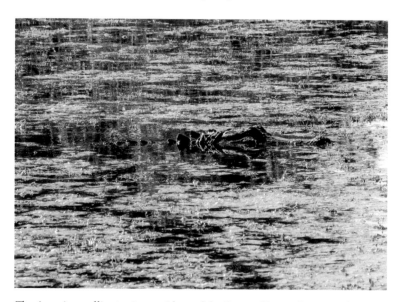

The American alligator is a resident of the Bayou City and surrounding area. This reptile can be intimidating and should be respected, although not necessarily feared. Alligators are fairly common in local waterways like Sheldon Lake, some parts of Lake Conroe, and Buffalo Bayou in the Katy area.

Ticks and Mosquitoes. Ticks and mosquitoes are prevalent throughout the Texas summer. Most of the time, these little pests are more of an annoyance than a legitimate concern, but it is still worth avoiding their tiny bites. When most people think of ticks, the first thing that comes to mind is the dreaded Lyme disease. Thankfully, Lyme disease is very rare in the Houston area. There are still other diseases that can be spread from tick bites, so to avoid having your blood sucked by either mosquitoes or ticks, it is wise to wear insect repellent. A spray known as permethrin is gaining popularity. Apply permethrin directly onto your clothes and boots about thirty minutes before putting them on. Let the permethrin dry onto your clothes. This product does an especially fine job at warding off ticks. Permethrin can also be used on dogs, but it is harmful to cats when still in its liquid form. If you have a house cat, spray your clothes with permethrin outdoors and make sure the liquid has fully dried before snuggling with Mr. Bigglesworth.

Fire Ants. Several species of fire ants exist in the Houston area. The bites and stings of these painful buggers should be avoided. The invasive fire ant species *Solenopsis invicta* is especially nasty. Fire ants build mounds of soft, loose soil. When their mounds are disturbed, the ants boil out of their nest by the hundreds looking to bite and sting the closest thing that's deemed a threat. Their stings leave small white pustules on the skin and are painful to the touch. All too often, unwary anglers walking the edges of bayous are oblivious to the fact that they disturbed a mound, until they feel the burning sensation of the fire ant stings. Wearing long pants, instead of shorts, helps protect your legs from the stings of fire ants.

Colonies of invasive fire ants can sometimes be seen floating on top of the water's surface after a flooding event. The ants make a raft with their bodies in order to float the colony to dry ground.

Stray Dogs. On more than one occasion, I've had run-ins with stray dogs. Most of the time, if you stand tall, lock eyes, point at the dog, and sternly yell, "Hey!" (or something like that), they will turn tail and run. Most of my encounters with strays have occurred when I brought along my own dog. My mutt was likely the unwitting culprit for bringing in the stray mongrels. A pack of strays is not a welcomed sight, especially when your only weapon of defense is a fly rod. After several unwanted encounters, I now carry a can of bear spray with me when I fish the urban waterways. If bear spray can stop a charging grizzly, it ought to do the same to a pack of stray dogs.

General Safety Tips for Urban Angling

Episode twenty-eight of the *Remote. No Pressure.* podcast, featured Houston-area native and fly fishing guide Danny Scarborough. At the start of the episode, Danny mentions to the host of the podcast, Jeff Troutman, that he is sitting in his truck while he's on the phone being interviewed. The audience can hear Danny put his keys into the ignition and start his vehicle. As the engine turns over, Danny says, "Some guy keeps coming up to my truck. I don't know what he's up to … All right, give me a second …"

After a brief pause, the audience can hear Danny say, "Get away from my truck, man."

Another brief pause follows, and then Danny resumes his conversation with Jeff by saying, "All right, I'm sorry. I'm in Houston, so you never know [what might happen] …"

Harris County (the county that contains the city of Houston) has more than four million residents. With the extremely rapid growth of this huge city comes typical big-city problems. It's an unfortunate fact, but levels of crime and homelessness do exist in Houston. As local anglers who fish urban waterways, we should be aware of these issues so we don't become victims of crime.

Theft. No matter whether you are fishing in the Pineywoods or in the urban concrete flats, always remember to hide any valuables that are in your vehicle before heading to the water. Thieves are always looking for an easy score, and if you leave a cell phone or computer bag in plain sight, you are providing an easy target. In addition to hiding obvious valuables, make sure to hide items like rod tubes, tackle boxes, and sling packs. Double-check your car doors to make sure they are locked.

Homelessness. Once you start exploring the urban fisheries, you'll eventually run across people who are downtrodden and, sadly, homeless. The vast majority of these poor souls are battling their own internal demons, and they will usually mind their own business as long as you mind yours. For the vast majority of the time, you won't have a negative encounter with these folks, but it is hard to stay inconspicuous while walking along the "concrete flats" carrying a 9-foot fishing rod. So, occasionally you may receive some unwanted attention. When urban angling, it is a good idea to fish with a buddy. Several overpasses and bridges closer to downtown contain homeless "camps." It's never a good idea to try your luck and go exploring under a dimly lit bridge or into one of these "camps." Stay in the open, within earshot and eyesight of your fishing buddy. Always be aware of your surroundings.

Don't put your fly line in your mouth when fishing in the urban waters. If your mother used to tell you, "Teeth are not tools," then it would be wise to heed her wisdom, especially if you're fishing Houston's bayous. Tying knots or cutting fly line with your teeth is a habit that many anglers have. I do it myself, but definitely **not** when fishing the urban waterways in Houston. Runoff from the streets, manicured lawns, dog parks, and industrial complexes all converge into our bayous. When you snip your fly line with those pearly white incisors, you are just putting the chemicals and bacteria from the urban waterways into your mouth. To avoid any kind of illness that could result, just use a pair of line snips and hemostats to change your flies and to tie your knots. If licking the sidewalk in downtown Houston sounds like a bad idea, then so should putting a fly line into your mouth.

Check your six before making a backcast. The reason behind the Houston Parks Rule 211.26 (Fishing prohibited in city parks) is safety concerns. The rationale behind this rule was that the city deemed it dangerous to have anglers casting sharp hooks at centralized urban parks where bikers and joggers might get hooked by errant casts. Fly rodders need more space for longer backcasts, so we also need to be more cognizant that our casts won't intercept unwitting joggers. Before you launch that beautifully executed double haul, take a peek over your shoulder and make sure the area behind you is clear of any park patrons.

Chapter 11

ETHICS OF FLY FISHING

AS FLY ANGLERS, WE AREN'T SIMPLY OBSERVERS OF THE natural world; we are participants. We bridge the gap between the aqueous animal kingdom and man's domain. We disrupt the daily routines of fish by fooling them into eating a hook, but we also do our part to understand and protect our cherished fish and their habitats. This is what we do as conscientious anglers.

There are a couple of simple guidelines that should be followed in order to maintain ethical standards. This is important so that our kids and grandkids can enjoy the same fishing experiences that we had. Follow these simple guidelines to ensure a bright and healthy future for fishing in the Houston area:

Fish legally and buy a fishing license. The money from purchased licenses funds land and water conservation, fisheries research, hatcheries, and the game wardens who enforce the state's game and fish laws. Anglers are required by law to have a fishing license if they fish anywhere within the state, with the only exception being a Texas state park. Fishing licenses can be purchased at big-box and sporting goods stores, many convenience stores near parks and lakes, and online at https://tpwd.texas.gov/regulations/outdoor-annual/licenses/.

Pack out what you pack in. Keeping our local waterways clean and free of litter should be our first priority as anglers. Always remember to pack out any trash that you might have brought in, including discarded fly line, tippet, and leaders. If you can spare the extra time, and the added weight in your sling pack, consider picking up some extra trash on your way out. A whole chapter has been dedicated to preventing further littering and cleaning up our bayous. See the chapter "An Angler's Role in Protecting Water Resources" for more information.

Be a considerate member of the fly fishing community. If you happen to run into other anglers while out on the water, never crowd the reach where they are fishing. The term "high holing" refers to the action of someone quickly leapfrogging around another angler and going just upstream so they can have dibs on a particular hole or section of water. Don't do that. If you simply stop and make small talk with another angler, you might find yourself a new fishing buddy.

Respect your quarry and the other creatures of the bayou. All creatures, big and small, deserve our respect. Some fly anglers choose to strictly practice catch and release. Every angler has their own journey, and just because one of us is determined not to harvest fish for the dinner table doesn't make the other wrong, so long as the fish taken is within the legal length requirement and daily bag limit. With that being said, consider practicing catch and release while fishing Houston-area bayous

Nick Heaverlo releases a dandy white bass.

Raccoons are often thought to be urban pests, but in their natural environment they compete with fisherman for their dinners.

and the streams of the Pineywoods, especially if the waterways being fished are small streams. Fish populations in small streams can easily be affected by the removal of fish for the dinner table. Please practice catch and release on smaller waterways.

Ethical Catch-and-Release Practices

There has been a long and ongoing debate in the angling world between two philosophies: "catch and release" and "catch to keep." The aim of this section isn't to pick a champion in this argument. Instead, the following paragraphs will focus more on how to do both ethically and also ensure that we have plenty of fish for future generations to enjoy.

Keep Fish Wet is an organization of anglers and scientists whose aim is to help increase the chances of survival for any fish that was caught and then released. Keep Fish Wet uses scientific data to provide anglers with a list of best practices that can be put to use when handling a fish

A white bass is released back into the waters of Caney Creek.

and returning it back to the water. Go to **keepfishwet.com** to check out its tips, articles, and studies. The following bullet points are merely a reproduction of the catch-and-release methods and tips endorsed by Keep Fish Wet:

Keep fish in the water as much as possible. All anglers know that fish breathe by bringing water, rich with dissolved oxygen, through their mouths and expelling it out through their gills. Therefore, a fish must be kept in the water in order to breathe. Landing nets are a great tool for keeping a fish fully submerged while the angler gets situated to either snap a photo or prepare for the release.

Avoid touching the fish with any dry surfaces. In addition to being covered in scales, fish are also covered in a layer of protective mucus. This "slime" protects fish from fungal infections and other diseases. If a fish comes in contact with a hard and dry surface, the layer of mucus can be scraped off, exposing the fish to infection. Before handling a fish, make sure your hands are dripping wet. This same rule applies for soft rubber nets or measuring boards. When you land a fish, either on the bank or in a watercraft, do not let the fish heedlessly flop around on the dry ground or deck of the watercraft. This will remove the protective mucus from the fish's scales.

Return the fish to water as quickly as possible. According to Keep Fish Wet, "It can take hours for a fish to physiologically return to normal once released." This means the longer you handle a fish, the more stressed it becomes. To speed up the recovery time, get the fish landed, unhooked, and released as quickly as possible.

Go barbless. We have all been there: you hook a small panfish or bass and the little guy absolutely inhales the fly. Then, using forceps, you have to tediously work the hook out of the gullet of the squirming fish. Most anglers feel a pang of remorse when a small fish is deeply hooked. We know that the chance of survival for that fish has been reduced, and it never had a chance to grow to its full potential.

To help reduce handling time and unnecessary prodding with pliers, make sure to crimp all the barbs on your hooks, or simply buy barbless hooks. This is especially important for those anglers who enjoy pursuing panfish. Many species of panfish have small and delicate mouths, a fact that we often forget given how aggressive and tenacious most panfish species are.

Dr. Robert Arlinghaus and Daniel Huhn published a scientific study that looked at mortality rates of fish caught with barbed versus barbless hooks. For barbed hooks, the average mortality rate was 14.6 percent. Not too bad. However, barbless hooks saw a mortality rate of only 8.2 percent. In addition to decreasing fish mortality rate, using barbless hooks can also be important from a safety point of view. On more than one occasion, I've seen friends howling with pain as they tried to remove a barbed hook from their flesh. Just think: had they fished barbless, the experience would have been far less unpleasant.

Use two hands when holding fish. In 2017, a study out of Florida was conducted on the techniques of handling largemouth bass and how they affect a bass's recovery time. The study found that a bass recovers faster if it is held with two hands. A largemouth bass that is held vertically, only by its lower jaw (lipping), has a recovery time that is drastically longer. To properly hold a fish (in this case, a bass), one hand holds the lower lip of the bass, while the second hand holds the fish under its belly, supporting the weight of the fish.

Ethical Catch-to-Keep Practices

I do enjoy angling for table fare on occasion, mostly for gar, catfish, and the occasional white bass and only on large waterways with plenty of fish. Most fly rodders do not keep what they catch because they simply like the sport of fishing and don't want the population of fish to suffer by their own hand. However, if you'd like to catch fish for dinner, always abide by the laws and bag limits set forth by the Texas Parks & Wildlife Department (TPWD). These regulations are based on population surveys and biological studies conducted by the state.

The regulations placed on certain species of fish are important because it helps ensure that healthy populations can survive year after year. Overharvesting fish, or harvesting fish that are too small, hurts the reproductive chances of particular species. You can find the size and bag limits for each species of game fish in the annually published "Outdoor Annual." This booklet is written by TPWD and contains the bag limits and laws for fish and game.

Additionally, it is a good idea to check the Texas Department of State Health Services to see whether any fish consumption bans or advisories are posted for the particular area you're fishing. There are many waterways in the Houston area that contain pollutants, and because fish also swim in these waterways, the Consumer Protection Division of the Texas Department of State Health Services issues consumption advisories against eating fish that are more susceptible to contamination. You can see a list of waterways with consumption advisories here: dshs.texas.gov/seafood/advisories-bans.aspx.

If you intend to eat some of the fish that you catch, please only harvest fish from large waterways. Killing fish from small waterways prevents future generations of anglers from enjoying the fun and productive small-stream fishing experiences that so many fly anglers seek. Be conscientious of your direct impact on our shared waterways, especially the small ones.

Anglers who use two hands to hold big bass ensure that the fish recovers quickly.

Rough Fish to Fine Dish

Gar are not often thought of as desirable table fare. But to anyone who has ever tried the mild-tasting meat, it is a wonder that these fish don't make it into the cooler more often. In order to properly clean these fish for eating, you will need a pair of tin snips. The armored scales of this fish can dull a knife in short order. Use the tin snips and make two crosscuts, one behind the head (from one gill plate to the other) and one above the base of the tail. Next, use the tin snips to cut down the length of the fish's back. Use a fillet knife and cut the white meat away from the inside of the scales. You can pull down on the scales to help peel it away from the flesh. Now use the fillet knife and cut parallel to the spine from the tail to the head. If you are familiar with removing the backstraps from a deer or wild hog, then this process will be familiar. Once the fillets are removed, you can brine them, batter them, or (my personal favorite) run them through a meat grinder and create gar meatballs. *Please note, gar roe (eggs) are* **very toxic to humans**. *Never attempt to eat the eggs from gar.*

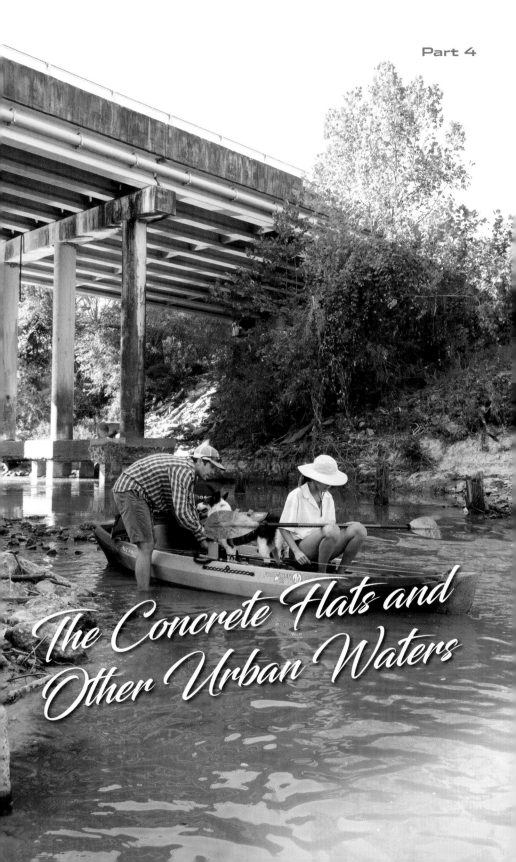

Part 4

The Concrete Flats and
Other Urban Waters

URBAN FLY FISHING

THESE WATERWAYS COME IN ALL SHAPES AND SIZES. SOME urban creeks run through forests, offering a feeling of tranquility, while others are lined in concrete and heavily urbanized. The fish in these waters vary just as much as the environments in which they swim. Native species like sunfish, bass, gar, and catfish can be found throughout the city. Numerous non-native species can be found throughout the city as well. Carp, koi, cichlids, and tilapia also call the Bayou City their home.

*Emily Scarborough
with a white bass from
Cypress Creek*

Chapter 12

CYPRESS CREEK

Suburban waterway with plenty of seclusion, steep and channelized banks make wading difficult, good paddling opportunities, spring runs of temperate bass.
Access Points: 4

THIS WATERWAY BEGINS AT THE CONFLUENCE OF TWO tributaries, Mound Creek and Snake Creek, and runs for 49 miles. From its starting point in Waller County, it flows northeast to its junction with Spring Creek. The large Houston suburb of Cypress (located along US 290/Northwest Freeway) is named after this creek.

Harris County's Precinct 3 and Precinct 4 Parks Departments have a master plan to eventually create a continuous trail system that runs the length of Cypress Creek. The trail will begin west of US 290 and run east, where it will end just downstream of the confluence of Cypress Creek and Spring Creek at Jesse H. Jones Park. The plan is to develop a network of hike and bike trails that connect the already existing parks that dot the length of Cypress Creek. This will form a natural riparian corridor for outdoor recreational use as well as flood mitigation.

The farthest upstream reaches of Cypress Creek flow through terrain that could be categorized as a mixture of woodlands and coastal prairie. As you go farther downstream, eastward, the creek gradually becomes more urbanized; however, the terrain adjacent to the banks of the creek still contains swaths of thickly forested lands.

For much of its length, the banks of Cypress Creek are very channelized. The incising of this creek yields steep banks of mud and silt. Wading certain reaches of this creek is a difficult chore at best and impossible at worst. With that being said, there are still plenty of locations along Cypress Creek that can be paddled.

This temperamental waterway can be a difficult nut to crack. The loamy and silty soils this creek flows through impart a muddy look to the waters, especially after a rain. The fine particulates can remain suspended in the water column for many days. Several tributaries and ditches that flow into Cypress Creek offer better water clarity and can be alternative small-stream fisheries for fly anglers. Tributaries like Faulkey Gully, Dry Gully, Theiss Gully, and others offer interesting opportunities, especially where they empty into Cypress Creek. One of the more prominent tributaries, Little Cypress Creek, will be outlined in more detail in the following pages.

Outside of the temperate bass spawning season, the lower reaches of this creek can be lacking in angling action. However, during the late winter and early spring months, white bass, yellow bass, and white crappie run upstream from Lake Houston and move into the lower portions of this creek. It is during this time of the year when Cypress Creek is at its best. To be a successful fly rodder on this creek, you'll need to practice patience and put forth a bit of effort.

USGS Stream Gauges along Cypress Creek

The stream gauge at I-45 (gauge number: 08069000) is the farthest downstream gauge on Cypress Creek. Low flows are around 40 cubic feet per second and a gauge height of approximately 64 feet.

Mercer Arboretum, Humble
30.03825, -95.38296
22306 Aldine Westfield Rd., Humble, TX 77338
24.5 road miles, 0:34 drive time
USGS Monitor Station: 08069000
Optimum flow: 40 cfs
Optimum gauge height: 64 ft.
Difficulty: Moderate to Hard

As previously mentioned, Cypress Creek can still appear cloudy even during low flows due to the suspended silt particles in the water. This waterway needs prolonged periods of time without inclement weather in order to clear up. Unfortunately, there are no turbidity gauges along this creek.

Try paddling this section of Cypress Creek during the white bass run. It is during this time of year when this portion of Cypress Creek offers the best fishing opportunities. With that being said, if you just want to go on a fantastic canoe or kayak adventure and fishing is secondary, then by all means float this creek any time of the year. If nothing else, this reach can be a fun and engaging paddle.

At optimum flows, the first 0.4 miles of this reach can simply be an out-and-back paddle. Beyond that, swift-flowing current will be encountered, making it challenging to paddle upstream back to the arboretum.

To get the most out of this section of water, consider floating downstream from Mercer Arboretum to Cypresswood Drive (30.02990, -95.33016). This trip is 4.1 miles. During the white bass run, bank fishing is popular at both Mercer Arboretum and at the take-out, Cypresswood Drive. However, if you are using a watercraft, you can access areas of Cypress Creek that see very little fishing pressure.

What You Will Find

Mercer Arboretum is approximately 400 acres and is maintained by the Harris County Precinct 4 Parks Department. This park is split into two sections. On the east side of Aldine Westfield Road, you will find the Mercer Botanical Gardens. On the west side, you will find the arboretum and various hiking trails, as well as access to Cypress Creek.

Prior to Hurricane Harvey, Mercer Arboretum had a well-maintained canoe launch under the Aldine Westfield Road bridge. Unfortunately, the flooding from Hurricane Harvey damaged the canoe launch beyond repair, and it is now condemned. The staff at Mercer Arboretum will tell you not to use the condemned canoe launch. Please abide by their request and don't launch your watercraft from the condemned launch. Instead, drag the watercraft down the sandy point bar, just on the east side (downstream) of the bridge. This launch site is steep but manageable. If you call the arboretum at (281) 443-8731, someone will open the gate and allow you to drive your vehicle to the edge of Cypress Creek. It is best to bring a kayak cart in your vehicle, just in case the gate to the canoe launch is closed. It is about 260 yards from the parking lot to the launch site.

Mercer Arboretum closes at 6:00 pm, and the gates will be locked by the staff. If you park your vehicle in the arboretum, be sure you are off the water before 6:00 pm, or you'll have to find another ride home. If you don't think you'll be off the water in time to retrieve your vehicle, another option is to park your vehicle on the north side of Cypress Creek at the CVS parking lot. This store is open 24 hours, so your vehicle will be safe here; just be sure to hide your valuables. Once you park at the CVS, simply walk along the sidewalk, across the bridge, and back to the entrance to the arboretum, about a third of a mile.

The original canoe launch at Mercer Arboretum has been condemned due to damages from flooding. You still may launch your watercraft here, but you must do so from the steeper sandy bank adjacent to the condemned launch.

Tanya Xu and Nick Heaverlo fish Cypress Creek.

16 Coyote Float (Paddling Downstream from Mercer Arboretum to Cypresswood Drive)

As soon as you launch your watercraft into Cypress Creek, you will be paddling through a deep pool. This is a great place to fish for white bass and black bass. Cast to the eddies and slack water on both sides of the creek, where the riffle empties into the pool.

For the next 0.4 miles, you will paddle through steep channelized banks. The clay shelves adjacent to the water offer habitat for bass. Cast to the sides of the banks and the submerged trees as you lazily float downstream. Be on the lookout for coyotes while you paddle this whole stretch. On more than one occasion while floating Cypress Creek, I've caught sight of these wily "yodel dogs." One summer, as we paddled Cypress Creek, we saw a coyote come leaping out from one of the large culverts along the edge of the creek.

This fast-flowing chute is probably the most "whitewater" you're going to find in the Houston area.

After the first 0.4 miles, you will float over a shallow riffle area. Here, the city has taken measures to reduce streambed erosion by lining the creek channel with what appears to be sandbags. However, these bags are likely geobags and are used frequently to mitigate erosion in sandy rivers.

In another 0.6 miles you will float under Treaschwig Road bridge. This is another popular bank fishing area and can also serve as an alternative access point (30.03410, -95.36712). Please note, the banks here are very steep, and more conducive for launching a paddlecraft rather than taking out a paddlecraft. If you plan on launching from this location, be prepared for a hard scramble.

Approximately 260 yards downstream from Treaschwig Road, you'll come to a large bend in the river followed by a set of riffles. If your watercraft has a shallow draft, you can easily shoot these small rapids, but before you do, make sure the rapids are clear of obstructions, like downed trees or overhanging branches. These can pose a hazard to paddlers.

For the next 0.3 miles, Cypress Creek flows over clay shelves and over small riffles. This section is best fished by beaching your canoe or kayak on the bank and walking downstream to fish the deeper chutes and holes.

The succeeding 0.5 miles is slow-moving and deep. There is a substantial amount of water to cover here, and unless you have a sink-tip line, much of this deeper flatwater can be skipped.

Once you come to another sharp bend in the creek, you will again see a section of small rapids. To be safe, it is best to beach your watercraft on the shallow clay bar, river right, and drag the watercraft over the rapids. You'll see that the creek makes a hairpin turn to the right, which can be hazardous to inexperienced paddlers. Just downstream of the rapid, you'll find a deep chute and pool.

The next 0.3 miles will be fairly shallow with interspersed pools and chutes. Eventually, you will enter back into a deeper section of water. Once in the deep water, you'll paddle for only about 200 yards and see

Emily Scarborough got four consecutive takes from a school of white crappie while fishing Cypress Creek during the white bass run.

a small waterway entering in from the right. This small stream is called Turkey Creek. A productive pool can be found at the confluence of Turkey Creek and Cypress Creek.

Once you paddle past Turkey Creek, the water becomes deep and sluggish. At this point you'll have approximately 1.25 miles left. This deep and flat section of Cypress Creek can be difficult to fish with floating line. By all means, bang the banks with flies, in the hopes of finding a largemouth, but for the most part you can continuously paddle through this section all the way to the take-out.

Once the Cypresswood Drive bridge is in sight, you may hear the whinnying of horses from the Cypress Trails Equestrian Center that lies on the high bank overlooking the creek. As you approach the bridge, stay to your left, along the outside edge of the creek. The current will sweep you around a shallow clay shelf. Once past the shelf, paddle for the sandbar on your right, upstream from the bridge. The take-out (30.03004, -95.33015) is undeveloped, so you'll be hauling your kayak or canoe up a sandy embankment to reach your vehicle.

Sections of Cypress Creek flow through secluded areas with towering trees on either side of the bank.

Keep in mind that the Cypresswood Drive bridge can also be used for a put-in location. At low flows, it is fairly easy to paddle upstream and then slowly float back down to the bridge.

Additionally, from the Cypresswood Drive bridge, it is a 2-mile paddle downstream to the confluence of Cypress Creek and Spring Creek. From the confluence, continue downstream on Spring Creek for 1.2 miles until

Sweepers and Strainers

Paddlers have a lot of nicknames for water hazards. Two of the most common are "sweepers" and "strainers."

Sweeper: A sweeper is an obstruction such as an overhanging tree or a tangle of branches that sits above the top of the water and can sweep a paddler out of their canoe or kayak.

Strainer: A strainer is an underwater obstruction. It can be a tangle of branches that lies below the surface of the water and can trap a paddler against the obstruction and hold them under water. Think of it like a giant sieve or colander where the paddler is the pasta.

you reach the kayak launch at Jesse H. Jones Park (30.02961, -95.29436). For more information on using the kayak launch at Jesse H. Jones Park, see the chapter on Spring Creek.

Getting There

From downtown, take I-45 North for about 17 miles. Take exit 66A toward Humble/Addicks/FM 1960. Turn right onto FM 1960 East. After nearly 3 miles, use the left two lanes and turn left onto Treaschwig Road. After 0.5 miles, turn left again onto Aldine Westfield Road. In 0.7 miles, you'll see a stop light and a street sign that reads "Mercer Park Entrance." Get in the left lane and make a left into the Mercer Arboretum on the west side of Aldine Westfield Road. Once in the park, make your first right. You will see a parking lot on your left. If you continue straight, past the parking lot, you will come to a gated road that will lead toward the Cypress Creek canoe launch.

Further Exploration

Little Cypress Creek flows southeast for approximately 14 miles before meeting Cypress Creek at a small community park called Maxwell Park. The water clarity in Little Cypress Creek is sometimes a bit clearer compared to Cypress Creek proper. The lower reaches of Little Cypress Creek are too shallow to offer much fishing opportunity. However, farther upstream, between Telge Road (on the west) and Longwood Trace Drive (on the east), there is section of water that offers a small-stream fishing experience. Park at Little Cypress Creek Preserve, just west of Telge Road (29.98994, -95.65378). The entire northern bank of Little Cypress Creek, from Telge Road downstream to Longwood Trace Drive, is part of the Harris County Flood Control District.

You can follow the creek under the Telge Road bridge and begin fishing the large pool, downstream from the bridge. The banks of Little Cypress Creek are high, which makes casting awkward, but there are several worthy fishing holes as you move farther downstream. There is a rudimentary hiking trail that runs along the top of the bank, river left, that can be used to quickly jump from hole to hole. Wading in the water is very difficult due to the steep, incised banks and deep holes.

About 0.3 miles downstream from Telge Road, you'll find a concrete ditch running into Little Cypress Creek from the north (river left). Where this ditch meets Little Cypress Creek, you'll find a riffle-pool-riffle section that holds crappie, bass, sunfish, and gar. Once you wet your line here, return to the bank and hike the primitive trail downstream to the next hole. As you continue moving downstream, the trail will eventually veer north, away from the water. You can call it quits here. If you wish to continue, you'll have to do so without a clearly marked trail.

This section of water can be a fun place to fish for an hour or two, especially if you live on the northwest side of the city. Because of the steep banks and difficult wading, don't try fishing this location if you are unsure on your feet.

Little Cypress Creek has very steep banks. This makes it necessary for anglers to scramble in and out of the water in order to fish this tributary throughly.

 Franklin's Tower

franklinstower.xyz

Franklin's Tower (4307 Treaschwig Rd., Spring, TX 77373) is located off Treaschwig Road between the cities of Spring and Humble. This establishment is within spitting distance of Cypress Creek. This eclectic beer joint and poolhall is sure to catch your eye with the many colorful murals painted on the side of the building and the Grateful Dead-themed school bus parked in the front yard. After a day of paddling Cypress Creek's Coyote Float, load up the kayaks and head over to Franklin's Tower for a cold brew. The friendly bartenders and fellow patrons are great for conversation. Franklin's Tower is open daily, noon–2 am.

Chapter 13

SHELDON LAKE

Fantastic paddling and opportunities for wildlife viewing, fun spring and summer topwater fishing for Florida largemouth, lots of gators. Access Points: 2

SHELDON LAKE WAS FIRST CONSTRUCTED IN 1942 BY impounding Carpenters Bayou, which flows into the historic Buffalo Bayou, about 11 river miles south of the reservoir. The impoundment flooded roughly 1,200 acres and resulted in a shallow wetland lake. The construction of Sheldon Lake was a federally managed project that was designed to supply fresh water to the wartime industries along the Houston Ship Channel during World War II.

In 1984, Sheldon Lake became a Texas state park. This park allows fishing, paddling, and wildlife viewing. This can be an excellent place to find an assortment of migratory waterfowl as well as shore birds. Gorgeous bald cypress trees tower over the water in many places throughout the lake. In the summer, a wide variety of aquatic plants

emerge, both invasive and native. The abundance of birds and wildlife makes it a great place to paddle around, even if you aren't interested in fishing.

Wading and swimming is prohibited in this reservoir due to the healthy population of alligators. The Texas Parks & Wildlife Department (TPWD) estimates that over 100 alligators reside in Sheldon Lake. Keep this in mind as you paddle around. Maintain a distance of 30 feet between you and the alligators. Never feed or harass alligators. If a gator becomes interested in a hooked fish that's on the end of your line, it's best to cut the line, and your losses.

Sheldon Lake boasts a healthy population of bowfin and large-mouth bass. Because of the stocking of Florida largemouth bass, this reservoir contains some lunkers. The all-tackle record for largemouth is 11.16 pounds. The fly rod record is 9.23 pounds. Crappie are also present, along with redear sunfish and bluegill.

A large alligator soaks up the sun on a fall afternoon. Texas Parks and Wildlife Department estimates that about one hundred alligators live in the Sheldon Lake State Park. Be respectful of these prehistoric reptiles and give them a wide berth.

Tanya Xu casts to the trunks of bald cypress trees in an attempt to entice a bass to strike her fly.

Although some bank fishing opportunities can be found along the southern levee and spillway (approximately 0.4 miles east from the Pineland Road boat ramp), the best fishing opportunities will be had from the hull of a canoe or kayak.

Because of this lake's close proximity to the city, it receives a substantial amount of fishing pressure. Many of the large bass in this lake are well educated and have seen just about every lure on the market, so don't be discouraged if you aren't connecting with any fish. Even if you only manage to land one or two fish, consider this an accomplishment. When a bass is fooled into eating your fly, it could be a hefty specimen. Because Sheldon Lake is a Texas state park, a fishing license isn't required to fish here.

Lake Levels

Sheldon Lake is a constant-level reservoir, meaning as the water level rises, it simply flows over the low-head dam on the southern end of the lake. Because of this, the lake level does not fluctuate much. According to a recent fish and habitat survey conducted by TPWD, the reservoir has a mean depth of 3 feet and a maximum depth of 20 feet.

Sheldon Lake, Garrett Road, Houston
29.88295, -95.18592
Garrett Rd., Houston, TX 77044
tpwd.texas.gov/state-parks/sheldon-lake
20.1 road miles, 0:27 drive time
USGS Monitor Station: N/A
Optimum flow: N/A
Optimum gauge height: N/A
Difficulty: Easy

Two designated canoe and kayak launch sites exist on Sheldon Lake. On the northern end, lake access can be found off Garrett Road (29.88295, -95.18592). This is a popular bank fishing location. The gravel lot allows for easy launching of kayaks or canoes. On the southern end, motorized bass boats can be launched from a paved boat ramp off Pineland Road (29.85105, -95.17444).

Travis Richards pops a foam frog among the lily pads on Sheldon Lake.

In the summer, many herons, egrets, and spoonbills nest in the cypress trees of Sheldon Lake.
Left: Great Blue Heron. Above: Roseate Spoonbill. Below: This Yellow-Crowned Night Heron had two juvenile chicks, still in the nest.

What You Will Find

In general, the northern end of the reservoir is the shallowest. In the summer, this end of the lake becomes choked in dense vegetation, which makes paddling a laborious chore.

Because this impoundment is so heavily vegetated, fishing topwater in the early spring and late fall is the most productive (and least aggravating) strategy. Hooks equipped with weed guards are a must-have on this lake.

17 Garrett Road Kayak Launch

It is best to launch on the western side of the parking area (on your right, if your back is to Garrett Road). This way, you will have immediate access to the open water. In the past, I made the mistake of launching my canoe on the other side (eastern side) of the parking area. I then had to sheepishly and apologetically paddle around the fishing lines of all the bank fishermen on my way to the open water. Save yourself a bit of embarrassment and launch on the western side of the parking area.

Sheldon Lake is not lacking in fishy habitat. Casting to the edges of weed beds is one strategy when fishing this body of water.

The John Jacob Observation Tower offers a commanding view of Sheldon Lake and the surrounding wetlands.

As soon as you leave the parking lot, you'll be paddling around large bald cypress trees with sagging limbs bending toward the water's surface. This makes for a novel fly fishing experience. If it weren't for the constant hum of the adjacent roadways, you'd think you were paddling through the backwaters of a secluded swamp somewhere in Louisiana.

The water depth in this area appears to be around 3 to 5 feet. The water is usually clear, or slightly stained from the natural tannins of the cypress trees. Paddle slowly around the edges of weeds and dense cover; you never know when you may come across a large bowfin.

In roughly 500 yards from the put-in, paddling along the "shore" of aquatic reeds and grasses, you'll see the reservoir open up before you. It's approximately 2.3 miles to the boat launch on the southern end of the lake if you continue south, paddling along the western shore.

The 82-foot-high John Jacob Observation Tower can be seen from the southern portion of Sheldon Lake.

Trey Alvarez displays a largemouth from Sheldon Lake. Topwater flies, like the blue BoogleBug, mimic an injured dragonfly fluttering on the surface.

As always when bass fishing, cast toward structure. A good spring and fall strategy is to lob topwater flies to pockets of open water (areas void of vegetation or algae). Once the cast is made, lightly wiggle your rod tip to impart slight movement to your fly, like a dying dragonfly. This should entice hungry bass to strike. It also has the added bonus of keeping your fly relatively weed-free.

Getting There

 From downtown, get on I-45 North. Follow the signs for I-10 east, toward Beaumont. Stay on I-10 east for over 12 miles. Take exit 781B for Beltway 8 North (Sam Houston Tollway). Take Beltway 8 north for just over 7 miles, and then take the exit for Garrett Road/CE King Parkway/ FM 526/Lake Houston Parkway. Make a right onto Garrett Road, taking it for just over 0.5 miles. You'll see the parking lot for fishing access and canoe launch on your right.

Sheldon Lake, Pineland Road, Houston
29.85105, -95.17444
Pineland Rd., Houston, TX 77044
tpwd.texas.gov/state-parks/sheldon-lake
17.0 road miles, 0:22 drive time
USGS Monitor Station: N/A
Optimum flow: N/A
Optimum gauge height: N/A
Difficulty: Easy

On the southern end of Sheldon Lake, off Pineland Road, a gravel parking lot and boat ramp can be found. This boat ramp is awkward because you have to back the boat trailer up and over a steep levee. The driver cannot see the water's edge and requires a buddy to help guide the trailer into position. Parking can also be a hassle because of the small size of the lot. However, fly anglers who choose to fish from a canoe or kayak will have no problem launching from this area.

Before paddling away from the boat ramp, make sure to hide any valuables in your vehicle and lock your car doors. A couple of years ago, there was a rash of vehicle break-ins at this boat ramp. Due to increased patrols from TPWD, the number of break-ins has decreased significantly.

What You Will Find

Although the summer months on Sheldon Lake bring an explosion of aquatic plants, there are still areas (primarily on the southern end of the lake) that remain relatively free of weeds. The water in the southern end of the lake runs deeper and is popular among bass boats. While operating a motorboat on the lake, it's against regulations to exceed headway speed (minimum speed necessary to maintain control of the boat).

18 Pineland Road Boat Ramp

Before paddling too far from the boat ramp, try poking around the islands that are in close proximity to the put-in (approximately 130 yards from the boat ramp). Plenty of structure can be found off the points of these man-made islands.

If you paddle toward the east, along the southern lake shore, you'll eventually come to the spillway (roughly 0.4 miles from the boat ramp, 29.85412, -95.16732). The spillway can be another area for bank fishermen to wet a line. Try making a couple of casts under the

There are several places along Sheldon Lake that can offer bank fishing opportunities. This fishing pier is on the south end of the lake, about 475 yards east of the boat ramp.

overhanging limbs in the corner of the lake, near the spillway.

Paddling the eastern edge of the lake is also a good strategy, and fish can be found under the overhanging limbs of bald cypress trees along the shoreline. Be sure to fish around the trunks of cypress trees. These sheltered areas attract all manner of fish. If you paddle the eastern shoreline up to the point where you are in line with the observation tower (John Jacob Observation Tower is an 82-foot-high viewing tower that is within Sheldon Lake State Park and offers a commanding view of the lake), then you will be about 0.7 miles, as the crow flies, from the boat ramp.

Getting There

 From downtown, get on I-45 North.–Follow the signs for I-10 east, toward Beaumont. Stay on I-10 east for over 12 miles. Take exit 781B for Beltway 8 North (Sam Houston Tollway). From Beltway 8 North (Sam Houston Tollway), take the exit toward US 90 West/Houston/90 East/ Liberty. Take the feeder road, crossing US 90, until the intersection with US 90 Business east (Beaumont Highway). Make a right. Continue on US 90 Business east for 0.7 miles, and then make a left onto Pineland Road. Travel north on Pineland Road for 0.2 miles. You'll see the boat launch on your right.

Sheldon Lake State Park Alligator Attack

Back in July 2014, ABC13 news reported that an elderly man was fishing in Sheldon Lake State Park. It is unclear whether he was fishing in one of the smaller ponds by the nature center or whether he was fishing in the lake itself. Nevertheless, he was happy to see his pole doubled over and bucking wildly. He had a fish on the end of his line, and he eagerly began reeling it to shore. Unbeknownst to the angler, an 8-foot-long alligator also had its eye on the hooked fish and trailed behind as the man reeled it in.

When the hooked fish neared the shore, the man noticed the pursuing gator, but because these reptiles are such a common sight at Sheldon Lake, he thought nothing of it and bent down at the water's edge to unhook the fish. That's when the gator lunged forward, fully emerging from the water. The man turned to run, but he tripped and the gator was on him. Its powerful jaws snapped down on the back of the man's leg and then again on his arm.

A courageous woman who witnessed the attack ran over and pulled the man to safety. The angler's injuries were not serious, and he was treated at a local hospital and released the same day. This was the first, and only, alligator attack to occur at Sheldon Lake State Park since the park opened in 1984.

 Spindletap Brewery

spindletap.com

Spindletap Brewery (10622 Hirsch Rd., Houston, TX 77016) is roughly 10 miles west of Sheldon Lake. This brewery makes some delicious beers. The warehouse and taproom boasts an outdoor sports complex where customers can get together with friends to play mini golf, basketball, and soccer. Needless to say, there is plenty of outdoor seating. Its taproom is open Tuesday and Wednesday from 4 pm to 9 pm, Thursday through Saturday from 11 am to 9 pm, and Sunday from 12 pm to 7 pm.

Chapter 14

Urban waterway with healthy fish populations. Mixture of concrete-lined channels and natural banks. Upper reaches contain chunky largemouth bass, lower reaches offer opportunities for gar and carp. Access Points: 8.

WHITE OAK BAYOU IS ANOTHER MAJOR WATERWAY THAT FLOWS through urbanized areas of Houston. White Oak Bayou rises northwest of the city and flows for 31 miles before running into Buffalo Bayou, north of downtown, at the historic Allen's Landing. The upper half of White Oak flows through banks covered in natural grasses and other wild flora. The lower half (downstream from West Tidwell Road) mostly runs through a concrete-lined channel until the bayou reaches Hogg Park, east of I-45. Here the bayou returns to a more "natural" state, with the channel being lined with large rocks and earth.

In addition to White Oak Bayou proper, Little White Oak Bayou is another waterway that will be addressed in this chapter. This small

At this location, the banks of White Oak Bayou transition from a natural state to a concrete-lined channel. A smaller tributary, Cole Creek, runs in from the west (left side of the picture). Inset: A well-fed White Oak Bayou largemouth

stream is a tributary that contributes a significant amount of water to the White Oak system. The confluence of these waterways can be found along the White Oak Bayou Greenway Trail on the western side of I-45.

In recent memory, Tropical Storm Allison (June 2001) brought unprecedented amounts of rain into the White Oak Bayou watershed. This storm event caused major flooding, which killed at least five people.

Decades later, while the city of Houston continues its rapid expansion, efforts are continuously made to reduce the risk of flooding along the

length of this waterway. Construction in the form of flood mitigation and erosion prevention has been an almost continuous occurrence over the past several years. As an angler, this can be frustrating. But as a homeowner in this flood-prone city, it is also welcomed. At the time of this writing, construction efforts are still underway along White Oak Bayou in the vicinity of Sam Houston Tollway (Beltway 8) and upstream in the community of Jersey Village. It's an unfortunate fact, but this has muddled the waters considerably, even for several miles downstream of the construction. Unfortunately, this has altered the fishing in many stretches of this bayou. It is the hope of many local fly fishers that water clarity will return to normal once the construction has finished.

Travis Richards makes a cast into White Oak Bayou with the Houston skyline looming in the background.

Over the years, a concerted effort has been made to incorporate this bayou into an enjoyable greenspace. The White Oak Bayou Greenway Trail runs along the lower reaches of the waterway for 17 miles. The trail begins at the confluence of White Oak Bayou and Buffalo Bayou, running upstream to North Houston Rosslyn Road in the neighborhood of Inwood. The White Oak Bayou Greenway Trail connects popular parks like T.C. Jester, Stude Park, and Hogg Park with trendy neighborhoods like Houston Heights.

To many local fly fishers, White Oak Bayou and Little White Oak bayou are thought of as fisheries for carp and bass. While there are good populations of both, these aren't the only fish that swim in these waters. Both spotted gar and alligator gar have been angled from these waters, along with freshwater drum, panfish, and even Rio Grande cichlids. The upper portions of White Oak Bayou have surprisingly girthy largemouth.

Generally, the largemouth bass have an affinity for the areas of White Oak that have naturalized channels. That is, upstream from West Tidwell Road. Of course, there are exceptions to this rule, but for the most part, if it's bass you're after, try the sections of White Oak that aren't lined in concrete.

Carp can be found throughout White Oak Bayou. They inhabit sections that are channelized in concrete as well as the naturalized banks. Fishing for carp along the concrete-lined sections can be fun because of the opportunities to catch these fish in an urbanized setting. However, much of White Oak Bayou upstream of Taylor Street and Stude Park doesn't offer a "concrete flat" for sight fishing. At normal flows, the concrete apron of the channel

Jack Boyd caught this grass carp using a deer hair hopper just upstream from West Tidwell Road.

is above the waterline. However, downstream of Taylor Street there is a concrete flat, but it's not quite as wide as the flats of Brays Bayou.

Safely Fishing the Concrete Flats

When the concrete banks of White Oak Bayou get wet, from either rain or humidity, they become slick. Be very careful when fishing the concrete flats after a rain. Consider fishing with a friend or not venturing out at all until the concrete dries. White Oak Bayou can rise very quickly and flow at a swift pace during rains. Know your limits and use your best judgement when fishing the concrete-lined channels of White Oak Bayou.

USGS Stream Gauges along White Oak Bayou

A total of three USGS stream gauges can be found along White Oak Bayou, plus one along Little White Oak Bayou. The farthest upstream gauge is at Alabonson Road (gauge number: 08074020), near the neighborhood of Inwood. If you plan on fishing the uppermost sections of White Oak, this is your only option for trying to get a grasp on flow rates. A discharge rate of around 15 to 20 cubic feet per second and a gauge height of 60 feet is optimum. For the lower reaches, try checking out the gauge at Heights Boulevard (08074500). Low flows are around 30 to 40 cfs, and look for around 8 feet for the gauge height. The final gauge can be found upstream from the confluence of White Oak Bayou and Buffalo Bayou. This gauge is located at the crossing of North Main Street (08074598), and it only records gauge height. Little White Oak Bayou

Jack Boyd is fond of using his bicycle to cover water along White Oak Bayou.

Biking for Carp

For 17 miles, White Oak Bayou Greenway Trail runs adjacent to the water. Local carp fanatic Jack Boyd is fond of taking his fly rod with him when he rides his bicycle along this portion of White Oak Bayou. When Boyd spies a carp from the bike trail, he hops off his bike and stalks in on his quarry. "Biking along White Oak is my favorite way to fish this bayou," says Jack Boyd. "I can cover miles of water. The best day I had fishing White Oak from my bike was when I managed to catch twenty-five carp. They were mostly grass carp."

If you'd like to try urban carp fishing from a bike, but you don't have a bicycle or you're just visiting the Bayou City, don't worry. Bike rentals can be found throughout the city at automated bike share stations called BCycles. It costs $3.00 for 30 minutes, plus a $26.00 charge that will be reimbursed in a week once the bike is returned to any of the automated BCycle stations. Stude Park offers a rental station (29.77915, -95.38562), which can be found at 2300 Forester, Houston, TX 77007. For other rental locations, go to houstonbcycle.com.

has one gauge that is located on Trimble Street, west of Moody Park (08074540). This gauge records height of the stream but only registers flow rates above 100 cfs, which only occur during high flows. Optimum gauge height is 19.3 feet.

West Tidwell Park, Houston
29.84738, -95.46175
West Tidwell Rd., Houston TX 77091
12.2 road miles, 0:21 drive time
USGS Monitor Station: 08074020
Optimum flow: 15 to 20 cfs
Optimum gauge height: 60 ft.
Difficulty: Easy to Moderate
Difficulty: Easy

Downstream from the West Tidwell Road bridge, the banks of White Oak Bayou transition from natural and grass-covered to channelized in concrete. From this location, anglers have the opportunity to walk either upstream or downstream along the White Oak Bayou Greenway Trail. By walking upstream, anglers have the opportunity to fish along natural banks.

What You Will Find

West Tidwell Park isn't much of a park. It is simply a greenspace with a couple of trees and a dirt parking lot. Patrons of the White Oak Bayou Greenway Trail often park in this empty lot. Before leaving your vehicle, be sure to take or hide any valuables.

Both bass and carp can be found at this location. Blind casting into the depths of the bayou, or casting to structures like rock piles, culverts, and bridge pylons, is a good way to find bass. Carp can be seen from the trail, usually feeding in the shallows, and grass carp can sometimes be seen eating from the surface.

19 Tidwell Wade (Wading Downstream from the Park)

From the parking area at West Tidwell Park, head toward the bayou. From the greenway trail, you should see a short riffle. The concrete fill that creates this riffle was placed in the bayou to mitigate erosion. If you're looking for bass, stand on the exposed concrete (only exposed during optimum flows) and launch casts upstream and downstream. Don't overlook the eddies that are formed along the downstream side of the fill.

Just a little more than 100 yards downstream is the West Tidwell Road bridge. It can be tricky fishing under this bridge because of the large boulders that line the bank. It's also hard to find room to make a decent backcast. Be cautious of walkers and bikers on the trail. Always check behind you to make sure your backcast is clear.

Once on the downstream side of the bridge, you'll notice a large culvert on the opposite bank (river left). A small pool is formed by a ring of rocks around the front of this culvert. This is an excellent place to find either a bass or a carp.

By now you will see where the concrete channel begins. The bayou shallows as you approach the end of the naturalized banks. Be on the lookout for carp in this shallow section. Move slowly, and meticulously scan the water for any carp in the shallows.

A little bit farther downstream, a tributary known as Cole Creek flows into White Oak Bayou from the right (river right). The flow of Cole Creek is magnified by discharge from a wastewater treatment facility. The water in Cole Creek is clear. It is worth taking a quick detour just to see if you can find a fish or two.

If you aren't having any luck downstream of the West Tidwell Road bridge, try walking upstream, past the parking area. There are several good riffles around the first bend, roughly 250 yards upstream from West Tidwell Park. When water conditions are clear, this can be a great area to find both bass and carp. Unfortunately, urban fly anglers might have to wait another year before the construction on White Oak Bayou is finished and the water clarity returns to normal

Anglers are encouraged to continue exploring along the greenway trail, either upstream or downstream. In order to traverse more water, consider exploring the upper reaches of White Oak Bayou by using a bicycle.

Parking can be found west of White Oak Bayou, on the north side of West Tidwell Road. This area is sometime referred to as West Tidwell Park.

Jack Boyd surveys the water along White Oak Bayou.

Getting There

 From downtown, head north on I-45. Stay on I-45 North for just over 5.6 miles. Take exit 54 toward Tidwell Road. Merge onto the North Freeway Service Road for approximately 0.8 miles before making a left onto East Tidwell Road. Continue heading west on Tidwell Road for 4.2 miles. Once you cross White Oak Bayou, slow down. West Tidwell Park will be your next right. It is a sharp turn into a dirt parking area in an open greenspace.

Stude Park, Houston
29.77989, -95.38241
White Oak Dr., Houston, TX 77009
houstontx.gov/parks/communitycenters/cc-stude.html
3.0 road miles, 0:08 drive time
USGS Monitor Station: 08074500
Optimum flow: 30 to 40 cfs
Optimum gauge height: 8 ft.
Difficulty: Easy

Stude Park is a recreational area with ball fields, community center, playground, and pool. The southern extent of the park borders White Oak Bayou. Starting at the Taylor Street bridge, the gently sloping bottom of the concrete-lined bayou is submerged, thus creating a concrete flat. This can be a fun spot for urban carpers attempting to sight cast to feeding grass carp. The farther downstream you go, the deeper the concrete flat becomes, making sight fishing more difficult.

What You Will Find

The above coordinates will take you to a gravel parking lot for the baseball field at Stude Park. Park in the gravel lot across from the large apartment building, Elan Heights Apartments. From the parking lot, head south along the paved walkway to the water. Keep in mind that you will be fishing in close proximity to the White Oak Bayou Greenway Trail. This trail is very popular for local residents. Be aware of your surroundings and always check behind you before making a backcast.

20 Stude Park Wade (Walking Downstream from the Park)

When you head south from the gravel parking lot toward White Oak Bayou, you will be upstream from the Taylor Street bridge by about 100 yards. Walk downstream toward the bridge. Once on the downstream side, the sloping concrete apron becomes submerged (at optimum flows) and forms a concrete flat on which the carp can be seen feeding.

Take your time as you move downstream from the Taylor Street bridge. The carp in this bayou tend to be pressured by local urban anglers, and they can be very wary. Local fly fisher and resident of the Houston Heights Joe Mills says that fishing for carp near the Taylor Street bridge can be productive, but at times it can be frustrating. "When the bite is on, it's really good. My favorite way to catch grass carp is on hopper patterns. If you can find grassers feeding on topwater, it's great watching them eat. If they aren't sipping on the surface, well-placed nymphs will usually work. Somedays, they aren't having any of it, which can make for tough fishing, but there's really no way to know without just going for it."

In a little over 300 yards from the bridge, you will see a small concrete ditch coming in on your left (river left). This ditch is often dry during optimum conditions. Before crossing the ditch, check along the corners of the concrete on both sides of the channel. Carp can often be seen at this location.

From this point, you can pick up the pace and cover ground as you head downstream. Still keep a watchful eye on the water's edge, just in

Joe Mills and Eric Ostrom point out a common carp cruising the shallows along Little White Oak Bayou near its confluence with White Oak Bayou proper.

case you see grass carp feeding on the surface, but it is nearly a half-mile walk to the next bridge, Houston Avenue.

Once you walk under the Houston Avenue bridge, it is a short 220-yard jaunt to where the waters of Little White Oak Bayou join with the proper White Oak Bayou. Blind cast to the mouth of Little White Oak Bayou, where it dumps into the main bayou. Be sure to fish upstream along Little White Oak Bayou. To successfully cover the lower section of this major tributary, it will be necessary to do some scrambling. It is easiest to access the water on the dirt path where the bridge spans Little White Oak. This section of water sees substantial fishing pressure from fly anglers and bait fishermen. Nonetheless, this can be a good place to find a largemouth bass, panfish, gar, or carp. There is a substantial hole that can be found where Little White Oak emerges from the high rectangular culvert, over which White Oak Drive spans the water.

If you simply wish to fish the confluence of Little White Oak and White Oak proper, parking can be found off White Oak Drive in close proximity to the intersection with North Sabine Street (29.78173, -95.37519).

At this point, you are about 0.2 miles from Hogg Park, which can be found farther downstream (29.77802, -95.36720). Accessing White Oak Bayou via Hogg Park is another option for anglers wishing to fish the lower reaches of this bayou. Local urban anglers like Joe Mills consider this lower section to be more of a bass and

Above, left: The largemouth bass that can be caught in proximity to Hogg Park aren't likely to be lunkers. But it is still an amazing experience landing in a bass with the cityscape of downtown Houston looming in the background. Left: Spotted gar from the waters of White Oak Bayou, downstream from Hogg Park

gar fishery, although finding carp through this section isn't uncommon. Any bass that is caught in close proximity to Hogg Park isn't likely to be a whopper, but landing a largemouth bass in sight of downtown Houston is something special in its own right.

From Hogg Park, you will see the end of concrete-lined channel about 140 yards downstream. From this point on, White Oak Bayou flows through naturalized banks to the confluence of Buffalo Bayou. Unfortunately, litter piles up at this location. Tie on a fly that you don't mind losing to a snag.

It's another 130 yards downstream to a bridge where the Heights Hike and Bike Trail crosses White Oak Bayou. On the upstream side of the bridge, a small black culvert protrudes from the bank (river left). You can cast to the bridge pylons with ease from this location. When you are finished casting on the upstream side of the bridge, move under

Olivewood Cemetery

From the eastbound lanes of I-10, between the exits 767A (for Studemont Street) and 767B (for Taylor Street), motorists can catch a glimpse of one of Houston's oldest cemeteries. The Olivewood Cemetery rests on the south bank of White Oak Bayou and the White Oak Bayou Trail. This historic cemetery is the burial site of Houston's earliest Black residents. Prior to 1875, this site was the resting place of many black slaves. Houston's first black alderman, Richard Brock, purchased the land in 1877 and established a cemetery.

the bridge and fish around the rocks and pylons on the downstream side. Again, watch your backcast. The bike trail is directly behind you.

Getting There

 From downtown, head west on Allen Parkway for 1.2 miles. Take the exit for Montrose Boulevard, heading north to Studemont/ Montrose. Montrose Boulevard turns into Studemont Street after 0.2 miles. Continue on Studemont Street for another 1.2 miles. You will drive over White Oak Bayou on Studemont Street. After crossing over the bayou, look for Usener Street on your right. Take Usener Street around the northern perimeter of Stude Park. Turn right at White Oak Drive and park at the gravel lot for the baseball field at the northern edge of White Oak Bayou.

Woodland Park, Houston
29.78350, -95.37064
212 Parkview St., Houston, TX 77009
4.2 road miles, 0:11 drive time
USGS Monitor Station: 08074540
Optimum flow: NA
Optimum gauge height: 19.3 ft.
Difficulty: Moderate to Hard

This little gem of a park is nestled among the trees. The waters of Little White Oak Bayou flow through a wooded area south of the community center and basketball court. This is a popular park because of its close proximity to The Heights, a fashionable Houston neighborhood. Primitive walking trails can be found in the trees at the back of the park. These trails lead down to Little White Oak Bayou and can be used to bounce between fishing holes.

What You Will Find

From the parking lot at Woodland Park, walk to the right side of the community center building along the paved walkway. When you get to the tree line, head into the forest on the dirt trail down the gentle slope. Once on level ground, you should see the bayou from the dirt path. This trail runs along the length of the stream.

21 Little White Oak Bayou at Woodland Park

Along this section of Little White Oak Bayou, there are several holes in which fly fishers can plunk their flies. Because of the diversity of fish in this waterway, it can be tough to decide which fly to tie on. Do you want to chase carp, bass, or panfish? When swapping flies, don't forget to use your nippers and hemostats to cut and tie your knots. Little White Oak Bayou is polluted, and you don't want to cinch down any knots with your teeth.

Heading upstream following the dirt trail, you'll eventually come to a large pool. Here the stream flows out of three large tunnels. This is the farthest upstream you can go in Woodland Park. Little White Oak Bayou flows from under I-45 at this location. The large pool at the mouth of the tunnels is a great place to throw streamers for bass and gar. In order to make a cast, it is easiest to scramble down the bank (river right) and cast from the water's edge. Be mindful of the overhanging trees. Use sidearm casts or roll casts to get your flies into the water.

Once you are done fishing this pool, turn around and walk back along the same trail. You will cross a makeshift bridge made from two boards that span a little wet spot on the trail. Once you cross these boards, head down the bank to the water. Here, a little pool often holds green sunfish, longear sunfish, bass, and the occasional grass carp.

Travis Richards stalks a pod of grass carp. With its unfortunate abundance of litter, Little White Oak Bayou isn't the most picturesque waterway, but holds a healthy fish population.

Downstream for the next 230 yards, the banks on either side of the waterway are steep and tall. On days when the water is clear, you will see gar and carp milling about. However, getting down to the water's edge to make a cast can be difficult along this section.

Despite the pollution and litter in Little White Oak Bayou, nature still finds a way. This spotted gar carried his prized longear sunfish around for at least an hour while we stood on the banks and fished for bass.

Little White Oak Bayou at Woodland Park

Marine biologist and professor Travis Richards says, "It is stunning that Little White Oak holds as many fish as it does, especially when considering how much trash is in that bayou."

Little White Oak Bayou is considered one of the most littered waterways in Houston, and it is ranked one of the top five most impaired waterways in the Houston area by the Bacteria Implementation Group. (BIG is a committee of local conservation groups and local governments that assess regional waterways and implement plans to reduce high concentrations of bacteria in those watercourses.) The bacteria levels that are found in this creek are fifteen times higher than the state water quality standard. When wetting a line in this small bayou, avoid wading in the water. Most of your fishing should be done from the bank. It's also a good idea to take a shower and wash your clothes after angling in this creek. With that being said, please don't be discouraged from visiting this waterway; the more that anglers are aware of the diversity of fish in this small creek, despite its subpar water quality, the more attention will be brought to cleaning up this unique lotic ecosystem.

Travis Richards launches a cast to the mouth of the tunnels along Little White Oak Bayou. Inset: Travis Richards holds a fat and healthy tilapia that was caught in Little White Oak Bayou.

Eventually you will see a large, washed-out concrete culvert laying in the middle of the waterway. During optimum flows, you can often stand next to the riffles that the concrete culvert is laying on. Make casts downstream into the deep pool. This is a good spot to find gar. The bridge that is downstream another 50 yards is Woodwright Street. Turn around and fish your way back upstream.

Getting There

From downtown, head north on Studemont Street. Once you cross under I-10, make a right onto Usener Street, which merges into White Oak Drive. Continue on White Oak Drive until the intersection with Houston Avenue. Make a left onto Houston Avenue, heading north for 0.2 miles. Make a right onto Parkview Street. You will see Woodland Park on your right.

Further Exploration

More fishing opportunities can be found in the smaller tributaries that flow into White Oak Bayou. Outflow ditches from wastewater treatment plants, along with minor streams, can be exciting waterways for small-water fly rodders.

Many minor tributaries can be found east and west of Sam Houston Tollway (Beltway 8) in the vicinity of Jersey Village. Use online aerial maps to do your scouting. Anglers can look for deep holes in smaller waterways, which are thermal havens for fish. Additionally, try fishing the areas where minor tributaries enter into White Oak Bayou. These confluences usually have deep holes associated with them.

One creek in particular that long rodders should visit is Vogel Creek, in the Greater Inwood area. Parking can be found north of West Little York Road in the Victory Disc Golf Course (29.86382, -95.46755). The thick vegetation growing along the banks of this creek offers plenty of habitat for insects as well as cover for the resident fish. Wear long pants if you intend on visiting Vogel Creek. You may have to do some bushwhacking through the tall grass adjacent to the water's edge.

Several mulberry trees grow along the banks of Vogel Creek. In mid- to late-spring, after the mulberries are fully ripe, they begin dropping into the water. This is an outstanding time to fish this small waterway. Grass carp can be found circling under the mulberry trees, waiting for the ripe berries to fall. Just about anything that plops into the creek (including a fly) is quickly eaten. Hopefully the city continues to let the mulberry trees grow and doesn't opt to cut them down due to flood mitigation efforts.

 Bobcat Teddy's Icehouse

If you are done chasing carp along White Oak Bayou, you may find yourself in close proximity to the Houston Heights. Head over to Bobcat Teddy's Icehouse (2803 White Oak Dr., Houston, TX 77007) for a cold beer. This is a laidback, come-as-you-are establishment with plenty of outdoor seating. Bobcat Teddy's doesn't serve food, but occasionally there will be a food truck parked behind the bar. There are also plenty of other restaurants in easy walking distance.

Chapter 15

BUFFALO BAYOU AND
ITS TRIBUTARIES

Historical urban waterway that runs through downtown Houston; steep and channelized banks require the use of watercraft. Poor water clarity in Buffalo Bayou but novel urban fishing opportunities in the adjoining tributaries. Access Points: 9.

IN THE YEAR 1836—THE SAME YEAR TEXAS WON ITS independence from Mexico—two brothers, John Kirby Allen and Augustus Chapman Allen, stepped off their boat onto the banks of Buffalo Bayou. The two brothers were land speculators from New York, and they had recently purchased more than 6,000 acres adjacent to the confluence of Buffalo Bayou and White Oak Bayou. This intersection of waterways would come to be known as Allen's Landing. It would become the first wharf of the city of Houston.

Ever since the Allen brothers developed Allen's Landing, Houston has been known as a port city. Currently, it is home to the largest port in the U.S. by tonnage. Many waterways weave across the landscape in close proximity to Houston, but Buffalo Bayou is chiefly responsible for giving this city its nickname, the Bayou City.

Before it empties into Galveston Bay, the lower reaches of Buffalo Bayou are dredged and widened regularly in order to maintain navigability for large cargo ships. This section of Buffalo Bayou is referred to as the Houston Ship Channel.

This historic waterway begins in the prairie lands west of the city, at the confluence of Willow Fork and Cane Island Branch. The region's loamy soils impart a cloudy and muddled look to the water. Even during periods of low flows and bluebird skies, Buffalo Bayou remains hazy. In total, these murky waters flow for 65 miles due east. The lower reaches run right through the heart of downtown.

On the western outskirts of the city, Buffalo Bayou flows through a low-lying bottomland. This area is known as Barker Reservoir and serves as flood control. A large earthen dike and spillway can be seen from the road while you are traveling along TX 6 south. The U.S. Army Corps of Engineers manages the flow of the bayou at this location. After the waters leave Barker Reservoir, it begins a winding course through a highly-urbanized environment. The farther downstream the bayou flows, the more metropolitan it becomes. A 26-mile stretch from the spillway at Barker Reservoir (29.76956, -95.64381) downstream to Allen's Landing (29.76458, -95.35958) is a designated Texas Parks & Wildlife Department (TPWD) Paddling Trail. For folks who are interested in floating this historic waterway, Bayou City Adventures (bayoucityadventures.org) offers kayak rentals, tours, and shuttle services.

Despite prior years of pollution and urban encroachment, Buffalo Bayou has seen a revitalization that has enhanced the aesthetics and ecological health of this important waterway. Through the efforts of the city, corporations, conservation groups, and local philanthropists, many county and city parks dot the length of this bayou. Hike and bike trails provide outdoor recreation but also double as riparian corridors for local wildlife.

After the flooding of Hurricane Harvey, controversies swirl on how to mitigate future floods along this bayou. Many local conservation groups are at odds for how best to address the environmental engineering efforts. However, when it all gets boiled down, one thing remains: everyone sees the importance of maintaining a healthy and iconic waterway.

When it comes to fly fishing Buffalo Bayou, wading in these mysterious waters is out of the question. The water is too murky, deep, and filled with submerged trees and other debris. Using a paddlecraft is the best way to access this watercourse. The trick is to hit the bayou when the conditions are just right. While paddling this bayou, cast to the mouths of feeder creeks, minor tributaries, and outflows from culverts. This is usually the best option for hooking into predatory fish like largemouth, gar, and channel catfish. Frankly, you won't catch tons of fish on the fly in the Buffalo Bayou proper, but fishing in this urban stream is too unique to pass up.

Buffalo Bayou proper is probably best known for its bait-fishing opportunities. Blue catfish, channel catfish, and flathead catfish have all been brought to hand using conventional tackle and bait. However, the most breathtaking species that swims in these murky waters is the gargantuan alligator gar. If anglers want to truly unlock the secrets of this waterway, put down the fly rod and pick up conventional gear. Soaking live bait or fresh cut bait will undoubtedly prove that river

Stavros Cotsoradis hangs on while an alligator gar makes an impressive leap. Cotsoradis went "all in" landing this beautiful specimen on the Buffalo Bayou. Stavros used conventional tackle and fresh carp cut bait to entice this fish.

monsters are lurking in the deep, dark recesses of this urban bayou. Maybe in the coming years, a resourceful fly fisher will figure out how to consistently target these massive alligator gar on the fly in Buffalo Bayou.

Local angler and fishing guide Alex Sosa (both a fly fisherman and gear fisherman) is well acquainted with the lower sections of this bayou. Alex fishes near downtown with the cityscape looming above. He uses fresh bait and conventional rods to catch large blue catfish, channel catfish, and alligator gar. If fly anglers want to put away their fly rods and pick up some heavy-duty bait-chucking gear, contact Alex Sosa through Instagram @buffalobayoufishingchamps.

Fly Fishers Should Focus on the Tributaries

Even though the mainstem Buffalo Bayou may seem like a difficult waterway to fly fish, anglers can still find opportunity at the mouths of small feeder creeks and along tributaries that flow into the main channel of

Fishing guide Alex Sosa and his client, James Marklove, hold a nice alligator gar that was pulled from the waters of Buffalo Bayou near downtown Houston.

Liam Smith holds a dandy flathead catfish that he caught in the Buffalo Bayou using conventional tackle and bait. Catching one of these fish on the fly is a rare occurrence.

Buffalo Bayou. These smaller watercourses tend to be more conducive to fly fishing and will be the main focus in the coming chapter. There are too many tributaries to describe in detail, so I would encourage you to look at aerial images online and scout any of the smaller waters that look intriguing. Some of these minor waterways, although small, can offer enjoyable small-stream opportunities. Streams like Turkey Creek, Horsepen Creek (north of Addicks Reservoir), Clodine Ditch (inside George Bush Park), and many more small creeks and ditches around Katy all have resident fish populations.

The select tributaries that will be introduced and discussed in some detail in the coming chapter are T-103 Ditch, Mason Creek, Bering Ditch, Spring Branch, and Niemann Branch.

The small tributaries that flow into Buffalo Bayou can be surprisingly clear and provide special urban experiences to fly anglers. In this chapter, these minor waterways will appear in order, starting with the upstream tributaries around Katy and then heading downstream towards the city.

USGS Stream Gauges along Buffalo Bayou

Once Buffalo Bayou leaves Barker Reservoir (in close proximity to TX 6 south), six stream gauges can be found along its length. For the purposes of this book, the ones to heed the most are the gauges at Barker Reservoir (gauge number: 08072600) and the gauge at Piney Point Village (08073700).

The gauge at Barker Reservoir (08072600) is always a good one to check because much of the flow of the bayou is dictated by this reservoir. When the discharge rate is around 51 cubic feet per second and a gauge height of 56.7 feet, that's about as low and clear as you're going to get. The gauge at Piney Point Village (08073700) should read around 110 cfs and a gauge height of about 28.1 feet.

George Bush Park, Westheimer Parkway, Houston

29.73610, -95.72268

Fun Fair Positive Soccer Complex, George
Bush Park, 20710 Westheimer Pkwy.,
Houston, TX 77094

26.8 road miles, 0:33 drive time

USGS Monitor Station: N/A

Optimum flow: N/A

Optimum gauge height: N/A

Difficulty: Easy

The T-103 Ditch flows from west to east alongside the George Bush Park hike and bike trail. This slow-flowing waterway is home to fish species like carp, gar, bass, and the occasional Rio Grande cichlid. A paved trail can be found along the bank, river left. In warmer months, watch your step while walking through the grass next to the bayou; cottonmouths have been spotted in this area. Also, on occasion, a large gator will be seen near the confluence of the T-103 Ditch and Buffalo Bayou.

What You Will Find

Parking for this location is found within the Fun Fair Positive Soccer (FFPS) Complex. Once in the park, head toward the back of the parking lot, past the soccer fields. When you get close to the tree line, you will see a paved sidewalk that leads into the woods. Walk along the paved trail

The George Bush Park hike and bike trail spans the width of the ditch.

for 0.3 miles until you come to a pedestrian bridge (29.74022, -95.72314). This is the T-103 Ditch.

From 2020 to 2021, the T-103 Ditch was under construction. The goal of the Harris County Flood Control District was to remove the silt and restore sections of the bank that had eroded. Since the construction began, this waterway fishes differently than it has in the past. It is still worth a trip because, for the most part, the fish are still there and still hungry.

This sign along the T-103 ditch serves as a friendly reminder that humans share this space with wild creatures. If you see an alligator in the T-103 ditch, please keep your distance.

 22 **T-103 Ditch** (Hiking Upstream from the Bridge)

The water flows at a very sluggish pace through this ditch. If you are standing on the paved pathway, looking at the pedestrian bridge, the water is flowing from left to right. It's a little more than a mile downstream where the T-103 Ditch meets Buffalo Bayou. However, the best fishing is in the opposite direction, upstream of the bridge.

Start by leaving the paved path and walk in the grass along the ditch. If the grass is high, be careful of where you step. Snakes have been seen here, and there are some fire ant mounds along the bank. Move upstream for about 115 yards. On the opposite bank, you will find another ditch, which brings in water from the north. Cast to the mouth of this ditch.

As you continue moving upstream, keep a close eye on the water. On days when the water is clear, you should be able to see carp, gar, and bass along the banks or in the shallows. Keep moving upstream until you see a culvert that discharges wastewater from a nearby treatment plant (29.74115, -95.72709). Fish tend to stack up in front of the concrete slab that the wastewater flows over. Water clarity is excellent in the vicinity of this discharge site. Baitfish can be seen swimming back and forth in the intermittent flow that discharges from the culvert. If the baitfish are there, bigger fish aren't far behind.

If you continue farther upstream for another 170 yards, you will see where rocks have been placed on the bottom of the

Top: Zach Wallace fishes for a late-evening bite along the T-103 ditch. Bottom: Wallace with a largemouth bass from the T-103 ditch

ditch to prevent erosion. Another small, cement-lined ditch flows in on your left (29.74162, -95.72892).

This is another excellent spot to make a couple of casts. Smaller bass and panfish seem to like the rocky substrate because it serves as a place to forage for food but also as a place to hide from predators.

Getting There

 From downtown, take I-45 North to exit 48B. Merge onto I-10 West (Katy Freeway). Continue on I-10 toward Katy. Head west for 20.8 miles. Take exit 747A toward Fry Road. Turn left onto South Fry Road. Stay on South Fry Road for 3.6 miles. Make a left onto Westheimer Parkway for 0.6 miles. The soccer fields can be seen from Westheimer Parkway. Turn left into the parking lot.

Prince Creek Drive, Katy
29.76681, -95.72870
20600–20615 Prince Creek Dr., Katy, TX 77450
25.9 road miles, 0:32 drive time
USGS Monitor Station: N/A
Optimum flow: N/A
Optimum gauge height: N/A
Difficulty: Easy to Moderate

Mason Creek is a tributary that flows into Buffalo Bayou upstream from Barker Reservoir. From 2020 to 2021, Mason Creek underwent construction in the form of channel widening and silt excavation. Prior to this construction, the waters of Mason Creek were relatively clear. Unfortunately, this recent construction muddled this waterway significantly. The hope is that this change will only be temporary and that fishing will return to normal. Even with the recent construction, largemouth bass, panfish, gar, and the occasional carp can be caught in this stream.

What You Will Find

When available, find street parking at the corner of Prince Creek Drive and Rustic Knolls Drive. Be sure you don't park in front of someone's driveway or mailbox. Once you find parking, head to the bridge where Prince Creek Drive crosses Mason Creek. There is a paved bike trail along the bank. From this location Mason Creek flows southeast for 0.8 miles before flowing under South Fry Road. Downstream from South Fry Road, the creek becomes significantly wider. It continues for another 1.5 miles before disappearing into the dense forests of Barker Reservoir.

23 Mason Creek (Wading Downstream from the Bridge)

Start at the bridge where Prince Creek Drive spans Mason Creek. Take a look upstream. You will see a large metal retaining wall that holds back both banks on either side of the creek. We will begin this wade by heading downstream, in the opposite direction from the retaining wall.

For the first 400 yards downstream, Mason Creek flows in a riffle-pool-riffle sequence. Prior to construction, and during times of low flows, small bass and panfish could be seen swimming about in these pools.

As you continue downstream, the flow becomes more sluggish. Multiple culverts protrude from either bank. Make yourself a personal rule to never walk past a culvert without making a cast to the mouth of the pipe. Structures like these are always good places to find largemouth bass or channel catfish.

By now, you should see a massive live oak tree that looms over the water on the bank, river right (29.762998, -95.723235). In the heat of the summer, this is always a welcomed place to take a quick break and drink some water or eat a snack. You may even find a bass or two in the shadow of this beautiful and ancient tree.

In a little less than 200 yards, you will begin to notice the channel widening. As you walk along the bank, look for carp feeding in the shallows. Be sure to make blind casts toward deeper pockets and pools.

By continuing downstream, you'll follow the bike trail under South Fry Road (29.75943, -95.71800). When going under this busy street, make a couple of casts to the bridge pylons. Be sure to watch your backcast for joggers or cyclists.

In another 560 yards downstream, you'll reach a pedestrian bridge that spans the width of Mason Creek. Cross this bridge to get to the northeast bank of Mason Creek. Just downstream of the bridge (river left), a wide ditch flows in from the north (29.75629, -95.71323). The water in this shallow ditch is usually clear. It's a good spot to make a couple of casts. Watch for snakes, especially if the grass is high.

This massive live oak can be found on the western bank of Mason Creek, downstream from Prince Creek Drive.

Flood mitigation and construction began on Mason Creek in 2020. Despite this, fish can still be found in this creek. After the construction wraps up, the fish populations will return to normal. Below: Largemouth bass like this one are a common fish in Mason Creek.

Getting There

From downtown, take I-45 North to exit 48B. Merge onto I-10 West (Katy Freeway). Stay on I-10, heading west, for 20.8 miles. Take exit 747A toward Fry Road. Turn left onto South Fry Road. Stay on South Fry Road for 0.7 miles. Make a right onto Kingsland Boulevard. After 0.2 miles, make a left onto Houghton Road. In less than half a mile, Houghton Road veers right and becomes Prince Creek Drive. Stay on Prince Creek Drive for about 0.5 miles. You will drive over Mason Creek just before the intersection of Rustic Knolls Drive.

Briarbend Park, Woodway Drive, Houston

29.74586, -95.50685

7926–7966 Woodway Dr., Houston, TX 77063

9.6 road miles, 0:22 drive time

USGS Monitor Station: 08073700

Optimum flow: 110 cfs

Optimum gauge height: 28.1 ft.

Difficulty: Moderate to Hard

Many of Buffalo Bayou's minor tributaries can be accessed on foot, but to get the full urban fishing experience, it is best to paddle down Buffalo Bayou itself. As was already mentioned, Buffalo Bayou can be a finicky waterway for fly fishing. For most of the year, the water is muddled, which makes fishing this waterway a difficult task. The following description will offer some insight into paddling and fly fishing this iconic waterway, but a focus will remain on the minor tributaries. This section of the bayou was chosen for this book because of the clear tributaries that join Buffalo Bayou along this reach. These feeder creeks include Bering Ditch, Spring Branch, and Niemann Branch.

Before launching a canoe into Buffalo Bayou, Ellen Dortenzo sits and surveys the water at the Briarbend Canoe Launch.

This nice bass was caught amongst the rocks and rubble at the mouth of Bering Ditch, where it enters the Buffalo Bayou.

What You Will Find

In total, this paddle is about 5.8 miles long. On TPWD's Paddling Trail website (tpwd.texas.gov/fishboat/boat/paddlingtrails/), the department estimates that the paddle will take between 3.5 and 4.5 hours. Of course, this doesn't factor time spent fishing. Realistically, this float could take anywhere from 6 to 8 hours, depending on how the fish are biting. Floating this section is a day-long commitment, so plan accordingly.

Although this bayou flows through a very metropolitan area, don't write this waterway off as an easy float. Parts of Buffalo Bayou can be surprisingly treacherous, especially for inexperienced paddlers. Submerged trees abound in these waters, and the bayou flows at a surprisingly quick pace. If you become complacent while paddling this waterway, you could very quickly find yourself in a bad situation. Be aware of water hazards, like sieves, that could entrap you or your boat.

Before you begin, you'll need to park a shuttle vehicle at the take-out. There is a gravel parking lot at the intersection of North Post Oak Lane and Woodway Drive (29.76502, -95.45698). From this gravel parking lot, a paved walkway leads to a well-maintained kayak launch on the downstream side of the Woodway Drive bridge (29.76448, -95.45801).

The put-in location is at Briarbend Park (29.74604, -95.50728). Here you will find streetside parking. The canoe launch is at the back of the park, in the tree line. The Houston Canoe Club and Bayou Preservation Association are responsible for developing this launch site. The path down to the water is quite steep with several switchbacks. Scout this launch site before attempting to take your kayak or canoe down the steep embankment. Be careful when you make your way down the stairs. The trail can be slippery if it's wet.

When fishing this section, consider bringing two rods. One rod can be loaded with a sink-tip fly line, and the other can be equipped with floating line. The rod with sink-tip can be used for blind casting into Buffalo Bayou, while the rod with floating line is great for plunking bugs into the smaller tributaries. Bring extra flies with you; the submerged timber in Buffalo Bayou has a tendency to steal all your hard-earned flies.

24 Briarbend Paddle (Paddling Downstream from the Park)

Once you shove off into the water, the first bridge you come to is San Felipe Street. This is only half a mile into the trip. From this bridge, it is another mile until Voss Road crosses the bayou. Once you travel under Voss Road, you will traverse along two bends. After the second, be on

Fish often congregate at the mouths of culverts like the one in this photo. This gar ate a black and white Mini Dungeon that was plopped down right in front of the culvert.

the lookout for a small tributary that flows in from the right side (river right). This is Bering Ditch (29.76193, -95.49642). You will notice large limestone boulders along the bank. Unfortunately, you'll also notice submerged shopping carts and other litter, so watch your step once you beach your watercraft on the sandbar, river right.

Make casts into the pools and eddies where Bering Ditch flows into Buffalo Bayou. Largemouth bass and channel catfish can be angled here. Additionally, carefully hop along the boulders upstream along Bering Ditch. About 20 yards from where Bering Ditch empties into Buffalo Bayou, a clear pool can be found that contains plenty of bass and green sunfish.

Cleaning Up Bering Ditch

For decades, Bering Ditch has been plagued with litter. Everything from shopping carts to Styrofoam cups to discarded tires have been heedlessly dumped into this waterway. Not only is this litter unhealthy for the environment, but it also creates flooding issues. Bering Ditch saw a major cleanup effort in 2011, thanks in part to Bayou Preservation Association. Then in 2020, Bering Ditch received a grant from Harris County Flood Control to remove accumulations of silt and even more litter. Efforts like this will help restore Buffalo Bayou to a beautiful and natural state.

From Bering Ditch, head downstream for another 2 miles. Along this stretch, you will see some huge mansions along the left bank. You will also hear golfers teeing off at the Houston Country Club on the right side of the stream. Be sure to cast to the mouth of any culvert you paddle past.

The next bridge spans the bayou at a small community of houses called Farther Point. Head under this bridge and float downstream for another quarter of a mile. You'll see a larger bridge for Chimney Rock Road. Just downstream of Chimney Rock Road, Spring Branch enters from the left. Swing your kayak into this creek and paddle upstream for 30 yards until you come to a sandbar (29.77402, -95.47921). You will likely see grass carp and mullet kicking up clouds of mud while they make their escape to deeper water.

Spring Branch is a clear little watercourse that flows over a streambed of hard-packed clay. Good populations of panfish exist, along with healthy numbers of bass and gar.

Once you beach your watercraft at the first available sandbar, make your way upstream to the large pool with a sizeable sycamore tree leaning over the water. This pool can be very productive for bass and panfish. Make casts toward the roots of the sycamore tree. Be ready for a bass to hit the fly on the drop.

Farther upstream, there are several more pools that can be fished. While hopping from boulder to boulder, watch out for the rebar that is protruding from some of the concrete fill that was dumped into the streambed.

After fishing Spring Branch, head downstream in your watercraft for another half mile. You will come upon an island that sits in the middle of Buffalo Bayou. Stay to the right side of the channel. Once you make it around the island, you will be faced with a set of small rapids (29.77217, -95.47431). At optimum flows, it is best to hit the first rapid on the left side and then cross to the right side and run the second.

Immediately after making it through the rapids, you will see a tiny tributary entering from the left (29.77229, -95.47398). Pay close attention, or you'll miss it. This is Niemann Branch. Paddle into the mouth of this creek. Once in the tributary, you will see that this stream is fed by an outflow from a private reservoir high on the bank, above Buffalo Bayou. Don't paddle too far into this tributary because you will spook the fish in the single clear pool. To thoroughly fish this little waterway, consider beaching your watercraft on the sandbar at the mouth of Niemann Branch and continuing on foot.

Once back on the mainstem of Buffalo Bayou, you will only have 1.3

Trey Alvarez battles it out with a nice spotted gar. Although it's a small waterway, Spring Branch can hold large bass and gar. Below: This gorgeous spotted gar was angled from the first pool, upstream from the confluence of Spring Branch and Buffalo Bayou.

miles left until the take-out. The next bridge you see is the Woodway Drive bridge. Float under the bridge and eddy out on the left side (29.76448, -95.45801). You will see a sandbar where you can beach your watercraft. It is a little over 100 yards up the paved walkway back to the parking lot and your shuttle vehicle.

Getting There

 From downtown, head west on Allen Parkway until Waugh Drive. Make a right onto Waugh, using the cloverleaf to merge onto Memorial Drive, heading west. Continue on Memorial Drive for over 3 miles, then make a slight left onto Woodway Drive. Stay on Woodway Drive for 3.5 miles until you come to South Voss Road. Make a left onto South Voss and stay in the right lane, crossing over San Felipe Street. The next street is Creekwood Drive. Make a right onto this street. Creekwood Drive turns into Woodway Drive. Take Woodway Drive through the neighborhood for approximately 0.4 miles. You will see Briarbend Park on your right. Park along the fence, but be mindful not to block any driveways.

Further Exploration

Even though the murky waters of Buffalo Bayou might not be conducive to the nature of fly fishing, the historic and modern-day ecological importance of this waterway make it worth wetting a line in. Who knows? As the health of this bayou continues to improve, maybe the next generation of fly anglers will be presented with an even more robust urban fishery.

Additional paddling opportunities abound for Houston's most famous bayou. I encourage you to strike out on your own and discover which sections of Buffalo Bayou you enjoy fishing. Personally, I have enjoyed

A freshwater drum (gaspergou) from Buffalo Bayou, along Terry Hershey Park

paddling through Terry Hershey Park (on Houston's west side) from the confluence of Langham Creek down to Sam Houston Tollway (Beltway 8). The bayou along this reach flows under a beautiful canopy of trees.

The put-in for this location is at the end of Memorial Mews Street (29.77367, -95.62328). The take-out can either be Dairy Ashford Road (29.76151, -95.60565) or Sam Houston Tollway (Beltway 8). Before attempting this section of river, scout the take-out site at Dairy Ashford Road to make sure you are up for the challenge of hauling your paddlecraft up the steep bank. The take-out is under the Dairy Ashford Road bridge, *before* the rapids. This paddle has yielded several species of fish, including gar, bass, gaspergou (freshwater drum), and crappie. Most of these fish were caught in the vicinity of feeder creeks and culverts.

At certain times of the year, fly fishing guide Mark Marmon offers float trips down Buffalo Bayou within the I-610 loop. Marmon suggests that anglers cast to any tributaries, ditches, or culverts that bring fresh water and morsels of food into the bayou. Marmon often begins his floats at Woodway Drive (29.76448, -95.45801). There are several take-out locations downstream of Woodway Drive. Hogg Bird Sanctuary (29.75856, -95.42186) is the next identified take-out downstream. Be forewarned that there isn't an established trail leading down to the bayou at Hogg Bird Sanctuary. You'll have to find your own way from the parking lot to the water. Try skirting the edge of the pedestrian suspension bridge.

For further reading on paddling Buffalo Bayou, visit the Houston Canoe Club website (thcc.clubexpress.com). Also check out Natalie Wiest's book, *Canoeing and Kayaking Houston Waterways*, for even more detailed route descriptions along this historic waterway.

Houston's Craft Breweries

Once you finish exploring the mysterious waters of Buffalo Bayou, you need to check out Houston's burgeoning craft beer scene. There are a ton of fantastic breweries within the I-610 loop where thirsty anglers can stop. There are too many breweries to pick just one, so I'll simply list some of my favorites. The following breweries have outdoor seating and won't care if you show up with a little bit of Buffalo Bayou mud stuck to your pants.

Small Breweries

Holler Brewing Co. (hollerbeer.com) This is a small brewery with a neighborly vibe. This brewery is connected to the Silver Street Art Studios and offers an outdoor patio and great-tasting beers.

Platypus Brewing (platypusbrewing.com) This is another small brewery with a laid-back, friendly atmosphere. There is plenty of outdoor seating under the covered patio at the back of the building. Try the IPAs.

Urban South – HTX (urbansouthbrewery.com) The original Urban South Brewery was born in New Orleans, Louisiana. The Houston brewery was opened in 2020 and serves as the company's research and development brewery. It's a constant revolving door of unique beers that are brewed at this location.

 ## Big Breweries

St. Arnold Brewing Company (saintarnold.com) This is a large brewery with tons of outdoor seating. St. Arnold boasts a commanding view of the downtown cityscape. It really is something to see. St. Arnold Brewing often hosts live bands, and it has even hosted the Fly Fishing Film Tour in past years.

Buffalo Bayou Brewing Company (buffbrew.com) You didn't think we could talk about the famous Buffalo Bayou and not mention Buffalo Bayou Brewing Company, did you? This locally famous brewery describes itself as "Houston's Most Creative Brewery," and it certainly has some unique beers to prove it. However, its mainstay brews are its copper ale, 1836; its Crush City IPA; and of course its imperial IPA, More Cowbell.

Chapter 16

BRAYS BAYOU

Iconic urban waterway. Home of the Houston concrete flats. Clear water with sight fishing opportunities for big carp. Plenty of catfish, gar, and other species, including exotics. Access Points: 7.

THIS 30-MILE-LONG WATERWAY BEGINS IN WESTERN HARRIS County and flows east until its confluence with Buffalo Bayou and the Houston Ship Channel. The upper portion of Brays Bayou flows through banks covered in grasses and other vegetation. Once the bayou reaches I-69/US 59 (Southwest Freeway), it begins flowing through a concrete-lined channel. When urban anglers think of Brays Bayou, it is this section that often comes to mind. This highly developed portion of Brays is recognized by local fly rodders as an iconic urban carp fishery.

Brays Bayou is a fairly clear waterway, which makes sight fishing possible. The deepest part of the channel runs through the middle of the bayou. This is the main travel corridor through which most fish swim up and down the watercourse. However, carp will move from the deeper water and feed on the shallow apron of the concrete-lined channel. This is called the "concrete flats." When the carp are feeding on the concrete flats, they can be spotted easily, but seeing these wary fish and catching them are two different things.

Carp are the most popular fish pursued by fly anglers in Brays Bayou, but this waterway holds a surprising array of aquatic life. In 2017, the Texas Parks & Wildlife Department (TPWD) conducted a fish survey of the lower portion of this bayou. The crew sampled the ubiquitous carp population but also found healthy populations of native fish like channel catfish, largemouth bass, and smallmouth buffalo. What's more, the lower reaches of Brays Bayou are tidally influenced, and the TPWD biologists captured several redfish and a sheepshead.

> "I find the urban concrete setting to be an interesting contrast to the fineries of fly fishing."
>
> —Shannon Drawe (texasflycaster.com) on fly fishing Brays Bayou

If you run into any bank fishermen while exploring this waterway, stop and talk with them. If they have been fishing Brays Bayou for any amount of time, you are bound to hear some stories about unique encounters with interesting fish species. Everything from blue catfish to alligator gar, American eels, and saltwater species like seatrout and redfish have all been caught in this unique bayou.

The Godfather of Urban Carp Fishing in Houston

Throughout the decades, Brays Bayou has appeared in magazine articles, newspapers, blog posts, and (more recently) YouTube videos. But before it was a locally famous fishery for carp fanatics, it was just a local fishing hole for desperate Houston fly anglers.

In 1999, Brays Bayou made its first appearance into the world of fly fishing. In the spring issue of *Warmwater Fly Fishing* (discontinued), author Phil Shook (author of *Flyfisher's Guide to Texas*, *Fly Fishing the Texas Coast*, and many others) penned an article about this urban fishery. The title of the article was "Houston's Urban Ditch Fishing." In it, Shook described one of the most influential figures responsible for starting the urban carp-fishing scene, Mark Marmon.

Even to this day, one cannot mention Brays Bayou without thinking of the part-time fly fishing guide, musician, and Episcopal priest.

Mark Marmon is considered the godfather of urban fly fishing in Houston. Also, to many contemporary fly rodders, Marmon is somewhat of a carp guru, especially when it comes to grass carp. He is likely one of the first fly fishermen in the country to pursue grass carp on the fly.

Marmon describes how it all began: "In Europe, fishing for carp with conventional gear was popular. But back then, I didn't know of anyone who was doing it with a fly rod. A lot of my early clients were Europeans who wanted to try fly fishing for carp. They would catch a flight to Houston for a business trip, and to kill an hour or two, they'd hire me to walk the bayou with them."

When asked why he started fishing Brays Bayou, Marmon says that he started because he liked fly fishing in saltwater, but he hated going to an empty field or a parking lot to practice his cast.

Mark Marmon with a common carp from Brays Bayou, circa 1979

He wanted to fish, not practice fishing. Marmon began fishing Brays Bayou out of necessity. He needed a place to fish, and Brays Bayou was just down the road from his house.

After making several trips to Brays Bayou to "practice" his casting technique, Marmon began toying with the species of fish that swim in the concrete-lined bayou. To date, Marmon has caught eighteen different species of fish from Brays, including largemouth bass, channel catfish, gar, and even an occasional white bass. But by far, the most notable fish, and the most popular, are the carp species. Three species have been caught in Brays Bayou: grass carp, common carp, and the coveted koi.

When asked how the bayou has changed over the years, Marmon says that aside from the ongoing flood mitigation efforts and construction, the biggest change is that the culture along the bayou has shifted. Marmon says that when he first began fishing Brays Bayou, the surrounding neighborhoods were different than they are today.

Marmon tells a story about when he was fishing in the bayou one evening, and he saw someone run down to the water's edge. The man threw a suitcase into the water. It floated downstream past Marmon, who used his fly rod to fish it out of the water. When he opened it, he was alarmed to find it full of drugs. Marmon wasted little time bringing it to the police station.

"But that was long ago," Marmon says, "Now, I see families walking or jogging along the bayou. I sometimes see young kids fishing with spinning gear."

Many local carp enthusiasts see Brays Bayou as a textbook urban fishery. Fly fishing guide Danny Scarborough says, "People don't realize that fish are in there, and that they can be up to 20 pounds, if not more!"

Danny caught the state fly rod record grass carp from Brays Bayou, in 2014. The big grasser weighed 16.5 pounds and was 32.5 inches long. Both Scarborough and Marmon claim that bigger fish have been hooked in the bayou.

How to Fish Brays Bayou and How to Do It Safely

The concrete-lined channel of this bayou is quite steep, and walking along the steep grade can be taxing on the ankles. It is easiest to walk along the level ground at the top of the channel. You can pretty easily walk the level berm where the concrete meets the grass. Also, from this height it is easier to see fish feeding in the shallows. Pay close attention to any nervous-looking water. If you see a single V-shaped wake, then it's likely a carp or smallmouth buffalo. If you see lots of smaller wakes making a wide swath of nervous water, it is probably a school of mullet.

When you do spy a carp feeding in the shallows, move down the slope of the concrete channel toward the water. Be as sneaky as you can. Crouch down and move slowly. When you make the cast, you may have to raise your casting arm high above your head in order to clear the top of the ditch on your backcast.

Although most of these locations along Brays Bayou have "Easy" access ratings, please be advised that the steep concrete sides of this bayou can be very slick when wet. The waters of Brays Bayou are surprisingly swift, especially after heavy downpours. Unfortunately, over the years, this waterway has claimed the lives of several people who fell into the water (usually during flooding events) and couldn't find purchase on the slick concrete sides of the channel to pull themselves to safety. This isn't meant to scare you into thinking Brays Bayou is a dangerous place to fish. It is not, but it's worth remembering that although this urban bayou has been heavily altered by the hands of mankind, there should be no doubt that Mother Nature is still in charge.

Before You Begin, Understand Grass Carp

If fishing for grass carp is a new endeavor for you, let it be known that these fish can be maddening at first. Take time getting acquainted with their nervous behavior and seemingly random antics. As time goes on, you will find more success fly fishing for them.

While you make your way along the banks of Brays Bayou, you will almost certainly see grass carp with regularity. They might be mixed in

Under certain conditions, grass carp can be found sipping food off the water's surface. They can eat grass clippings, bugs, berries, or in this case, flower petals from wild mustard plants. If you see grass carp feeding on the surface, tie on a dry fly. Hooking a grass carp on topwater is exhilarating.

Joe Mills poses in a stormwater drain with a dandy grass carp from Brays Bayou.

with groups of smallmouth buffalo or with a school of mullet. You might consistently see them in certain section of the bayou for weeks, and then one day, they'll be gone, having moved to a different part of the bayou.

Seeing grass carp and catching grass carp are two very different things. Some of these finicky fish may continuously reject well-presented flies. If this happens, don't sweat it; keep covering water and finding more fish. Eventually you'll cast to one that's willing to eat. Some days, when the stars align and all is right with the world, anglers may find the grass carp in a feeding frenzy, sipping bugs and algae off the surface with abandon. Needless to say, these are the days anglers remember fondly.

Often the best strategy for hooking a grass carp is to plunk a weighted fly, like Scarborough's Brasshawk or Marmon's Bellaire Bonefish Fly, a couple of inches in front of the fish. This may seem counterintuitive for some anglers because this action often spooks other species of fish. However, for Brays Bayou grass carp, the sound of something dropping into the water often results in the grass carp moving in to eat. If you find a pod of feeding grassers, they may even race one another to the fly. Sometimes, when a grass carp moves in to eat, it will lose track of the fly. Simply pick up your line and cast again. It may take three or four casts until the grass carp finally connects with your fly.

If an angler botches a cast or the grass carp gets lined in its face with tippet or leader, the fish will often bolt for the deeper channel. This is nothing to worry about. You'll have plenty more opportunities before the day is done. Houston native and urban carper Jack Boyd says, "Most of the time when you spook them, they swim downstream a couple of yards and hide in the deeper water. Go fish another section of the bayou, but make sure you come back. The carp you spooked earlier will probably be feeding again at the same spot."

USGS Stream Gauges along Brays Bayou

Consult the stream gauge that is located where Main Street crosses the bayou (gauge number: 08075000). Low and clear readings usually bounce between 120 and 150 cubic feet per second, with a corresponding gauge height between 16.6 and 17 feet. If you are fishing the downstream reaches by MacGregor Park, consult the gauge at Martin Luther King Boulevard (08075110). Optimum levels will bounce between 1 and 2 feet depending on the tides.

Intersection of S Braeswood Blvd and W Loop S, Houston
29.68034, -95.45869
Lot A, W. Loop South, Houston, TX 77096
12.0 road miles, 0:17 drive time
USGS Monitor Station: 08075000
Optimum flow: 150 to 120 cfs
Optimum gauge height: 17 to 16.6 ft.
Difficulty: Easy

At this location, I-610, South Post Oak Road, and several feeder roads cross Brays Bayou. The mass of bridges spanning the water offer habitat for a population of common carp and grass carp. There are several places to park. You can find parking along the streets of Meyer Park Drive (29.68372, -95.45569) or Frankway Drive (29.68387, -95.45459). Both of these locations are on the north side of the bayou. If you park here, you will need to walk south, cross North Braeswood Boulevard, and then head west toward the I-610 bridge. Another option is to grab a drink at the Starbucks (29.68246, -95.45795) located at the corner of North Braeswood Boulevard and West Loop South and leave your car in the parking lot while you fish. Additionally, there are parking lots under the I-610 bridge on the south bank of the bayou. These lots are owned by the Houston Metro Park & Ride. According to its website, the gates at the parking lot close at 4:00 pm, but this may not be accurate. I have parked here in the past and haven't had an issue with towing. With that being said, I'm not entirely sure whether parking at this location is legal.

What You Will Find

Both common carp and grass carp can be found at this location, although they don't seem to frequent this reach in the summer months. In the fall and winter, you might find them directly under the network of bridges or downstream from the bridges. If you get frustrated with the carp in Brays Bayou, just head downstream from the bridge, along the south bank (river right), and you will find a 5.5-acre detention pond that holds panfish, small bass, and tilapia.

25 610 Flats (Wading Downstream from the Bridge)
Starting under the bridge, you will notice lots of debris and a wide concrete apron. If you see any gaps or cracks in the concrete, look over

Stavros Cotsoradis scouts along the edge of Brays Bayou under the 610 bridge.

these areas thoroughly. These cracks fill with gravel and attract fish that are looking for aquatic bugs that burrow in the gravel. You will also notice that some of the bridge pylons protrude from the water. These pylons serve as breaks in the current and can hold fish on their downstream sides.

When moving along the bayou, under the bridge, work very slowly and keep a watchful eye on the water. Due to the shadows cast from the bridges overhead, it can sometimes be difficult to see the carp along the concrete flats under the bridge. Once you head downstream from the bridge, you will have roughly 200 yards of productive water to cover.

If you don't have any success with the carp, try heading to the detention pond south of the bayou. This is a fairly large body of water (5.5 acres), and you will likely find some fish willing to take your fly. Rock fill has been dumped along the northern edge of the lake, in close proximity to the cement embankment. This structure offers habitat for panfish and small bass.

The next location addressed in this book (Marmon Flats) can be found 0.3 miles downstream, starting where North Braeswood Boulevard crosses the bayou. You can easily combine these two wades into one

The complex of bridges that crosses Brays Bayou provides habitat and cover for the carp species.

continuous route. However, for the purposes of this book, they have been separated into two distinct descriptions.

Getting There

 From downtown, access I-45 South from Allen Parkway. In a little over 1 mile, take exit 46B for TX 288 South. You will head south on TX 288 for 4.5 miles. Take the exit for I-610 West and continue on for 3.7 miles. Take exit 4A toward Braeswood Boulevard/Beechnut Street. Once you exit the interstate, you will be on South Loop West. You can either find parking at the Houston Metro Park & Ride (at the intersection of South Loop West and West Loop South) or continue in the right lane, crossing Brays Bayou and making a right onto North Braeswood Boulevard. You will see the Starbucks on your left; park there or head east for 0.1 miles and hang a left onto Meyer Park Drive or Frankway Drive. You can find parking on either of these two streets.

Greenwillow Street, Houston
29.68412, -95.44920
9002–9098 Greenwillow St., Houston, TX 77096
10.8 road miles, 0:16 drive time
USGS Monitor Station: 08075000
Optimum flow: 150 to 120 cfs
Optimum gauge height: 17 to 16.6 ft.
Difficulty: Easy

Greenwillow Street is located south of Brays Bayou. This area is a convenient place to find streetside parking, and you won't have to worry about marauding tow trucks. This location can serve as a jumping-off point for an out-and-back excursion either upstream or down.

What You Will Find

Find street parking along Greenwillow Street or at the intersection with Cliffwood Drive. Be respectful of the homeowners in this neighborhood and don't park in front of driveways or mailboxes. Once you are safely parked, and your gear is rigged, head north on Greenwillow Street toward North Braeswood Boulevard. When you get to this busy street, instead of crossing it and heading to the water, head west (left) toward the bridge, where North Braeswood Boulevard crosses the bayou. From this high vantage point, you can look upstream to see whether any grass carp are feeding on the surface. To get down to the water, cross North Braeswood Boulevard to the north side of the street and walk down the grass-covered slope to the concrete-lined channel.

Travis Richards makes his way along the water's edge while a train barrels across the bayou.

26 Marmon Flats (Wading Downstream from the Bridge)

Mark Marmon has spent decades fishing this section of Brays Bayou. His willingness to share his knowledge about this unique waterway is something that the urban fly fishing community won't soon forget.

Start fishing under the North Braeswood Bridge. Try to locate the carp along the concrete flats or feeding on the surface. If you don't see anything, head downstream.

On the far bank (river left), look for any culvert or break in the monotony of the concrete—anything that looks out of the ordinary. Piles of debris or a break in the concrete often attract fish.

A mere 200 yards downstream from the bridge, two pipelines span the length of the channel. If you happen to see a carp in the vicinity of these pipelines, use every advantage of stealth that you can to hide your approach, including the vertical stanchions that support the pipeline. Screening your movements from feeding carp can increase your odds of remaining undetected while you make a cast at these spooky fish. Another 65 yards downstream, you'll see where water is discharged from an adjacent water treatment. This can be a good location to find fish, especially in the wintertime, as the discharged water is warmer than the bayou.

Mark Marmon surveys Brays Bayou for any sign of rising grass carp.

Mark Marmon and the Coffee Bean Fly

One of Mark Marmon's favorite flies for grass carp is the coffee bean fly. In the eyes of many fly fishermen, the coffee bean fly is taboo because it is made from edible organic material. In other words, it is considered bait. Mark Marmon describes why he chose to adopt the coffee bean fly into his carp fly box: "At the time [1980s], I didn't have any fly tying materials or a tying vice, and finding flies that worked for carp was tough because no one was fishing for them. I saw the coffee bean fly in a magazine and knew I could replicate it easily without having any fly tying tools. I grabbed some coffee beans out of the pantry and started gluing them to hooks."

For those fly anglers who don't mind using the coffee bean fly, Marmon says that it is a very effective pattern for grass carp. "Maybe the carp think it is a beetle? I'm not sure. But I've seen grass carp swim up and poke the fly with their nose. After they catch a whiff of the scent they say, 'It's java! It's java!'"

Don't forget to check under the railroad bridge, just a bit more downstream. If a train should pass overhead while you are walking under this bridge, be mindful of any falling gravel that could come down from the trestle.

Getting There

From downtown, head south on I-45 from Allen Parkway. In 1.5 miles, take the exit 46B for TX 288 South, toward Lake Jackson. Continue on TX 288 South until I-610 West. Use the right three lanes to take the exit toward I-610 West. Stay on I-610 West for 4.2 miles. Exit the interstate at 4A toward Braeswood Boulevard/Beechnut Street. After the exit, be looking on your right for the first side street, Cliffwood Drive. Turn right onto Cliffwood Drive and proceed through the neighborhood until it intersects with Greenwillow Street. Find street parking on Greenwillow Street.

Nick Heaverlo uses every bit of cover to his advantage while approaching a grass carp. Inset: A fine urban grass carp

Bevlyn Drive, Houston
29.69032, -95.43047
8500–8598 Bevlyn Dr., Houston, TX 77025
7.6 road miles, 0:19 drive time
USGS Monitor Station: 08075000
Optimum flow: 150 to 120 cfs
Optimum gauge height: 17 to 16.6 ft.

Difficulty: Easy

This spot is usually worth checking out. You might see carp here, but then again you might not. Nevertheless, it is still worth parking the vehicle and walking down over the bank to check the water.

What You Will Find

You can easily find street parking along Bevlyn Drive, Timberside Drive, or Castlewood Street. Once parked, you will need to cross South Braeswood Boulevard and then cross the Brays Bayou Greenway Trail. You should be able to see the bayou and a large concrete outflow that enters into the bayou.

27 Bevlyn Flats (Confluence of Concrete Outflow and Brays Bayou)

After you cross South Braeswood Boulevard, head down the bank toward the bayou. The concrete outflow that joins the waters of Brays Bayou should be on your left. Check the concrete flat near the confluence of the outflow. You will certainly see plenty of mullet, but you may see tilapia and channel catfish as well.

It is roughly 250 yards downstream to a wide bend in the bayou. Be on the lookout for grass carp through this entire section. The concrete flat is wide and fairly deep, giving grass carp ample room to move and feed in the shallows. It is generally not worth going beyond the bend in the bayou. If you make it downstream to the bend without seeing any grass carp, turn around and head back upstream.

Travis Richards makes a stealthy cast to a grass carp along Bevlyn Flats.

Striped mullet feed along the surface of Brays Bayou. Inset: Striped mullet on the fly

Getting There

From downtown, take I-610 West, take exit 3 for Stella Link Road. Once you exit the highway, be prepared to take an immediate right onto Timberside Drive. Head north on Timberside Drive to Linkwood Drive (just past the church on your right). Make a right onto Linkwood followed by a left onto Bevlyn Drive. Take Bevlyn Drive north toward the intersection with South Braeswood Boulevard. Find parking along Bevlyn Drive.

Brompton Road, Houston
29.69762, -95.42344
7599–7555 Brompton Rd., Houston, TX 77025
7.3 road miles, 0:19 drive time
USGS Monitor Station: 08075000
Optimum flow: 150 to 120 cfs
Optimum gauge height: 17 to 16.6 ft.
Difficulty: Easy

This is simply a spot to park the car and see whether fish are swimming about. At this location, a tributary known as Poor Farm Ditch flows in from the north. Catfish, carp, and tilapia are commonly found at the confluence of Poor Farm Ditch and Brays Bayou.

What You Will Find

You can find street side parking along Brompton Road. After you park, you'll need to head south toward the bayou. Safely cross North Braeswood Boulevard and head west along the Brays Bayou Greenway Trail. You will come to a pedestrian bridge that spans the width of Poor Farm Ditch.

28 **Poor Farm Ditch** (Confluence of Poor Farm Ditch and Brays Bayou)
Head down the steep embankment at the confluence of Poor Farm Ditch and Brays Bayou. Approach the water cautiously because the fish at this location see plenty of pressure from both fly anglers and bait fishermen.

Mark Marmon casts into Brays Bayou at the mouth of Poor Farm Ditch.

If fish are present, you should see their silhouettes on the bottom of the channel. If no fish are here, try heading either downstream, past the concrete chute, or upstream, toward the Buffalo Speedway bridge.

Getting There

From downtown, take Allen Parkway west until it turns into Kirby Drive (at the intersection of Shepherd Drive). Continue on Kirby, following the road as it gradually veers south. After about 4.5 miles, turn right onto North Braeswood Boulevard. Take North Braeswood Boulevard for only 0.3 miles, and then turn right onto Brompton Road. Find parking along the curb.

Bayou Parkland, Hermann Park, Houston

29.70766, -95.38430

6532–6538 Almeda Rd., Houston, TX 77021

hermannpark.org

5.6 road miles, 0:10 drive time

USGS Monitor Station: 08075000

Optimum flow: 150 to 120 cfs

Optimum gauge height: 17 to 16.6 ft.

Difficulty: Easy

Bayou Parkland is a small section of Hermann Park that was originally established to foster native plants and wildlife. This 80-acre minipark is connected to the main area of Hermann Park via a pedestrian bridge called Bill Coats Bridge. The Bill Coats Bridge spans Brays Bayou downstream from the parking lot. Bayou Parkland has public restrooms next to the parking lot.

The parking lot at Bayou Parkland can fill up fast, especially on the weekends. Additional parking can be found in the heart of Hermann Park, in Lot H (29.71503, -95.38836). If you park here, use the Greenway Trail to head southeast through the park. Once you cut through the park, you'll come to North MacGregor Way. Simply cross the road and head down to the water. Another location for parking exists at the corner of South MacGregor Way and Almeda Road (29.71195, -95.38192). This lot is shared by two restaurants. Park at the back of the lot.

What You Will Find

The Brays Bayou Greenway Trail runs along both sides of the bayou. There will be plenty of people out on the trails, either riding bikes or walking. The concrete-lined channel is almost 60 feet across in some places. It can be challenging to cast toward fish on the opposite bank, especially if there is a strong wind. If you can't quite make the cast to the opposite bank, simply find the nearest bridge and cross to the other side of the bayou. NEVER attempt to cross the bayou by wading through the water. The current is swift, and there is hidden debris along the deep channel. Also, the sides of the concrete-lined channel are incredibly slick from the algae.

 Hermann Park Flats to 288 Flats (Wading Downstream from South MacGregor Way Bridge)

It doesn't matter whether you parked in the heart of Hermann Park or at Bayou Parkland. Either way, you will head to the bayou and walk downstream under the bridge of South MacGregor Way. As you walk along the edge of the concrete channel, scan the flats on either side for any carp that have moved onto the shallow apron of the channel.

Downstream from the South MacGregor bridge, the bayou bends to the east before heading under Almeda Road. Just before the Almeda Road bridge, you will see a gap in the concrete about 2 feet wide. Local carp anglers refer to this as "The Crack." Bits of gravel and other debris wash into the gap in the concrete channel and this attracts various species of fish. Carp and catfish can often be found milling about here looking for food that is trapped in the gravel.

The next network of bridges downstream is the crossing of TX 288 (South Freeway). This monstrous network of concrete usually has a couple pods of grass carp, mullet, or gar swimming about, either upstream or downstream. You may even see a saltwater species called a needlefish (*Strongylura marina*) at this location.

Jack Boyd shows off a whopper of a common carp from Brays Bayou.

Liam Smith holds a Brays Bayou grasser.

After crossing under the bridge, you will likely begin to notice another carp-like fish (although it isn't a carp), the smallmouth buffalo. These native fish can be a frustrating quarry for anglers, even more than grass carp. However, they will occasionally eat a fly, so it's still worth casting to them every once and awhile. You will likely notice grass carp mixed in with schools of smallmouth buffalo, so be sure to meticulously scan pods of smallmouth buffalo with a keen eye.

Downstream from TX 288, the channel flows straight for nearly a quarter of a mile before it makes a wide bend and flows in a southerly direction. The first bridge you will see is the Columbia Tap Rail-Trail pedestrian bridge. Just upstream from this bridge, a pipeline crosses the bayou. This can be a productive spot to pick up either a common carp or grass carp.

Next is the Ardmore Street bridge. Carp can be found in close proximity to this bridge. As you continue downstream from the Ardmore Street bridge, you will begin to notice substantial numbers of smallmouth buffalo. They seem to be fond of this section of the bayou. Some urban carp anglers refer to this section as "Buffalo Bend." Once again, be sure to scan groups of buffalo meticulously. More often than not, you can find a grasser among the herd.

At this point, you are a little more than 1 mile from the Bayou Parkland parking lot of Hermann Park. Feel free to turn around and fish your way back upstream.

Getting There

 From downtown, take I-45 South and then take exit 46B for TX 288 South. Stay on TX 288 South until you see the exit for North and South MacGregor Way and the Texas Medical Center. Turn right onto North MacGregor Way, and then make your first left onto Almeda Road. Head south on Almeda Road for 0.4 miles. You will see the parking lot for Bayou Parkland on your right.

Further Exploration

In addition to the previously described wades, there are two more locations that are absolutely worth checking out. MacGregor Park (29.71092, -95.34086) (MacGregor Loop Dr., Houston, TX 77021) is a city-owned park that can be found at the terminus of the concrete-lined channel. Downstream from MacGregor Park, the bayou flows between natural banks until it meets the Houston Ship Channel. The transition from the concrete channel to the natural one offers a change in habitat that fish seem to like. Bank fishermen seem to like it too. On any weekend, you are likely to see at least a couple of bank anglers using bait to catch many different species of fish (saltwater and freshwater).

Above: Brays Bayou runs along the western edge of Arthur Storey Park. Below: At MacGregor Park, the banks of Brays Bayou transition from concrete-lined back to natural.

One of the most interesting fish spotted at this location is the anadromous American eel (*Anguilla rostrata*). I have not heard of anyone successfully

catching one on the fly, but it is still worth a trip to this location to see what odd fish one might be able to find.

Another location to check out is on the west side of the city at Arthur Storey Park (29.69630, -95.55771) (7400 W. Sam Houston Pkwy. S., Houston, TX 77036). Brays Bayou runs along the southwestern border of this county-owned park. A paved walking path runs along the bayou for nearly a mile. At this location, the waterway is not lined in concrete, so it's usually murky. With that being said, you can still find grass carp feeding on the surface and spot an occasional koi.

 Baileson Brewing Company

bailesonbrewing.com

Baileson Brewing Company (2322 Bissonnet St., Houston, TX 77005) is open on the weekends, from Fridays to Sundays. Check its website for hours of operation. This small brewery has an amazing staff and great-tasting beers. The taproom is small but provides an intimate setting. If you'd rather sit outside, there is plenty of seating under the shaded picnic tables along Bissonnet Street. If you are fishing Brays Bayou during the summer, Baileson Brewing's pilsners will cool you off.

Chapter 17

URBAN PARK PONDS AND LAKES

Winter trout stocking, additional stockings of bass, catfish, and panfish. Easy access. Access Points: 6

MANICURED PARK PONDS AND LAKES ARE NOT THE FOCUS OF this guidebook. With that being said, park ponds offer easy access and are great for kids, for beginner fly fishers, or when the local streams are flooded. Many of these ponds have fishing piers that provide access for patrons who have mobility impairments. Several of these lakes have canoe or kayak launches that make it a breeze to load and unload your paddlecraft.

Fishing is allowed in most parks operated by Harris County; however, the parks operated by the city of Houston do not allow fishing—with the exception of Hermann Park, as long as anglers fall within the age restrictions (twelve and younger and sixty-five and older). Be sure to abide by all local park regulations and state fishing laws.

In many Harris County parks, stocking programs exist for warmwater species like bass, panfish, and catfish. Additionally, during the winter months, the Texas Parks & Wildlife Department (TPWD) dumps rainbow trout into many of the local ponds and lakes. Catching trout for the dinner table is encouraged because these fish can't survive the Texas summer. For a list of waterbodies that are stocked with rainbow trout, go to TPWD's website, or use the following URL: tpwd.texas.gov/fishboat/fish/management/stocking/trout_stocking.phtml.

The following list of ponds and lakes is not comprehensive by any means. These six waterbodies were chosen for their regional locations and because they are open to the public for fishing. Countless fishing opportunities exist in green spaces, riparian corridors, detention ponds, and neighborhood ponds (some are private; respect the rules and regulations).

To explore additional stillwater opportunities, try looking at online aerial images in and around the city. Start by looking along the riparian corridors of major waterways like Spring Creek, Cypress Creek, and the West Fork San Jacinto River. If you find a hidden pond or oxbow lake that requires a little hike, even better. The use of a subscription-based mapping software that annotates publicly accessible lands, like onX Maps (onxmaps.com), is also advisable. Another helpful resource is the book *The Original Guide to Family Fishing Holes Within 120 Miles of Downtown Houston* by Lorraine Leavell. Unfortunately, this book is out of print, but it is occasionally found in used bookstores. This book outlines 109 bank fishing locations, both saltwater and freshwater.

Strategies for Park Ponds

Manicured park ponds and lakes see substantial fishing pressure. This is especially true on the weekends and during the winter months when TPWD stocks trout. In order to avoid the crowds, try fishing these waterbodies during the week or early morning on the weekends.

When you arrive at one of these ponds, it should be obvious which areas are frequented by bank fishermen. You will see paths leading to the water's edge and bare patches of earth where people stand to make casts. It is also likely you will see lures and fishing lines hanging from trees. It is a good idea to give these spots a cursory check and maybe make a cast or two, but do not hesitate to move to other areas where bank fishermen don't venture. This is easily accomplished if the local waterbody allows the use of a watercraft.

*A wet evening on the
Kickerillo-Mischer Preserve*

During the warm summer months, weeds and vegetation can be an annoyance for fly anglers. Try using flies with weed guards. If a pond is particularly choked in vegetation, use a stout rod and strong tippet to keep fish from running into the grasses and breaking off. Topwater flies are essential during the summer and can provide endless fun when fishing for panfish and bass. Foam poppers, Gurglers, hopper patterns, mouse patterns, BoogleBugs, and Muddler Minnows all work well.

The Ponds and Lakes

A cursory overview will be provided for six park ponds managed by Harris County. The following waterbodies are listed in order, starting with the most distant (in terms of road mileage) from downtown Houston.

Burroughs Park, Tomball, TX

30.13521, -95.57724

9738 Hufsmith Rd., Tomball, TX 77375

hcp4.net/parks/burroughs

37.2 road miles, 0:44 drive time

Optimum flow: N/A

Optimum gauge height: N/A

Difficulty: Easy

30 Burroughs Park

A heavily wooded 320-acre park situated in northern Harris County. This park has plenty of hiking trails and borders Spring Creek to the north, although at this location the creek appears too muddy and the banks too steep to be worth fishing. Instead, direct your attention to the picturesque 8.2-acre pond within the park. Catch-and-release fishing is required for all bass. The pond is stocked with Florida largemouth bass, bluegill hybrids, and channel catfish, along with an annual winter stocking of rainbow trout.

The landscape along the southern and western banks of the pond is devoid of any tree cover, making it open enough for fly casting. On the eastern and northern sides of the pond, the tree line is too close to the edge of the water, making casting difficult. On the southern end of the pond, a peninsula juts out into the water; this is an excellent place to rip a couple of casts. Lily pads and grasses are prolific in the summer.

In the summer, the pond at Burroughs Park has a lot of aquatic plants. Consider fishing with heavy tippet to avoid losing fish.

Use a stout rod and heavy tippet (10 to 12 pound) to winch any bass out of the weed line.

Getting There

From downtown, head north on I-45. You'll be on the interstate for just over 22 miles. Take exit 70B for Spring Stuebner Road West. Next, you will merge onto TX 99 (Grand Parkway),

This small largemouth from Burroughs Park hit a Mini Master Splinter Mouse.

heading west. Remain on TX 99 for roughly 3.5 miles. Take the exit for Kuykendahl Road/Spring Stuebner Road. Turn right onto Kuykendahl Road. Stay on this road for 3.7 miles. Make a left onto Hufsmith Road. After traveling on Hufsmith Road for nearly 1.5 miles, you'll see the entrance to Burroughs Park on your right. Follow Burroughs Park Road all the way to the end, where you will find the pond.

Northshore Park, The Woodlands, TX

30.16896, -95.47574

2505 Lake Woodlands Dr., The Woodlands, TX 77380

thewoodlandstownship-tx.gov/facilities/facility/details/
northshorepark-112

33.0 road miles, 0:36 drive time

Optimum flow: N/A

Optimum gauge height: N/A

Difficulty: Easy to Moderate

31 Northshore Park

A beautiful park lies on the northwestern shore of Lake Woodlands, a 200-acre lake popular with the residents of The Woodlands. The park is equipped with a boat ramp and serves as a launch site for kayaks, SUPs, and small sailboats. You can find some bank fishing opportunities from the docks and shoreline, but to up your odds, it is best to use a paddlecraft and explore more areas of the lake.

From Northshore Park, paddle north for a little more than a half mile to the mouth of a small creek called Panther Branch (30.17586, -95.47181). In the summer, the mouth of this creek can be filled with aquatic plants, but paddling through the vegetation is easy. Continue upstream and paddle under Research Forest Drive. Here, it appears like the waterway forks. Stay to your left and explore the backwater sloughs. The farther back you paddle, the tighter the waterway will become as you enter into Panther Branch. Largemouth bass, gar, bluegill, and redear

Lake Woodlands is a popular spot for paddlers, especially in the summer.

sunfish can all be found in the backwater areas of Panther Branch and Lake Woodlands.

Kayak and SUP rentals can be found at Riva Row Boat House at Town Green Park (rivarowboathouse.com), or at Lakes Edge Boat House at Hughes Landing. Renting from Lakes Edge Boat House will put you on the lake, almost directly across from the Northshore Park.

A beautiful healthy redear sunfish from the mouth of Panther Branch and Lake Woodlands

Getting There

 From downtown, head north on I-45 for 27.5 miles. Take exit 76B for the Woodlands Parkway. Head west on the Woodlands Parkway for 2.3 miles. Turn right onto East Panther Creek Drive. At the T-intersection, make a right onto Lake Woodlands Drive. As you approach the lake, you'll see Northshore Park on your right. It is before the bridge.

Mary Jo Peckham Park, Katy, TX
29.80474, -95.82035
5597 Gardenia Ln., Katy, TX 77493
pct3.com/Parks/Mary-Jo-Peckham-Park
31.6 road miles, 0:40 drive time
Optimum flow: N/A
Optimum gauge height: N/A
Difficulty: Easy

32 Mary Jo Peckham Park

Situated north of Katy. The 4.85-acre pond within the park is stocked annually with rainbow trout during the winter. Fly casting can be accomplished easily along the shoreline of this pond, but be aware of your surroundings. This park can get crowded with anglers during the stocking season. In addition to the stocking of trout, this pond also contains largemouth bass, channel catfish, and bluegill.

Mary Jo Peckham Park is a popular neighborhood lake for many folks living in the Katy, Texas area.

Getting There

 From downtown, head north on I-45. After traveling on I-45 for about 0.9 of a mile, take exit, 48B, to merge onto I-10 West toward San Antonio. Remain on I-10 West for 17.5 miles. Take exit 741 for US 90 West/Katy Mills Boulevard/Highway Boulevard. Make your first right after exiting the off-ramp. This is Highway Boulevard/Old Katy Road. Stay on this road for only 0.2 miles before making a right onto Katyland Drive. Stay on Katyland Drive until the intersection with Franz Road. Make a left onto Franz Road. After 0.5 miles, make a right onto Katy City Park Road. Take this road to its terminus. You'll see the entrance to the park.

Lake Friendswood Park, Friendswood, TX

29.47975, -95.18087

2533 Davis Prairie Ln., Friendswood, TX 77546

ci.friendswood.tx.us/482/Lake-Friendswood-Park

29.6 road miles, 0:35 drive time

Optimum flow: N/A

Optimum gauge height: NA

Difficulty: Easy

33 Lake Friendswood Park

The gorgeous 33-acre lake was once the site of a sand pit mine, but now it is a picturesque lake with clear, turquoise water in a newly-established park in the Friendswood community. The lake is equipped with a kayak launch and two fishing piers. Anglers with mobility impairment will find plenty of room for casting from these piers. There are some bank fishing opportunities along the northwestern bank (bank closest to the parking lot) and the northeastern bank. The southern shoreline is protected by dense trees, which makes bank fishing nearly impossible. However, if you are fishing from a paddlecraft (highly recommended for this lake), you'll definitely want to paddle along the southern shoreline while casting to the bank. The water in this lake is crystal clear. You may want to consider fishing with lightweight tippet if you notice the fish aren't responding well to your flies.

Lake Friendswood Park offers a wonderful kayak launch for park paddlers.

Travis Richards fishes the shoreline at Lake Friendswood Park.

Getting There

From downtown, head south on I-45 (Gulf Freeway) for 21.5 miles. Take exit 25 for FM 528/NASA Parkway. After exiting the highway, make a right onto FM 528 Road. Continue on this road for 3.9 miles before making a left onto South Friendswood Drive. After 1.2 miles, turn right onto West Boulevard. Stay on this road for nearly 1 mile before turning left onto Davis Prairie Lane. Take Davis Prairie Lane through the neighborhood until you see the lake. Make a left into the parking lot of Lake Friendswood Park.

Kickerillo-Mischer Preserve, Houston, TX
29.98790, -95.56340
20215 Chasewood Park Dr., Houston, TX 77070
hcp4.net/parks/kmp
25.9 road miles, 0:30 drive time
Optimum flow: N/A
Optimum gauge height: N/A
Difficulty: Easy to Moderate

34 Marshall Lake

The lake is approximately 31.7 acres and is the main outdoor attraction within the Kickerillo-Mischer Preserve. The edge of the lake is lined with trees, which makes casting from the bank very difficult. This waterway is best explored using a paddlecraft. A ramp for launching kayaks and canoes is found at the end of the access road leading into the preserve (29.98793, -95.56334). There are three fishing piers that can be accessed by those with mobility impairment.

This lake is stocked with catfish fingerlings but also gets an annual winter stocking of rainbow trout. There are decent populations of largemouth bass too. Bass fishing is catch and release only. From a kayak or canoe, try focusing on areas of the lake that bank fishermen cannot access. This is mostly around the island in the middle of the lake as well as the southern shoreline. From time to time, alligators are spotted in Marshall Lake.

The large lake at Kickerillo-Mischer Preserve is difficult to fish from the bank. Using a paddlecraft is highly recommended.

Getting There

 From downtown, head north on I-45 for 12.5 miles. Take exit 60C for TX 8 (Sam Houston Tollway) and head west. Continue driving west on TX 8 for 5 miles. Take the exit for TX 249 North toward Tomball. Remain on TX 249 for 4.8 miles before exiting the highway at Chasewood Park Drive/Compaq Center Drive. Make a right onto Chasewood Park Drive, and then immediately make another right into the Kickerillo-Mischer Preserve. You'll see the lake on your right as you drive into the preserve.

Tom Bass Regional Park Section III, Houston, TX

29.59053, -95.35373
15108 Cullen Blvd., Houston, TX 77047
hcp1.net/TomBassPark
15.9 road miles, 0:22 drive time
Optimum flow: N/A
Optimum gauge height: N/A
Difficulty: Easy

35 Tom Bass Regional Park

The park is split into three sections. Section III contains a 23-acre lake that is open to bank fishing. There is a fishing pier on the southern shoreline for folks with mobility impairment. This lake is stocked with rainbow trout annually. Catfish and panfish are also stocked regularly, but TPWD makes no claims of stocking largemouth bass on its website.

However, if you visit this lake, you will likely see (or even catch) a largemouth bass, although it isn't likely to be big. The majority of the lake is deep, but shallow edges and coves can be found. Bank fishermen hit this lake pretty hard, and you'll likely notice that many of the fish are skittish. At the very least you should be able to find a couple of willing panfish in the shallows. A paved trail encircles the whole lake, making access easy.

Getting There

From downtown, merge onto I-45 South. After 1.2 miles on I-45 South, take the ramp 46B for TX 288 South. Continue south on TX 288 for about 10 miles. Look for the exit for TX 8 Frontage Road. Take this exit. At the intersection, go straight through the first light, but make a left at the second light onto the frontage road for TX 8 (Sam Houston Tollway) East. Stay on the frontage road for 1.1 miles. Make a right onto Fellows Road. Continue on Fellows Road for almost a mile; then you'll see an entrance to the park with a sign reading "Clear Creek Golf Course." Make this right. You'll see the lake on your left as you drive into the park. Continue down the park road and make your first left. Continue down this road, and you'll see a parking lot on your left. Park here to access the lake.

The lake at Tom Bass Park has plenty of room for casting.

Part 5

Sporting Fishes of
Southeastern Texas

A GRAB BAG OF FISHES

TEXAS BOASTS A DIVERSE POPULATION OF SPORTING FISHES. This is one of the reasons why fly fishing in this state is so much fun. The fish that chomps down on the end of your line could be anything from a tiny and colorful panfish to a carp that weighs double digits. Fly fishers who are willing to push the envelope on "traditional" sport fishes will find even more opportunities as they explore the waters of southeastern Texas.

If one thing can be said about fly anglers in Houston, it's that they aren't beholden to the rules of fly fishing tradition. The same thing can be said for the fish species that are pursued by fly anglers in the Bayou City. All manner of non-native and native fish species are seen as possible sporting quarry in the eyes of local fly fishers.

Take a look at the following pages and familiarize yourself with some of the traditional and non-traditional fish species that can be angled from Houston-area waters. If you'd like to further your knowledge of these fishes and their ranges, I highly recommend *Peterson Field Guide to Freshwater Fishes* by Lawrence M. Page and Brooks M. Burr. Another fantastic resource for exploring different fish species is the website Fishes of Texas (fishesoftexas.org). This website is a compilation of scientific data from the Hendrickson Lab at the University of Texas at Austin. Other organizations, such as the Texas Parks & Wildlife Department (TPWD) and the Texas Commission on Environmental Quality, have also lent their support to this fantastic website.

Chapter 18

KING OF THE BAYOUS: THE BLACK BASSES OF SOUTHEAST TEXAS

IT ISN'T A SURPRISE THAT **LARGEMOUTH BASS** (*MICROPTERUS salmoides*) get the spotlight when it comes to fishing in Texas. The state has a rich history of monster bucketmouths, and just about every farm pond and reservoir in Texas has been stocked with largemouth bass at some point. The state all-tackle record for largemouth sits at 18.18 pounds, with the fly rod record coming in at 14.14 pounds.

Two species of largemouth bass exist in southeastern Texas. The native subspecies is the **northern largemouth** bass, *Micropterus salmoides salmonids*. The larger and non-native **Florida largemouth** (*Micropterus floridanus*) has been stocked in many lakes and reservoirs throughout the state, including Lake Conroe and Sheldon Lake.

Outside of the stereotypical bass ponds and reservoirs, largemouth also patrol the waters of Houston-area bayous and creeks. Although studies tend to show that largemouth bass prefer lacustrine (lake) environments, *Travis Richards displays an excellent spotted bass from the West Fork San Jacinto River.*

they do still exist in plentiful numbers in the low gradient and slow flowing bayous and creeks in the Houston area.

The seemingly ubiquitous presence of largemouth is owed to the fish's hardiness. They can withstand harsh environments and are voracious predators. Juvenile largemouth often eat insects (aquatic and terrestrial) and small fish, while larger adults primarily eat fish and the occasional crawfish, depending on their abundance. In addition to their typical diet, largemouth bass are notorious for eating all sorts of oddities. Never shying away from a meal, there have been records of largemouth bass eating snakes, turtles, lizards, mice, small ducks, and even squirrels. Basically, if a largemouth bass thinks a prey item will fit into its mouth, it's going to try to eat it.

Another species of black bass also lives in the waterways of southeastern Texas, the **spotted bass** (*Micropterus punctulatus*). This species of bass doesn't often grow to the hefty size of largemouth, but it is certainly a hard-hitting and aggressive fish, especially when angled on lightweight tackle. The fly rod record for spotted bass is 1.92 pounds.

Spotted bass (sometimes referred to as Kentucky bass) are native to this region of Texas. They often live in lotic environments and prefer creeks and rivers with streambeds composed of sand or gravel. Spotted bass, or "spots,'" are partial to waterways that have a moderate flow rate, usually too swift for a largemouth, although in many waterways their habitats overlap. Spots are the choice black bass species for anglers who explore the small creeks and streams of the wooded terrain of the Pineywoods.

Not only can largemouth bass be found in the local lakes and bayous of southeastern Texas, but they also lurk in the urban waterways of Houston.

Spotted bass, a native stream-dwelling fish of East Texas, is a favorite of many local blue-lining creek stompers.

Spotted bass, much like their big-jawed cousins, are not overly picky when it comes to diet. However, several studies have shown that spotted bass tend to eat more crawfish and insects than the largemouth. This is likely because many aquatic insects and crayfish prefer to live in the lotic environments of clear streams with gravel bottoms and steeper gradients, an environment that is shared with the spotted bass.

Both largemouth bass and spotted bass can be caught on a wide assortment of flies. Classic subsurface flies like the Clouser Minnow and Woolly Bugger rarely fail to entice a bass to strike. Additionally, specific subsurface patterns that have proven to be excellent on bass include Bennett's Brunch Money and Carp-It Bomb; Bailes' Hatchling Craw; variations of Whitlock's squirrel-hair nymph and Waking Minnow; and many other baitfish, streamer, and crawfish patterns.

Fishing topwater is another fantastic and adrenaline-pumping way to catch bass. Popping topwater flies across the surface of a lake or creek can produce ferocious attacks from both largemouth and spotted bass alike. Fishing topwater is especially deadly in the warmer months. Some classic topwater fly patterns include the gurgler, BoogleBug, and deer hair poppers.

Spots and Largies: Understanding the Difference between the Black Bass Species in Southeast Texas

Most fly fishers are well aware of the semi-cult following that small-mouth bass (*Micropterus dolomieu*) have. There is little doubt that this strong-fighting fish deserves the admiration of anglers. While Houston-area flyrodders don't have a population of smallmouth to chase, our own creek-dwelling bass species, the spotted bass, also enjoys a bit of a cult following among Houston-area anglers.

Because the preferred habitats of largemouth bass and spotted bass overlap, it can be hard to tell the difference between the two. To make matters worse, on occasion, largemouth bass will hybridize with spotted bass, making the differentiation impossible. But there are several distinguishing features between the two species that can help determine what type of bass is on the end of your line.

1. Consider the environment in which you angled the fish. Was it in a chute, channel, riffle, or any section with flowing water? Or was it in a sluggish backwater or eddy with plenty of aquatic vegetation? Remember that largemouth prefer slack water pools with plenty of weeds, whereas spotted bass prefer moderate current with a sandy or gravel streambed.

2. Look at the belly of the fish under the lateral line. Do rows of black dots exist on the belly? If so, you likely have a spotted bass. However, water clarity often dictates how visible these belly spots are. If you're having a hard time seeing rows of spots on the belly, you can check a couple of other physical features.

Largemouth bass

"Tooth patch" is absent.

Back of the jaw extends well beyond the back of the eye.

3. Take a look at the mouth. With wet hands, gently close the mouth and see whether the back of the jaw extends past the rear margin of the eye. If the jawline stops at mid-eye, or at the back of the eye, then you likely have a spotted bass. If the jawline extends well past the back of the eye, then it's a largemouth.

4. Open the mouth of the fish and take a look at the tongue. Spotted bass have a distinct rectangular tooth patch. Largemouth do not.

5. Still can't tell? There's one last thing to check: the dorsal fin. The first dorsal fin on spotted bass has a minor convex shape and is clearly connected to the second dorsal fin. Imagine that the empty space above the connection of the first and second dorsal fins forms the letter *U*. A largemouth's first dorsal fin has an exaggerated convex shape, almost like a triangle, and is nearly separate from the second dorsal fin. The empty space above the connection of the dorsal fins forms the letter *V*. *(See next page for fin illustration.)*

For further information on determining the difference between the two species, check out the scientific paper titled "Morphological Models for Identifying Largemouth Bass, Spotted Bass, and Largemouth Bass X Spotted Bass Hybrids" which will be cited in the "Sources and Further Reading" section at the back of the book.

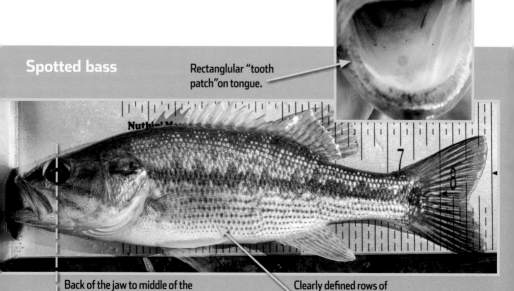

Spotted bass

Rectanglular "tooth patch" on tongue.

Back of the jaw to middle of the eye, or slightly past the middle.

Clearly defined rows of spots along the belly.

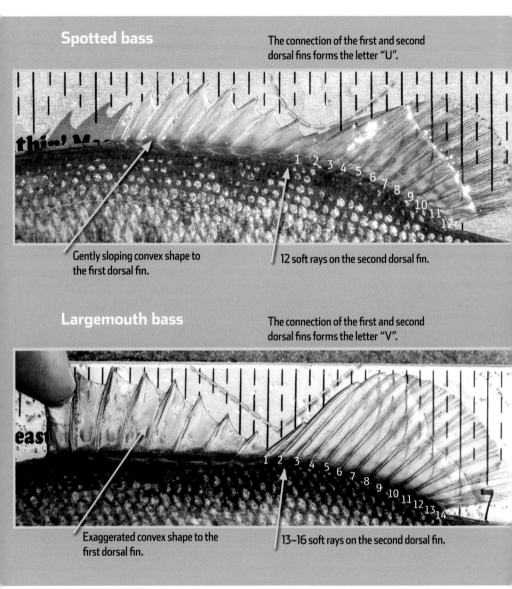

Spotted bass

The connection of the first and second dorsal fins forms the letter "U".

Gently sloping convex shape to the first dorsal fin.

12 soft rays on the second dorsal fin.

Largemouth bass

The connection of the first and second dorsal fins forms the letter "V".

Exaggerated convex shape to the first dorsal fin.

13–16 soft rays on the second dorsal fin.

Chapter 19

PANFISH: THE SCRAPPY FLYWEIGHTS

"This challenging little game fish is the Rodney Dangerfield of the fly-fishing world; he has never gotten the respect he deserves."

—JACK ELLIS, *The Sunfishes*

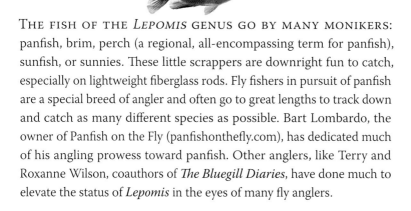

THE FISH OF THE *LEPOMIS* GENUS GO BY MANY MONIKERS: panfish, brim, perch (a regional, all-encompassing term for panfish), sunfish, or sunnies. These little scrappers are downright fun to catch, especially on lightweight fiberglass rods. Fly fishers in pursuit of panfish are a special breed of angler and often go to great lengths to track down and catch as many different species as possible. Bart Lombardo, the owner of Panfish on the Fly (panfishonthefly.com), has dedicated much of his angling prowess toward panfish. Other anglers, like Terry and Roxanne Wilson, coauthors of *The Bluegill Diaries*, have done much to elevate the status of *Lepomis* in the eyes of many fly anglers.

When it comes to fly patterns, panfish can be caught on miniaturized versions of common bass flies. Panfish primarily eat aquatic and terrestrial insects. Some panfish-specific patterns that work well in the Houston area are Lombardo's Woolly Worm and Triangle Bug, Puck's Squrat, and the Wilsons' Bully Bluegill Spider. When fishing creeks in the Pineywoods area, try using buggy streamer patterns in size 10. This seems to be the sweet spot for enticing both panfish and creek-dwelling bass. Additionally, classic trout flies like the elk hair caddis, Parachute Adams, and Rat-Faced McDougal are a blast when the topwater bite is on.

The morphology of particular panfish species varies based on their environments, which can make them hard to identify. Add to that their tendency to hybridize, and it's no wonder many anglers use all-encompassing terms like "sunfish" and "bluegill" to describe all species of the *Lepomis* genus.

In the Houston area, there are six species of sporting panfish that can be angled with some degree of regularity. They are bluegill, green sunfish, longear sunfish, redear sunfish, redspotted sunfish, and warmouth. Other smaller species like dollar sunfish, spotted sunfish, and bantam sunfish are often too small to be caught on the flies most anglers are casting.

Surprisingly, one of the more common panfish species in the Texas Hill Country, the redbreast sunfish (*Lepomis auratus*), is seldom caught in Houston-area waterways. This non-native panfish is virtually absent from the San Jacinto River watershed. There is at least one tiny creek in the Sam Houston National Forest that is known to have them. However, this creek eventually meanders its way into the Trinity River, not the San Jacinto River.

The following descriptions of panfish should help anglers determine the different species among the *Lepomis* genus. Keep in mind that hybridization is fairly common, so don't bang your head against the wall if you can't figure out a particular species of panfish. Just chalk it up as a hybrid and release it back into the water.

A chunky bluegill from Lake Conroe

Bluegill (*Lepomis macrochirus*) are probably one of the best-known species of panfish. They can be found in many waterways throughout most of the country. They can grow to substantial proportions (the current Texas all-tackle record is 2.02 pounds) and are hard fighters on the fly rod. Bluegill often, though not always, exhibit blue coloring toward the base of their gill cover. Fish living in clear waters exhibit vertical barring along their sides. Most bluegill have an olive-colored back and yellowish bellies.

Bluegill are a common fish that can have many different morphs. Their colors can range from bright yellow to a drab olive.

The pectoral fins on bluegill are long and pointed. If you fold the pectoral fin of a bluegill forward, toward the head, the tip of the fin extends past the eye. The ear flaps on bluegill are black and stubby, although they grow longer with age. Lastly, the bluegill has a distinguished and small mouth, with the upper jaw not extending to the front of the eye.

Green sunfish (*Lepomis cyanellus*) are a hardy species of panfish that the Texas Parks & Wildlife Department (TPWD) claims can handle wild swings in environmental conditions. Trophy-sized green sunfish can push the one-pound mark. The most distinguishing features of the green sunfish are its large mouth (upper jaw extends to the eye) and its olive-green to yellowish coloring. Usually, the anal, pelvic, and pectoral fins are all edged with bright yellow coloring.

Green sunfish are a hardy species that can often be found in the urban ditches around the suburbs of Houston.

Blue-green, wormlike markings extend from the edge of the mouth back under the eye. The pectoral fins are round and short. The ear flap is short, stiff, and mostly black (although some adults have a yellow edge around the outside of the ear flap). Because of their large mouths, "greenies" will often pursue bigger flies usually intended for bass.

Longear sunfish are some of the most beautiful panfish in North America.

Longear sunfish (*Lepomis megalotis*) are one of the most beautiful and iconic creek-dwelling fish in the Houston area. Their bold and vibrant colors match their tenacious attitude. Despite their smaller size (usually not growing larger than eight to nine inches), they grapple well above their weight class. The mouth is fairly large, extending to under the front of the eye when closed. The ear flap is long and usually dark green to black, although adults will often display a thin, pale line around the edge of the flap. Brilliant blue, wormlike markings extend from the front of the cheeks back across the gill cover. Longears often have a bright orange or yellow belly that gradually fades to a rich red color toward the tail. Their sides are often a hue of blueish green. The pectoral fin is rounded and stubby, not reaching past the eye when bent forward. They're sometimes called the "brook trout of the south" because of their beauty and ability to survive in very small waterways. Bringing a longear to hand is always a treat.

Redbreast sunfish are very rare in the San Jacinto River watershed. On occasion, they can be angled from the small streams in Sam Houston National Forest.

Redbreast sunfish (*Lepomis auritus*) are uncommon in the waterways immediately surrounding Houston. Therefore, we won't spend much time on them. However, because of their presence in the Trinity River watershed (east of Houston), as well as watersheds west of Houston (Brazos River watershed and farther into central Texas), it is worth making a brief mention of them. Redbreast sunfish are a non-native fish in Texas but still very popular with fly anglers due to their aggressive nature and ability to grow to a hefty size (the Texas all-tackle record weighed in at 1.63 pounds). Because of their extremely long ear flap, which extends midway down the length of the body, they are often confused with the longear sunfish. The belly on the redbreast is usually yellow to orange in color. The pectoral fin is long and pointed, extending well past the eye when bent forward

Redear sunfish (*Lepomis microlophus*) are excellent fighters on the fly rod. This chunky sunfish can grow to impressive size. The Texas state record is a whopping 2.99 pounds. The namesake of this fish comes from the reddish coloring at the edge of the otherwise-black ear flap. The mouth of the redear sunfish is small; the jawline doesn't reach the eye when the mouth is closed. The pectoral fins of the redear are long and pointed and do extend to the eye, or past, when bent toward the head. Redear sunfish

Redear sunfish are a fairly common panfish, but they can be difficult to catch on the fly due to the deep waters they tend to inhabit. Redears spend most of their time feeding at or near the bottom of lakes.

are nicknamed "shellcrackers" because of their affinity for devouring small aquatic snails. Rarely will redear sunfish feed on, or near, the surface of the water. These panfish can be caught by fishing deep with damselfly patterns or with other patterns resembling aquatic insects.

Redspotted sunfish (*Lepomis miniatus*) are the smallest sunfish species that will be outlined in this chapter. However, because of their beauty and willingness to chase down larger flies, they deserve a seat at the table with the rest of the "sporting" panfish. Redspotted sunfish are less common than many of the other creek-dwelling panfish, and hooking into one should be cause for celebration. They have rows of

Redspotted sunfish are small but beautiful. These feisty little fish can be found in the secluded waters of the Pineywoods. They seem to be especially fond of the East Fork San Jacinto River.

spots along their sides, ranging in colors from bright red to yellow. They also display a reddish-orange spot just above their small, stiff ear flap. Most of the local redspotted sunfish have a bright red iris and also have a blue line just under the eye, as if they were wearing a bit of eye shadow. The pectoral fins are short and rounded, not extending to the eye when bent forward. These sunfish spend much of their time hunting along the streambed for aquatic invertebrates. If you fish the creeks of the Pineywoods long enough, you'll eventually find one on the end of your line.

The drab and mottled colors of the warmouth make it an excellent ambush predator. Warmouth can be found around woody debris and vegetation.

Warmouth (*Lepomis gulosus*) is an apt name for this fish. Its mouth more closely resembles that of a bass than a panfish. When the mouth is closed, the upper jaw extends well under the eye. Black or brown lines radiate from the back of the eye across the gill plate, although sometimes these lines are faint. The overall coloring of the warmouth is mottled, with olives, browns, and yellows being the primary colors. The ear flap is short, stiff, and black. Adult warmouth usually have a small red dot at the outer edge of the ear flap. Warmouth are ambush predators, and they can often be found in dense cover, where they wait to attack prey like minnows and small crayfish. This is a highly prized and coveted fish for local panfish anglers.

Chapter 20

CARP: DITCH TARPON

"Then the line went tight, the rod bent and tried to wrench itself from my hands, and I managed to get out 'Oh my G ... ' as the leader passed its maximum weight capacity and my strip of rabbit fur and 1/0 Gamakatsu hook were gone forever."

—MARK USYK, *Carp are Jerks*

DESPITE THE COMMON CARP'S INTRODUCTION TO AMERICAN waterways over a century ago, anglers have never fully accepted them into the ranks of North American "sport" fish. Common carp have long been the source of consternation. This worry was created from the idea that the hulking, invasive fish would be the ruin of aquatic habitat and the destruction of waterways. With several exceptions, this thinking has more or less been exaggerated. In fact, if it wasn't for these incredibly resilient and enduring fish, many urban fisheries throughout the United States wouldn't receive any recognition at all. To illustrate this point, authors Rob Buffler and Tom Dickson, in their book *Fishing for Buffalo*, make a beautiful point:

Either ignorant of or blind to the damages they themselves had wrought on the landscape, people looked past the dredged and straightened channels, drained wetlands, eroded riverbanks, and waters laden with human and industrial waste, saw carp roiling in the shallows, and accused them of wrecking the water.

Common carp have mouths on the bottoms of their heads (sub-terminal). Common carp also have barbels on both sides of their mouths to help detect food.

Thankfully, over the past several decades, common carp have seen a surge in popularity as a game fish in North America, something European anglers have long embraced. For many fly anglers, common carp are seen as one of the ultimate freshwater fish to target with a fly rod. When hooked, they are incredibly powerful fighters and will make explosive runs. Currently, the state fly rod record is from Lady Bird Lake in Austin. The behemoth common carp weighed 33 pounds!

The term "carp" is often used as a blanket term for the larger species of the taxonomic family *Cyprinidae*, also known as the "true minnows." In addition to the common carp, other varieties from the *Cyprinidae* family can be found in the Houston bayous, including grass carp and koi.

Common carp (*Cyprinus carpio*) are easily identified by their large size and shimmering golden scales. The mouth of the common carp is found on the underside of its head (subterminus). The mouth is positioned so the fish can easily scarf up food along the streambed. Common carp have two barbels on each side of the mouth that are used to help detect food. Carp do not have teeth in the traditional sense; however, they do have a set

Danny Scarborough with a common carp from Lake Conroe

of pharyngeal teeth in their throat that helps grind food.

Common carp are omnivores and eat plants, seeds, berries, aquatic bugs, crayfish, mussels, clams, and occasionally small baitfish. When carp are actively feeding, it is called "mudding." When mudding, they are attempting to scrounge around on the stream-bed for aquatic insects, worms, or anything else they can digest. When an angler sees a common carp feeding, it is best to try and make a cast in front of the fish using a heavily weighted fly. Many times, carp will respond to the fly being plunked in the water in front of them.

Danny Scarborough holds a fantail common carp from Brays Bayou. This mutation produces elongated caudal (tail) and pectoral fins. Koi and common carp can exhibit this mutation.

If they don't make a move for the fly, attempt to bring the fly into the carp's feeding lane by slowly stripping it. If you do it successfully (without spooking the fish), the carp will often swim over to the fly and suck it into its mouth. Danny Scarborough has developed some deadly fly patterns for Houston-area carp. His most well-known pattern is the Brasshawk. In addition to that, Scarborough has also developed the Carp Booger. Several other patterns work well for common carp, including Pat's Rubber Legs and Bennett's Carp-It Bomb.

Carp will occasionally mutate, which can result in oddities with the appearance of the fish. One of the most common mutations found among Houston-area carp is the "fantail" carp. This is a mutation where the pectoral fins and caudal fins become long and flowing, almost like the carp is dragging around golden ribbons. Koi can also exhibit this mutation. Catching a fantail carp should be a proud moment for any urban angler.

Grass carp (*Ctenopharyngodon idella*) were originally introduced in the United States as biocontrol for invasive aquatic vegetation. Sexually sterile (triploid) grass carp are still stocked in Texas waterways by the Texas Parks & Wildlife Department (TPWD). Populations of grass carp

A nice profile shot of a grass carp showing the typical elongated body and terminal mouth. This fish was angled by Travis Richards.

that are able to reproduce (diploid) have escaped captivity over the years and are established in many of the waterways in Houston.

Lake Conroe has a diploid grass carp population that was originally established in either the 1960s or 1970s to help control the spread of the invasive aquatic plant hydrilla. As the name suggests, grass carp eat a variety of plants, but they will also eat insects, berries, and seeds. Morphologically, grass carp are long and slender compared to the common carp. However, grass carp can grow to huge proportions. They have a very wide head with a terminal mouth (mouth sits at the front of the head). The color of the local grass carp is silver on the back to white on the belly. Their large scales fade from silver to dark gray at their base. Grass carp can be notoriously picky and skittish, but much like common carp, they will often respond to a fly being plunked down right in front of their face. Local fly rodder Joe Mills describes what it is like

Jack Boyd holds a uniquely colored grass carp from White Oak Bayou. This fish likely had some kind of genetic mutation that gave it these unique colors.

casting to a grass carp: "When I fish for grass carp, I'm not worried about getting a good drift, mending line, or doing all the things you would normally do for a trout. Instead, what you are trying to do is plop the fly just off the carp's nose. When I cast to a grass carp, I'm aiming for their face. If they don't eat the fly within that very short window, I'll pick up my line and try again. If they still don't eat after a couple of tries, I'll just move on and find the next carp."

Grass carp respond well to small nymph-like flies like Scarborough's Brasshawk. Frequently, grass carp can be observed feeding on the surface. When this feeding behavior is observed, a well-placed hopper pattern (tied on a stout hook) can trick a grass carp. Sometimes, grass carp will be seen feeding ravenously after a hard summer rain. Rains will wash insects, grass clippings, and seeds into the local ditches, where the grass carp will go crazy for them.

Koi (*Cyprinus rubrofuscus*) can occasionally be found in Houston waterways. These fish likely came to the ditches by way of flooding or by intentional release. Koi are a desirable quarry for local fly rodders because of their novelty. These fish can be tricked into eating a fly in the same way that common carp can. In fact, koi can sometimes be seen schooling with common carp and mudding alongside them.

Above and below: Jack Boyd displays two interestingly colored koi.

Koi are cautious and can be easily spooked (try being a bright red, orange, or white fish in an otherwise brown environment). Be stealthy when approaching them. The same flies that are used on common carp can be used on koi.

The various carp of the *Cyprinidae* family have sustained healthy populations in most Houston-area waters. Because

of their abundance, size, and strength, they are an important game fish for local fly rodders. As further proof of their importance to the local angling scene, from 2017 to 2019, Danny Scarborough and Bayou City Angler hosted the Holy Carp Tournament. This tournament was a citywide event where anglers attempted to catch as many carp as they could in a ten-hour window. The Holy Carp Tournament was a blast for local fly fishermen. The final year the tournament was held was in 2019. Perhaps someday this enjoyable event will be rekindled.

Smallmouth Buffalo (*Ictiobus bubalus*)

The Smallmouth Buffalo may resemble the non-native carp species, but that's where the similarities end. Smallmouth buffalo are not carp. They are a true native North American fish. Smallmouth buffalo have a small head with large eyes. They lack the barbels that are found on common carp, and they are often a light cream color compared to the golden hue of common carp. Smallmouth buffalo can be fished in a similar manner to common carp, but these fish are notoriously picky. They are a common sight in many urban bayous in Houston, but getting one to eat can be excruciatingly difficult. Their finicky nature makes them a fish that's pursued by only the most patient of fly anglers. The fly rod record in Texas weighed 59 pounds and was angled from Lady Bird Lake in Austin.

Chapter 21

GAR AND BOWFIN:
THE DINOSAURS

Both gar and bowfin have similar primordial beginnings. These fish can trace their origins back to the Late Jurassic age, roughly 150 million years ago. These fish have evolved over the ages, but they still retain many of their ancient physiological characteristics.

Gar and bowfin are "bimodal," meaning they can breathe both air and water. This adaptation is accomplished by using a gas bladder. This organ has dual purposes: it helps the fish stay buoyant, but it also serves as an additional way to get oxygen to the bloodstream. Anglers often see gar and (to a lesser extent) bowfin breaching the water's surface to gulp air. This is done to replenish the gas bladder. This bimodal advantage allows these dino-like fish to thrive in waters deficient of oxygen. This is one of the reasons why both gar and bowfin have survived over the eons.

Since the middle of the twentieth century, gar and bowfin have been unjustly accused of being a detriment to populations of sport fish. It was mistakenly thought that gar and bowfin outcompeted fish like largemouth bass. There is no better example of

Above: The author with an alligator gar

this vitriol than the following quote, taken from *The Fishes of Illinois,* 1920, written by Stephen A. Forbes and Robert E. Richardson:

> *The time will doubtless come when thorough going measures will be taken to keep down to the lowest practicable limit the dogfish [bowfin] and the gars—as useless and destructive in our productive waters as wolves and foxes formerly were in our pastures and poultry yards.*

In recent years, research has concluded that the impact gar and bowfin have on other bite-sized populations of fish like bluegill and crappie is actually positive. These fish experience enhanced growth rates in waters shared with gar and bowfin. In an article appearing in the *Fisheries* publication, Dennis Scarnecchia writes, "Gars and bowfins have been shown to eat mostly small fish, thereby reducing prey fish numbers but increasing the growth rate of survivors."

Gar and bowfin are just another cog in the ecologic wheel and should be afforded the same respect that is given to other game fishes. Heck, since time immemorial, bowfin and gar have been cruising the bayous and swamps. Much longer, in fact, than the beloved bass species. Add to that that these prehistoric fish are truly native to Southeast Texas, unlike the introduced Florida largemouth bass.

The Three Gar Species in Southeastern Texas

Gar are easily identified. They have long slender bodies with a distinctly pointed head. Their mouths contain many sharp and needlelike teeth. The dorsal and anal fins on all gar species sit far back on the body, close to the tail. Three species of gar can be found in the Houston area: the longnose gar, spotted gar, and alligator gar.

It's usually a good idea to have a pair of leather gloves in your backpack if you go gar fishing. In this photo, the author uses protective gloves to hold the mouth of a longnosed gar open to display it's needle-like teeth.

Spotted gar (*Lepisosteus oculatus*) is probably the most common species of gar in the Houston bayous. They have long snouts, but not nearly the length of long-nose gar. As the name suggests, spotted gar have spots, ranging from light brown to black, along the length of their body including their heads. Often, the presence of spots can be hard to see (water turbidity may dictate this), but after close inspection, they become more apparent. Spotted gar are the smallest species of gar in the Houston waters, but they can still grow to be around 3 feet long.

Trey Alvarez shows the sleek profile of a spotted gar he caught on Lake Conroe.

Right: Spotted gar can be distinguished from other gar species by the presence of dark spots on the fish's head.

Longnose gar (*Lepisosteus osseus*) have a snout that is narrow and long, twice as long as the length of the head (adults only). The head of longnose gar is absent of any dark spots, but they do have spots on their rear fins. Longnose gar can be difficult to angle because of their narrow jaws. In general, this species grows larger than the spotted gar, but still not as large as the gargantuan alligator gar. With that being said, longnose

Longnose gar can grow to substantial size. This one was hooked from a deep hole in the West Fork San Jacinto River.

After looking at the head of an alligator gar, one doesn't need an imagination to see how this fish got its name.

Nick Heaverlo angled this alligator gar from a saltwater marsh in Galveston Bay, south of the city.

gar can still grow to an impressive 5 feet in optimum conditions.

Alligator gar (*Atractosteus spatula*) are the most iconic of all the gar species. Alligator gar have a distinctive head that resembles, well, an alligator's. They can grow to staggering proportions, reaching lengths of 6 and 7 feet, occasionally bigger, and commonly weighing 100 to 200 pounds. Gar can live as long as 60 years in the wild, an astounding age for a freshwater fish.

Alligator gar (sometimes called "gator gar" by locals) have lower rates of reproduction than other gars and are more closely regulated by the Texas Parks & Wildlife Department (TPWD). Attempting to land a gator gar is no easy task. This is the kind of fish that can cause injury to an angler if he or she isn't prepared to deal with its power. Serious hardware is required to land one of these beasts. Not only must the rod, reel, and line be strong enough (think saltwater tackle), but other hardware is also required. Anglers should consider bringing a sturdy rope to lasso the fish, as well as leather gloves to control the toothy mouth.

Local fly angler Alan Antonson has successfully matched wits with alligator gar on the fly in the Trinity River (northeast of Houston). Antonson recalls that it took multiple hours of nonstop casting to eventually find a gator gar willing to eat. To date, Antonson has successfully landed several gator gar on the fly. For the most part,

anglers who tangle with alligator gar do so primarily with conventional equipment and fresh bait.

Catching any species of gar on the fly can be tricky. When water temperatures are cool, gar can often be seen lying immobile on the bottom of a waterbody in a state of lethargy. When gar are in one of these docile "moods," you can bounce a fly right in front of them, and they'll still refuse to eat. Usually, as the water temperatures increase, so does the gar's willingness to take a fly. By the time summer rolls around, these fish tend to chase and attack almost anything you put in front of them. They move with heart-pounding speed after baitfish patterns and make slashing sideways takes.

There are a couple of tricks that can increase the chances of successfully landing one of these powerful fish. Hooks must be sharp and able to pierce their tough mouths. Tying a smaller trailing hook, called a stinger, onto the hook bend of the main fly can increase your chances of a hookup as well.

Another option is using frayed nylon rope. This "rope fly" tangles around the sharp teeth of the gar and ensnares the gar's mouth. The only drawback to the rope fly is

This Trinity River alligator gar angled by Alan Antonson. These are very powerful fish and should be treated with a healthy amount of respect. Do your research on how conventional anglers land these river monsters before attempting to fish for these behemoths on your own.

that anglers must be sure that all strands of the rope are removed from the gar's mouth before releasing it back into the water. If this is not done, the mouth of the gar will once again become entangled in the remaining strands of nylon rope, preventing the fish from opening its mouth. This eventually results in starvation. If anglers choose to use the rope fly, it's absolutely imperative that all remnants of the nylon rope are removed from the gar's mouth before it is released.

In the past couple of years, a hybridized style of rope fly has become popular for gar anglers. These flies are often tied with a combination of nylon rope, as well as one or more hooks. Angler Joey Ramirez has designed a fly specifically for pursuing gar (although it also hammers bass too). He calls it the Gar Funk (G Funk) Fly.

Bowfin (*Amia calva*) are a unique North American fish, with many equally unique nicknames: mudfish, dogfish, and swamp trout. Many folks native to East Texas refer to the bowfin by its regional nickname,

Ancient Fish in the Atomic Age

Biologists have long counted growth rings, or annuli, in gar otoliths (ear bones), but as the fish age and the rings become more densely packed, the count becomes uncertain. In 2020, a crew of scientists from University of Hawaii at Manoa and TPWD used radiocarbon dating techniques to determine accurate ages for several alligator gar specimens. Using the worldwide increase in background radiocarbon due to atomic bomb testing in 1958 as a reference, the scientists were able to verify annuli counts to within just a couple of years. Of all the gar sampled in the study, the oldest one was estimated to be 68 years old. That is an incredibly old fish, especially for fresh water. In recent years, more studies have been coordinated to better understand this interesting, and sometimes misunderstood, fish.

Alligator gar are at the top of the food chain, so their numbers are few compared to other sport fish. Not only that, but females don't reach maturity until five to ten years old and they only reproduce a handful of times each decade. TPWD estimates that a sustainable harvest rate for gator gar should not exceed 5 percent. Luckily for Texans, the Lone Star State still has healthy populations of alligator gar that swim in our local rivers. This is a boast that many other states with native populations of gator gar cannot make. In years long since passed, these fish were subjected to unwarranted hatred. They have been accused of having a detrimental impact on more desirable fish species like bass, and they have even been accused of attacking humans. Luckily, through education and outreach, many of these myths have been dispelled. The alligator gar should be seen as just another native Texan.

"grinnel." Bowfin have a large head and elongated body. The dorsal fin stretches almost the entire length of the body. They have short tubelike nostrils protruding from their face. In spawning males, the fins become a vibrant emerald green, temporarily turning the male bowfin into a stunningly beautiful piscivorous predator. Often, bowfin will have a black dot, or eye spot, near the base of the tail fin. On young fish, the black dot is ringed with a yellow or orange halo. As the fish gets older, this distinct spot fades.

Bowfin are "demersal," meaning they live near or on the bottom. They prefer sluggish waters like reservoirs or slow-flowing bayous. They are usually found in weedy back-waters, lying in patches of vegetation or along gently sloping banks. They have a unique method of locomotion that is unforgettable the first time it is witnessed. Undulations of their entire dorsal fin propel the fish in a slow and stealthy manner, almost like a ghost slowly hovering across the

Top right: Male bowfin exhibit vibrant green fins during the spring spawning season.

Right: Bowfin have a black spot at the base of the caudal fin.

Below: Danny Scarborough with a beautiful female bowfin from Lake Conroe

seafloor. Bowfin can swim backward just as easily by reversing the undulations of the dorsal fin.

When a bowfin moves quickly after its prey, it does so with a full-body, eel-like motion and attacks with lightning-quick speed. Bowfin are opportunistic feeders, mainly consuming small baitfish, although crawfish and frogs have also been documented. When hooked, these fish are incredible fighters. It is puzzling why they don't receive more respect from the bass fishing community.

Fly fishing for bowfin is most readily accomplished from a canoe or kayak. With a watercraft, the angler can have a bird's-eye view of weed beds and shallow mud flats. Spotting a bowfin in its lie takes a keen eye. Remember to work slowly across the water with quiet methodical strokes of the paddle.

Danny Scarborough has guided bowfin-specific trips for years and is a local expert on these ancient fish. "Sometimes you'll just see their nose sticking out of the weeds," Scarborough says. "They'll lay in the thick vegetation and watch as you paddle by. They're very bold and curious."

Luckily for fly anglers, bowfin don't spook easily. While you're drifting over a weed bed in a kayak, a bowfin might become startled and swim out of cover, but often they will stop, still within casting range, and can be duped into eating a well-presented fly.

Scarborough has often told the story that while he was out kayaking, he watched a bowfin swim into a mass of vegetation and disappear from sight. To test the inquisitive nature of the bowfin, Danny sloshed his kayak paddle back and forth on the surface of the water. Sure enough, the bowfin came swimming out of the weeds and right over to him.

"He swam right up to my kayak to see what all the racket was about," Scarborough recalls. "When you're the biggest predator in the backwaters, what do you have to worry about?"

The spring and fall are usually the best times of the year to target bowfin. This is because the aquatic vegetation that bowfin hide among is either dying or hasn't bloomed yet. An angler has an easier time spotting them in these conditions.

Most flies that mimic baitfish patterns work well on bowfin. It is important that the fly sinks in order to get down to the bottom, where the bowfin dwells. Clouser Minnows, Scarborough's Weedless Baitfish, and small streamers with dumbbell eyes like Bennett's Lunch Money, will all be scarfed up by hungry bowfin.

Chapter 22

WHITE AND YELLOW BASSES: THE "TRUE" (TEMPERATE) BASSES

TWO SPECIES OF "TRUE" BASSES CAN BE FOUND IN THE HOUSTON area: yellow bass and white bass. These fish spend most of their time in large rivers and lakes. However, every spring (February through April), these fish can be found moving upstream into smaller tributaries in an effort to spawn. It is during the spawning season that fly anglers have ample opportunity to catch them.

The way Texas anglers view the white bass run is similar to the way Northerners in the Great Lakes region view the steelhead run. The fish are not comparable in size, of course, but the zeal with which the white bass are pursued is just as intense. When the white bass are running, it's a great time to be a Texas fly fisher. Grab the long rod and hit the creeks.

White bass (*Morone chrysops*) in particular are highly prized by many Texans. Due to their popularity as a sport fish, white bass have been introduced to many waterways and lakes

Above: A nice white bass.

White bass are exceptional fighters. Anglers usually have a great time catching these fish in the local creeks when they run upstream during their annual spawning season.

throughout the state. Their historical native range was mostly contained to the Mississippi River basin and the Red River in the northeast corner of the state.

White bass look similar to their cousins, the yellow bass, but have some distinct features. White bass have four to seven dark grey lines on either side of their body. Only one of these lines extends the entire length to their tail. They have a distinct tooth patch on their tongue and two separate dorsal fins. In general, white bass are larger than yellow bass, making them a more desirable game fish. They fight hard and are a lot of fun when angled with lightweight tackle. Prior to spawning, males run upstream into the tributaries first, followed by the larger females. Once spawning begins, they swim in schools and move from deep hole to deep hole, feeding along the way. Once spawning is finished, the fish usually return to the lakes or reservoirs; however, finding holdovers in the deeper holes in local creeks is fairly common.

Yellow bass (*Morone mississippiensis*) are closely related to white bass and are sometimes confused for them. Like white bass, yellow bass also have dark lines on either side of their body, but the lines on yellow bass are more distinct. The lines closest to the belly, just above the anal fin, are usually broken and offset. Another distinguishing feature of yellow bass is that the first and second dorsal fins are connected. Also, yellow bass lack the tooth patch on their tongue. The native range of yellow bass is primarily the Mississippi River basin; however, the watershed of the San Jacinto River is one of the farthest western watersheds that yellow bass occupy. They do not swim in the waters west of the Brazos River (with the exception of an introduced population in Arizona), making them a fish unique to the eastern half of the state.

Yellow bass are usually smaller than white bass. These fish are native to the Houston-area waterways and spawn in large numbers along with their cousins, the white bass.

Striped bass hybrids, sometimes called sunshine bass, palmetto bass, or "wipers," can be angled with a fly rod on occasion. These fish were originally "created" in South Carolina in the 1960s by crossing striped bass with white bass. Since then, they have been stocked throughout the Southeast. The Texas Parks & Wildlife Department (TPWD) stocks palmetto bass in Lake Conroe. Periodically, lucky anglers may find a rogue wiper in the West Fork of the San Jacinto River. These fish are likely escapees from Lake Conroe.

Above: Striped bass hybrids commonly called, sunshine, palmetto, or "wiper" bass.

Inset: Hiro Yamamoto holds a dandy palmetto bass that he angled from the West Fork San Jacinto.

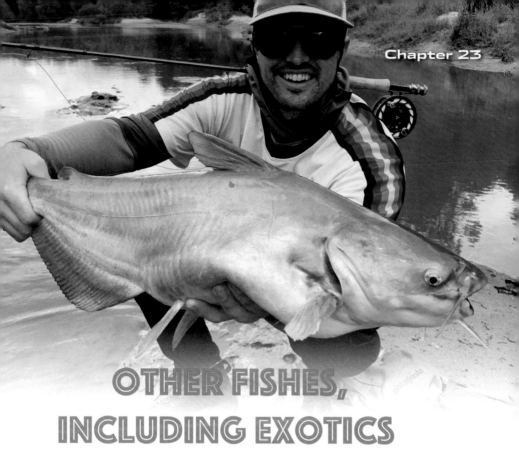

Chapter 23

OTHER FISHES, INCLUDING EXOTICS

In addition to the previously mentioned fishes, there are several more species that fly anglers will encounter in the Houston-area waters. Most of the fishes that will be mentioned in the coming paragraphs are native to the area, but there are several exotics worth mentioning that also swim in the Houston bayous.

Catfish

Overall, catfish are a very popular game fish for many Texans. Most anglers who pursue catfish do so with baited lines that sit on the bottom of a waterway. Because catfish are predators, catching them on streamer patterns is something that happens regularly. When it comes to catching catfish on the fly, fly anglers usually fall into one of two camps. You either love 'em or you hate 'em. Thankfully, for many Houston fly fishers, the catfish is treated with the same respect as all other fish. Fighting a catfish on

Above: Nick Heaverlo holds a blue catfish that weighed in at 8 pounds 1 ounce. This stout fish was angled from the West Fork San Jacinto River using a 5-weight rod equipped with sink-tip line and a Clouser Minnow.

a fly rod is nothing short of a good time. When these predators move in for the take, they do so with gusto.

Channel catfish

Channel catfish (*Ictalurus punctatus*) are the most common species found in the area. They are partial to flowing water but can still be found in large reservoirs. Channel catfish have a dark grey body and a lighter-colored belly. Their tail is deeply forked, and they have a rounded anal fin, a feature that can be used to tell them apart from a blue catfish. Younger channel catfish will display small black spots on their sides. These fish are opportunistic and will eat anything, including fish, crawfish, insects, crustaceans, and even plants. Channel catfish will chase down streamers and nymphs, but they will also occasionally take topwater flies. These fish, although bemoaned by some, are a welcomed catch by many local long rodders. On several occasions, what almost became a fishless day was saved when a channel catfish turned up on the end of my line.

Heaverlo's blue catfish that weighed in at 8 pounds

Blue catfish (*Ictalurus furcatus*) closely resemble channel catfish, but their anal fin is usually straight. Blue catfish also lack the small dark spots that are found on younger channel catfish. One of the most distinguishing characteristics of this fish is that they can grow to proportions twice as large as channel catfish. The state fly rod record for blue catfish is 35.5 pounds, whereas the fly rod record for channel catfish is 16 pounds.

Flathead catfish (*Pylodictis olivaris*), also called yellow catfish, are also found in the waters of southeastern Texas. These large fish are mostly piscivorous and nocturnal. During the day, flatheads seek the shelter of logjams, rock piles, and any other dense structure which makes them hard to target with a fly rod. However, incidental catches do happen, especially when you're using a sinking fly line. The current fly rod record is 49.5 pounds.

Rio Grande Cichlids

Populations of Rio Grande cich-lids exist throughout the bayous and creeks in the Houston metro area. These fish do not occur in the same quantities that can be found in Central and South Texas, but where present, they have established healthy popu-lations. The Rio Grande cichlids are the only species of cichlid that is native to North America. However, the ones found in Houston streams are a long way

Travis Richards caught this gorgeous Rio Grande cichlid in Little White Oak Bayou. Pockets of cichlids exist throughout the Bayou City.

from their native range along the Rio Grande and Pecos Rivers. Rio Grande cichlids are a unique and strikingly beautiful fish. They are often dark-colored, grey to dark brown, but have a smattering of light colored spots. Variations in their color seem dictated by water clarity in the Houston waterways. Often, the more turbid the water, the lighter-colored these fish are. Small nymphs and crawfish patterns work well on cichlids. Try tossing Bennett's Rio Getter, Bailes' Hatchling Craw, or Scarborough's Brasshawk to tempt one of these fish.

Crappie

Black crappie (*Pomoxis nigro-maculatus*) and **white crappie** (*Pomoxis annularis*) can be angled from various water bodies in the metro area and Pineywoods. Black crappie tend to live in ponds and reservoirs, whereas white crappie can be found in both len-tic and lotic environments. White

Black crappie can usually be found in ponds and lakes. Lake Conroe boasts a healthy population of black crappie.

White crappie can be found in local creeks and rivers. They are often caught in the early spring, along with temperate bass.

crappie usually have faint vertical barring extending down their sides. The sides of the black crappie have a random smattering of black spots. Both of these fish have large mouths and will readily take bass flies, like Clouser Minnows, or other streamer patterns. Most of the time, crappie can be found in schools, so if you hook into one, there's a good chance at finding more in the general vicinity.

Drum

Freshwater drum (*Aplodinotus grunniens*) or **gaspergou**, as they are sometimes called, are an excellent fighting fish on the fly rod. These fish spend most of their time close to the bottom, feeding on mollusks, insects, and crawfish, but they will also hunt down and strike streamer patterns. These fish are closely related to the salty and beloved Texas redfish (*Sciaenops ocellatus*) and black drum (*Pogonias cromis*). Tight-line nymphing with beadhead nymphs along the bottom of deep pools is a great way to find a "gou." The state fly rod record for a freshwater drum was taken in Grapevine, Texas. The drum weighed 11.7 pounds and was 27.7 inches in length.

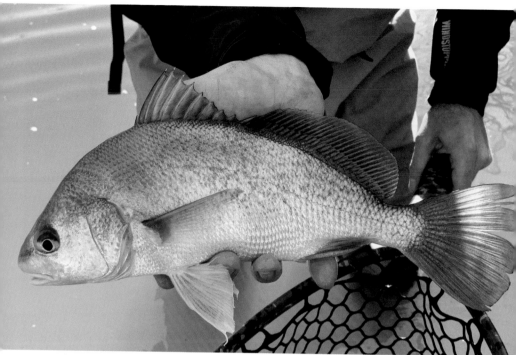

Freshwater drum (also called gaspergou, or "gou" for short) are a stout and powerful fish. These hard fighters can be found throughout southeastern Texas.

Pickerel

Grass pickerel (*Esox americanus vermiculatus*) can occasionally be found in the waters of the Pineywoods north and east of the city of Houston. Although related to the large and powerful northern pike and musky, this species of *Esox* is much smaller, only reaching a length of 12 to 15 inches. They appear to be the most active during the colder months and prefer hanging out in weedy and sluggish backwaters. Hooking into a grass pickerel in the waters of the Pineywoods would be a real treat.

Exotics

Armored catfish of the family *Loricariidae* are a common sight in the urban bayous. These invasive fish from South America are also called pleco catfish, suckermouth catfish, or algae-eaters. As the latter name suggests, these fish eat only algae and can be found "grazing" on the sides of cement ditches or along the bottom of streams. They have an elongated dorsal fin and a flat head with the mouth positioned underneath the head. The ones in Houston are usually darker in color with intricate cream-colored patterns across the back. They can grow to two feet in length. Likely, these fish came to swim in the local waterways by illegal dumpings of aquariums. In their miniature form, these are the same fish that can be seen stuck to the sides of aquariums, sucking the algae off the glass. They are especially destructive to the local waters because they burrow into the banks to nest, which damages the integrity of the waterways. These fish are very rarely caught by hook and line. Most of the time, when a pleco finds the end of a fly rod, it is through sheer luck or snagging.

Tilapia, of the genus *Oreochromis*, can be found in numbers throughout Houston's bayous. These invasive cichlids are from Africa and have a similar shape and build to Rio Grande cichlids, but they can grow much larger (up to 21 inches). The tilapia that swim in Houston are a drab, light color with faint barring on the sides. Tilapia have relatively small mouths but still eat a wide variety of foods. Everything from small baitfish to insects and occasionally vegetation are on the menu. Try fishing small buggy patterns in sizes 10 to 12 when you encounter tilapia.

Over the years, there have been reports (and pictures to prove it) of other exotics taken from Houston-area waters. **Red-bellied pacu**, a plant-eating species from South America, have been occasionally caught. More recently, an angler soaking stink-bait in the Buffalo Bayou hooked into a **redtail catfish**, another invasive species from South America.

Liam Smith with a nice tilapia from Brays Bayou. These fish are not native to the Houston area but they seem to thrive in the local bayous.

Part 6

Farther Afield: Village Creek

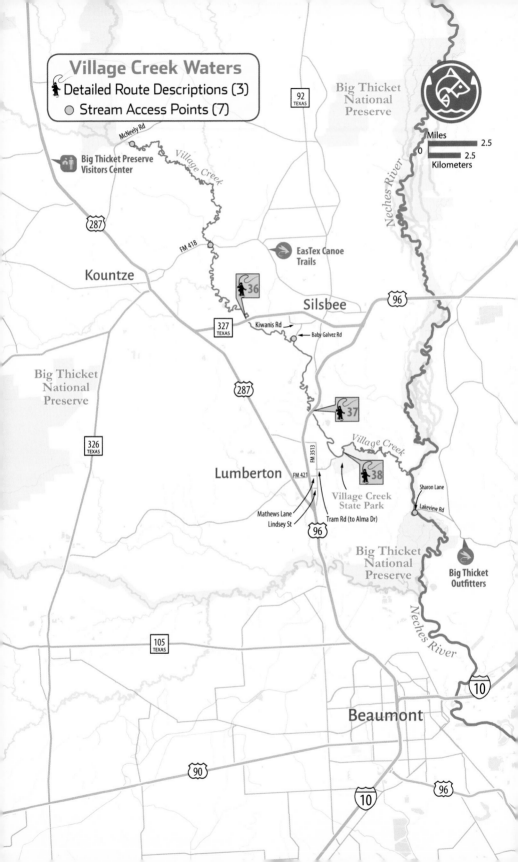

Village Creek Waters

Detailed Route Descriptions (3)
○ Stream Access Points (7)

Big Thicket National Preserve

92 TEXAS

McNeely Rd

Big Thicket Preserve Visitors Center

Village Creek

287

FM 418

Kountze

Neches River

96

EasTex Canoe Trails

36

Silsbee

327 TEXAS

Kiwanis Rd

Baby Galvez Rd

Big Thicket National Preserve

326 TEXAS

287

37

Village Creek

Lumberton

FM 421

FM 3513

38

Village Creek State Park

Sharon Lane

Lakeview Rd

Mathews Lane
Lindsey St

Tram Rd (to Alma Dr)

96

105 TEXAS

Big Thicket National Preserve

Big Thicket Outfitters

Neches River

10

Beaumont

90

10

96

Miles
0   2.5

Kilometers
         2.5

A BRIEF HISTORY OF
THE BIG THICKET

Roughly one hundred miles east from downtown Houston, there exist some of the most unique ecological environments within the Lone Star State. This region is known as the Big Thicket National Preserve, and it's exactly as the name suggests: one big thicket. It's also a place of beauty, wild and secluded creeks, and unique flora and fauna.

While this book is certainly about the art of fly fishing, and focuses mainly on waterways around Houston, it's worthwhile to give a brief introduction into this Big Thicket area and why it's important for Houstonians who are interested in the natural world.

Before it was designated a national preserve, the Big Thicket region was a place of mystery. As Lorraine G. Bonney puts it in *The Big Thicket Guidebook*, "It was as legendary as the Llano Estacado or the Mustang Desert." It was (and still is) a crossroads of ecology. It is different from the Pineywoods but also unique from the ecosystems of the coastal prairies of the Gulf. The Big Thicket is an expansive region of creeks and rivers, forests, baygalls (blackwater swamps), and lush vegetation; a mishmash of endemic plants like orchids and carnivorous pitcher plants, mammals, reptiles, and history.

Much of the Big Thicket region is shrouded in mystery. Historically, the area was nearly impossible to penetrate overland. After a three-year-long tour of Mexico, New Mexico, and Texas, Cayetano María Pignatelli Rubí Corbera y San Climent, the third Marqués de Rubí, suggested in his 1768 report that the Spanish government should not bother claiming southeastern Texas (especially the Big Thicket area) as part of the Spanish Empire. In writing to his superiors, Rubí stated, "In this vast area there was not a settlement or semblance of one, nor hope of any being established."

However, various groups of Native Americans did reside (whether temporarily or permanently is still debated) within the area. Their main method of transportation was via the many waterways in the region. Spanish explorers and French traders eventually gained access to the area by paddling Pine Island Bayou, Neches River, Village Creek, and the other waterways of the region.

Travis Richards presents a fly to the base of the cypress trees that line the banks of Village Creek.

Early in the nineteenth century, the Big Thicket's reputation as an inhospitable place was furthered by the arrival of scurrilous characters like smugglers, horse thieves, and fugitives. The reason for their influx into the Big Thicket region was the U.S. Army's crackdown on the criminals who had been hiding in an area called the Neutral Ground, a densely forested area along the present-day boundary of Louisiana and Texas. After 1821, the western boundary of the Louisiana Purchase (originally signed in 1812) was finally established. The United States claimed lands up to the Sabine River (the current border between Texas and Louisiana), and the U.S. Army moved into the Neutral Ground to weed out the remaining criminals. Many of this sordid lot simply jumped the Sabine River and headed west, establishing themselves in the Big Thicket region.

In 1836, after the Texas Revolution, Anglo-Americans from the Appalachian Mountains of the eastern United States immigrated to the outskirts of the Big Thicket area. After settling on the outskirts, groups of daring families pushed deeper into the overgrown and hostile region by using the local waterways. Prior to the establishment of railroads in the area, river transportation was the easiest way to travel through the Big Thicket region.

Timber was an important industry in Big Thicket. In the days before the railroads, many of the creeks and rivers were used to float logs downstream to the town of Beaumont, where they could then be milled into lumber. As railroads started making their inevitable penetration into the otherwise impregnable region, smaller mill towns began springing up. Towns like Silsbee, Kountze, and Lumberton all came into being on the backs of the railroads. The highly prized longleaf pine was the first tree species to be cut. Cutting of this particular species of pine occurred with reckless abandon. Now, much of the East Texas landscape that once boasted prolific numbers of this species is devoid of this tree. In recent years, there has been a determined effort to restore the longleaf pine to much of its native range.

Oil was another important commodity that was discovered in the vicinity of the Big Thicket. The historic Spindletop Oil Field, south of Beaumont, was discovered in 1901. The discovery propelled the world into the age of oil. Other oil discoveries occurred farther north, closer to the ecologic region of Big Thicket. The town of Sour Lake, sometimes referred to as "The Gateway to the Big Thicket," saw prolific oil production that lasted from 1901 to 1948.

In the latter half of the twentieth century, efforts were made to define the ecologic region of the Big Thicket in order to better understand the area's environmental importance. In 1967, Dr. Claude A. McLeod defined the Big Thicket region as an area of 1.5 million acres, expanding across the East Texas counties of Jasper, Polk, Tyler, San Jacinto, Liberty, Hardin, and parts of Montgomery.

Local conservation groups began to form in order to lobby for some kind of environmental protection for the Big Thicket area. Negotiations between conservation groups, timber companies, and governments (local and federal), continued for many years. In 1974, President Gerald Ford signed into law the creation of the Big Thicket National Preserve, which at that time was only 84,550 acres. In 1993, an additional 10,766 acres were added to the preserve by incorporating the lands adjacent to Big Sandy and Village Creeks.

The Big Thicket Preserve is broken into several different units. Many of these separate units are connected by creeks or rivers that have established riparian corridors that are designated as part of the national preserve. These protected waterways include parts of Neches River, Turkey Creek, Big Sandy Creek, Menard Creek, Pine Island Bayou, and Village Creek. Of these streams, Village Creek will be addressed in greater detail in the following section.

If you'd like to learn more about the Big Thicket National Preserve, check out the visitor's center located at 6102 FM 420, Kountze, TX 77625 (30.45819, -94.38709). Here, you can peruse exhibits, find maps of the various hiking trails, and learn about the unique ecology of this region. Be sure to check out the exhibits on the carnivorous plants. North America has a total of five types of carnivorous plants, four of which are found in the Big Thicket region. To get a more intimate look at some of these special plants, you can hike Pitcher Plant Trail (30.58216, -94.33569), an easy one-mile loop outside of Warren, Texas.

There are too many intriguing things to cover about Big Thicket National Preserve, and it is easy to become distracted by it all. Many books have been written about this area, including *The Big Thicket Guidebook* by Lorraine G. Bonney and *Reflections on the Neches* by Geraldine Ellis Watson. Of course, the book you're reading now is about fly fishing, so let's cut to the chase.

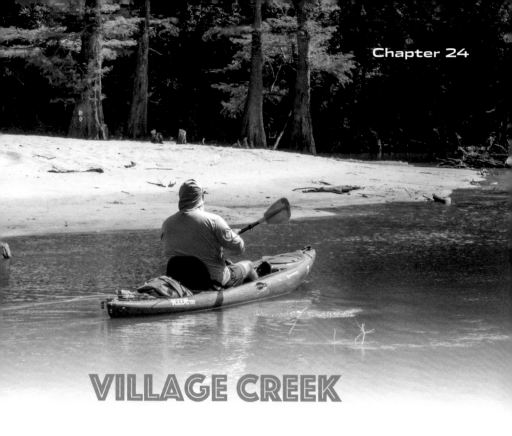

Chapter 24

VILLAGE CREEK

Secluded wilderness waterway with pristine white sandbars, popular TPWD Paddling Trail, and part of the Big Thicket National Preserve; panfish galore, spotted bass, largemouth, and catfish. Access Points: 7

IN 2016, A FRIEND OF MINE WAS DOING SOME SPRING CLEANING at his apartment in Houston. He offered to give me several old issues of *Southwest Fly Fishing* magazines that he had scattered around his place. I was happy to take some of the magazines off his hands. Later that evening, while thumbing through the September/October 2013 issue, I came across a short article written by Robert Sloan. The article outlined an intriguing East Texas waterway called Village Creek. In the article, Sloan states, "If ever there was a backwoods Texas stream made for fly fishing, this is it."

That was all I needed to read. The next day at work, I showed the article to another fly fishing friend. He read it eagerly and quickly decided to join me on the water the following weekend.

Due to the ruggedness of the surrounding forests, much of the area adjacent to Village Creek has remained undeveloped and wild. No man-made impoundments exist along the length of this 41-mile stream.

Village Creek begins at the confluence of Big Sandy Creek and Kimball Creek in northern Hardin County, west of TX 287 and the community of Village Mills. The waterway flows in a southeastern direction, eventually dumping into the Neches River east of the town of Lumberton.

For most of its length, the banks of Village Creek are steep and lined with towering pines, cypress trees, and hardwoods. Fly fishing from the banks is extremely difficult, which makes fishing from a watercraft your best option. Multiple white sandbars exist along this creek, which are perfect places to stop to eat lunch or take a quick swim.

The tea-colored tannic waters flow with a slightly reddish hue. Because Village Creek is spring-fed and flows under a dense canopy of trees for much of its length, the water temperature is fairly cool. In fact, it tends to be too cool for even alligators and mosquitoes. According to the website for EasTex Canoe Trails, which offers a canoe-rental service on Village Creek, "While alligators do exist in the Big Thicket, they are rarely ever seen on Village Creek, but we do occasionally see small American Alligators on our Neches River Wilderness trips."

A couple enjoys a leisurely paddle along Village Creek.

A nice specimen of spotted bass from the waters of Village Creek

Village Creek is a gem of a waterway, which makes it popular with weekend warriors. The slow current is perfect for beginner paddlers and for families. Overnight camping excursions are popular on this waterway. Numerous white sand point bars offer picturesque campsites. At least two canoe rental companies operate along Village Creek. EasTex Canoe Trails (eastexcanoes.com) has been running a rental service out of Silsbee, Texas, since 1978. Big Thicket Outfitters (bigthicketoutfitters.com) also rents canoes and kayaks, as well as camping gear.

Much of the upper reaches of Village Creek are impassible by watercraft due to numerous downed trees spanning the width of the creek. The official Texas Paddling Trail doesn't begin until the crossing of FM 418. The 21-mile-long paddling trail ends at Village Creek State Park, which lies upstream of the confluence of the Neches River by about 6.5 miles.

Since my initial trip to Village Creek in 2016, I have made multiple excursions to this remote wilderness stream. After each trip, I am reminded of the secretive beauty of East Texas and the Big Thicket region. If you live in Houston and still haven't visited this waterway, you owe it to yourself to make a trip.

USGS Stream Gauges along Village Creek

For paddlers, the most important gauge to check before hitting the water is located on FM 418 between the towns of Kountze and Silsbee (gauge number: 08041500). Flow rates around 375 cubic feet per second or lower usually bode well for clarity. Gauge heights in the range of 4 to 5 feet usually mean clear and low water. If gauge heights are lower than 4 feet, you can expect to drag your kayak over a couple of shallow sandbars if you explore some of the backwater areas. But for the most part, you won't need to drag your kayak too much.

TX 327 Bridge, Kountze

30.34690, -94.23949

TX 327, Kountze, TX 77625

92 road miles, 1:50 drive time

USGS Monitor Station: 08041500

Optimum flow: 375 to 275 cfs

Optimum gauge height: 4 to 5 ft.

Difficulty: Easy to Moderate

If this is your first time on Village Creek, this float is a perfect introduction. The total length from the boat ramp at TX 327 (put-in) to Baby Galvez Landing (take-out) is approximately 3 miles. You can take as much time (or as little) paddling, fishing, and exploring as you want.

The boat ramp at TX 327 is a popular place for swimming and for launching canoes and kayaks. During the summer weekends, the section of water can get a little crowded. Try fishing this during the week, or start early in the morning.

Village Creek is a unique and beautiful waterway.

This section has some deep holes lined in towering cypress trees but also shallow chutes and white sand beaches. Casting is easily accomplished because of the high banks and wide riverbed. Consider bringing two rods with you. Rig one rod with a small streamer, like a Clouser Minnow, and the other with a dragonfly nymph or topwater pattern.

What You Will Find

During the summer, both the launch site and take-out can get crowded with swimmers and paddlers. If you hit the water during the workweek or early morning, you will likely have the water all to yourself. Assuming that you have your own paddlecraft and aren't renting from the local outfitters, you'll need

How Baby Galvez Landing Got Its Name

The popular swimming hole and canoe launch Baby Galvez Landing was once part of a larger resort, which offered bath houses and a pavilion that served as a dance hall. The building itself (long gone from various floods) was situated high on a bluff overlooking the creek. You can drive past the general area where the resort once stood. It was located at the sharp bend on Lindsey Road, which intersects Baby Galvez Road. Patrons could use the bathhouses at the resort to don their swimming garb and then walk the short distance to the creek. Later on, the pavilion was converted to a honky-tonk, which the *Silsbee Bee* (the local newspaper) says "had a bad reputation." The name "Baby Galvez" is a play on words meaning "Little Galveston," an homage to the popular resort island of Galveston, Texas.

to run a shuttle vehicle to the take-out, which is at the end of Baby Galvez Road, outside of Silsbee (30.33455, -94.20396). This will only take 15 minutes or so. When you arrive at the boat ramp at Baby Galvez Landing, do not park in the wide gravel turnabout in front of the boat ramp. This area is needed to load and unload canoes and kayaks. Instead, park along the shoulder of the gravel road on the way into Baby Galvez Landing.

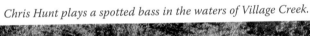 **Baby Galvez Float** (Paddling Downstream from the Bridge)
After you shove off, you'll paddle through a deep stretch of water. This section can be fished by making casts to the trunks and knees of the bald cypress trees that line the banks. During the summer months, rig your fly rod with a hopper-dropper. Use a large foam terrestrial like Kevin Hutchinson's Llano bug and a dropper that mimics a dragonfly nymph. Tried-and-true droppers could be Josh Smitherman's Draggin' Nymph, Wilson's Bully Bluegill Spider, or the San Jac Squirrel.

Once you paddle downstream for about 0.3 miles, you will see the first sandy beach on your right (river right). Fish around the sunken trees on your left next to the cutbank. Lob a couple of casts to the shallow

Chris Hunt plays a spotted bass in the waters of Village Creek.

eddies that are formed behind the logs and debris in the riffles opposite the sandbar.

Continue downstream for another 1.4 miles, being sure to cast to overhanging banks, downed trees, and the trunks of cypress trees as you float along. You will pass two more sandy beaches. Eventually, you will see a particularly nice white sand beach, river left, and several cypress trees jutting out from the water. The creek makes a hard turn to the right just after this beach. If you decide to keep paddling through this section, pay attention because debris in the form of logs and downed trees gets caught on the trunks of the cypress trees. These could pose a hazard to unwary paddlers. Immediately downstream of the sandbar, on your left, a small creek called Mill Creek enters into Village Creek. If you stopped on the aforementioned sandbar (as you should have), you can fish the mouth of Mill Creek.

This picturesque sandbar is found at the confluence of Mill Creek. This is a fantastic place to swim, eat lunch, or camp for the night.

After paddling nearly 0.5 miles more, you will see another large sandbar on your left with an interesting backwater section, also on your left. It's worth making a quick detour back into this secluded backwater, even if it's just to look at the cypress trees. Keep an eye out for various herons and egrets tucked in amongst the trees.

Head downstream another 0.4 miles, and you will see where Village Creek diverges around a large island, forming two different channels. The majority of the water flows through the channel on your left (river left). This route is the quickest way to the take-out. If you go this route, be aware of the sweepers and snags that pile up around the first bend and farther downstream. Be extremely careful as the water flows swiftly through this section and there are plenty of downed trees that could rake you out of your paddlecraft. Make casts to the eddies as you round the first bend; spotted bass and longear sunfish have been caught at this location in the past.

If the gauge height of Village Creek is somewhere between 4 and 5 feet, try paddling the other channel, river right. This is the original stream channel and a more circuitous route to the take-out, but it is absolutely gorgeous and can offer some great fishing opportunities. The water tends to be skinnier, but there are plenty of deep holes, chutes, and woody debris. If you are floating this section in the summer, this is where the hopper-dropper shines. As you float downstream, cast to the banks or various logjams and allow your paddlecraft to match the speed of the current. Let your hopper-dropper match the current as well, just like you would if you were fishing trout on a big river out West. Be ready to set the hook as soon as you see the hopper go under. Beautiful spotted bass and longears have been landed using this technique.

Once you finish floating around the large island, you will rejoin the other channel. High on the bank, river left, you will see a rope swing. The take-out at Baby Galvez Landing is immediately downstream from the rope swing, river left (30.33455, -94.20396).

A typical bass from Village Creek

Getting There

The GPS will likely tell you to take I-10 East to Beaumont and then head north on US 96 North through Lumberton. This route is roughly 10 miles longer than if you take US 90 East toward Dayton and Liberty. I recommend this latter route because it is not subject to I-10 traffic and the delays from ongoing construction. Plus, you get to see more of East Texas and pass through some unique small towns along the way.

From downtown Houston, head north on I-45 to I-10 East. Remain on I-10 East for 4.7 miles. Take exit 775B for US 90 East toward Liberty. You will stay on US 90 East for 38.5 miles. You will cross the mighty Trinity River and then drive through the towns of Dayton and Liberty. Once you pass through Liberty, be on the lookout for MLK Road (TX 105 East) in the small community of Ames. Make a left onto MLK Road and cross the railroad tracks. Stay on MLK Road until the

T-intersection with FM 770 North. Take a left onto FM 770 North. Stay on this road for 6.8 miles until the intersection with TX 105 East. Make a right onto TX 105 East, which runs along with FM 770. Stay on TX 105 E/FM 770 N for 2.9 miles. Once you see West Hardin High School on your right, slow down; you are making the left at the intersection and following FM 770 North. You'll stay on this road for 15 miles until the intersection with TX 326 North. Make a left, taking TX 326 North into the town of Kountze. Keep right at the intersection of TX 326 and US 287/US 69. There will be a Brookshire Brothers supermarket on the right at this intersection. You will head out of Kountze on US 287 South/ US 69 South. Continue on for 4.3 miles. Look for the signs for TX 327 toward Silsbee. Get in the left lane and make the left turn onto TX 327 East. Continue on for 2.3 miles. The boat ramp is on your right. Slow down as you approach the bridge; the turn is sharp, and it's down a steep embankment.

US 96, Lumberton
30.28568, -94.191465
885 N. Main St., Lumberton, TX 77657
96 road miles, 1:46 drive time
USGS Monitor Station: 08041500
Optimum flow: 200 to 300 cfs or less
Optimum gauge height: 4 to 5 ft. or less
Difficulty: Moderate

There is a bit more water to cover along this section of Village Creek, but long rodders will be able to find plenty of fish (especially panfish) by targeting logjams and other structure. From the put-in at US 96 (also called North Main Street) to the take-out at Village Creek State Park, the paddle is roughly 3.2 miles. Assuming you aren't arranging a shuttle service from one of the local outfitters, you will need to park a shuttle vehicle at the kayak launch in Village Creek State Park (tpwd.texas.gov/ state-parks/village-creek). It costs $4.00 to enter the park. From the park entrance, follow the main road through the park until it dead-ends at Village Creek (30.25496, -94.17120). There is plenty of room for parking.

What You Will Find

The width of Village Creek along much of this float is roughly twice as wide as the section from TX 327 to Baby Galvez Landing. Don't let the vastness of this waterway dissuade you from fishing it. Use your fishy intuition and pick apart the water in the same manner you would with any other stream.

37 Panfish Paddle (Paddling Downstream from the Bridge)

As you head downstream from the put-in at US 96, you will paddle through a wide and deep section of water. Make casts to the banks and to all woody debris. Remember not to overwork the fly. Use small (size 6 to 8) Clouser Minnows, or nymph patterns in the summer.

This deep section of water is a little over a half mile in length. Once you round a slight right-hand bend in the creek, the water will shallow. A large sandbar can be seen river right with a small stream entering just behind this sandbar. Cypress trees jut vertically from the middle of Village Creek, and plentiful logjams exist along the cutbank, river right. This is a good place to beach the paddlecraft and fish the logjams and pools from the bank.

Village Creek offers wonderful scenery and plenty of fish habitat.

As you continue downstream, look river left, and you will see a beautiful backwater area flanked on either side by tall cypress trees. By now you should see the railroad bridge downstream that crosses the creek. As you paddle under the railroad bridge, you'll see the remnants of the old bridge pylons sticking out from the water's surface. This is another wide and deep section of water.

Downstream from the railroad bridge, a little over half a mile, the water will shallow again. You will see a split in the creek channel (30.26772, -94.18040). Some of the water branches off to the right, flowing down a tight corridor crisscrossed by fallen timber. The main channel continues on, river left, flowing around sandy beaches. This is another spot to beach your watercraft. Fish the eddies at the head of the side channel, river right. If you're feeling adventurous, you may even decide to hike down the channel a little way. If you do, be careful because the sandbars may shift under your weight, causing your feet to become stuck. It's an uneasy feeling, but nothing to be overly alarmed about. There is not nearly as much actual "quicksand" in the world as our childhood reading and TV viewing led us to believe.

Doubled up with longear sunfish on Village Creek. Fishing with lighter tackle on Village Creek is a great way to enjoy the fight of sunfish species.

Continue down the main channel, swerving around the meanders and various sandbars. By now you will encounter cottages and camps along the left bank. This is a productive stretch of water. Once you have paddled about three quarters of a mile, you will come to another large pool. Village Creek bends to the left, flowing due south. The previously mentioned channel that branched off farther upstream enters back into the main channel on your right. This is another good place to pick up some fish.

At this point, you are just under one mile (0.8 miles) away from the take-out. You will continue to see houses on either side of the creek until you enter Village Creek State Park. Look for a steep sandy embankment, river right. You will see a blue sign high on the bank that denotes the end of the paddling trail. Keep a watchful eye; the sign is small, and you may miss it. The take-out at Village Creek State Park is steep. Consider bringing a rope with you to attach to the bow of your paddlecraft to help haul it up the bank.

Getting There

 From downtown, head north on I-45. Take exit 48A for I-10 East, toward Beaumont. After 6 miles on I-10, take exit 775B for US 90 East toward Liberty. You will be on US 90 East for approximately 34 miles. Once you enter into the town of Liberty, continue east on US 90. You will pass through the community of Nome before coming to an intersection with TX 326 North. Make a left onto TX 326 North/Old US 90. Continue on for 11.3 miles, passing through the town of Sour Lake, until the intersection with TX 421 East. Make a right onto TX 421 East. Continue on for 13.1 miles. Once you enter the town of Lumberton, TX 421 will come to a T-intersection with US 96/South Main Street. Make a left onto US 96 North/South Main Street. Take this road north for 3.4 miles, leaving the town of Lumberton. You will drive across Village Creek. As soon as you see the creek, be prepared to make a right-hand turn to the boat ramp.

Village Creek State Park, Lumberton
30.25496, -94.17120
8854 Park Rd. 74, Lumberton, TX 77657
tpwd.texas.gov/state-parks/village-creek
94 road miles, 1:40 drive time
USGS Monitor Station: 08041500
Optimum flow: 200 to 300 cfs or less
Optimum gauge height: 4 to 5 ft. or less
Difficulty: Moderate

Village Creek State Park is open from 8 am to 10 pm. It costs $4.00 per person to enter. The State Park borders the southern shore of Village Creek. This is the last bit of public land that allows access to the creek before it flows into the Neches River another 6.5 miles downstream. Village Creek State Park offers camping, cabin rentals, and hiking trails and is the final stop along the Village Creek Paddling Trail. It is a 3.2-mile paddle from US 96 (located upstream) to Village Creek State Park.

Additionally, paddlers can launch at Village Creek State Park and paddle downstream 6.5 miles to the confluence of the Neches River. Once on the Neches, it is another 1.9 miles to the take-out at Lakeview Sandbar (30.21655, -94.11665). Strong paddlers will find it is quite possible to launch their watercraft at the state park and paddle upstream (the current is not very strong) and then float back to the park.

What You Will Find

Be aware that the canoe and kayak launch at the state park is steep and sandy. You might consider using a rope tied to the bow of your paddlecraft to help with launching and retrieving. The width of Village Creek in the immediate vicinity of the State Park is roughly twice as wide when compared to the section of Village Creek from TX 327 to Baby Galvez Landing.

 **Village Creek State Park** (Paddling Upstream or Downstream in Close Proximity to the State Park)

This is a description of the immediate water around Village Creek State Park, as if a paddler launched their watercraft at the park and paddled around in close proximity to the launch. There are more than enough opportunities for fishing to be had in close proximity to the park.

From the launch, try fishing the cutbank immediately upstream (river right). You can easily paddle upstream from the boat launch and lazily drift back down while making casts to the cutbank and sunken trees.

If flows are low (gauge height of less than 4 feet), you may find additional chutes and drop-offs that you wouldn't have noticed if the water level was higher. Look for these chutes, especially if cypress trees border them or if sunken logs are present. Woody debris is a perfect hiding place for panfish and spotted bass to wait for food as it gets swept down the chutes. Again, using a hopper-dropper rig works wonders in the summer.

If you venture downstream from the launch, just know that you may have to drag your canoe or kayak upstream if the flows are low. There is a wide and deep backwater area (river left) about half a mile downstream from the state park. Before heading downstream, be sure you know your physical limits. When you decide to turn around and paddle back upstream, you can easily become exhausted fighting against the current. Consider attaching a bow line to your paddlecraft and lining your canoe or kayak upstream along the sandbars.

In Robert Sloan's *Southwest Fly Fishing* article about Village Creek, he mentions that fishing can be fantastic along the 6.5-mile-long reach

The blue sign marks the final launch/take-out site for the Village Creek Paddling Trail. It may be wise to use a rope tied to the bow of your paddlecraft to help with getting it in and out of the water.

below the state park, upstream from the creek's confluence with the Neches River. If you plan on floating this downstream area, consider allotting yourself two or more days to complete the float. Just as elsewhere along Village Creek, you may camp on the prolific sandbars along this portion. You can find a take-out on the Neches River, downstream from the confluence of Village Creek, at the National Preserve's Lakeview Sandbar, found at the end of Sharon Lane, Vidor, Texas (30.21655, -94.11665). Call the Big Thicket Visitor's Center at (409) 951-6700 before attempting this paddle to ensure the Lakeview Sandbar is open. The Neches River can be unruly at times and will flood even when the surrounding tributaries have returned to normal flows.

Getting There

From downtown, start by heading north on I-45. Take exit 48A for I-10 East. After traveling about 6 miles on I-10, take the exit for 775B toward US 90 East and the town of Liberty. You will be on US 90 East for roughly 34 miles before coming to the town of Liberty. From Liberty, you will continue on US 90 East for about 22.6 miles. You will come to a little community called Nome, where you will make a left onto TX 326 North. Continue on for 11.3 miles, heading through Sour Lake. Make a right onto TX 421 and continue heading east for another 13 miles. Eventually, TX 421 will come to a T-intersection with US 96/South Main Street in the town of Lumberton. Make a left onto US 96 North/South Main Street. You will be on this road for a mere 250 feet before making a right onto Matthews Lane. Take Matthews Lane to the end, where it intersects with FM 3513 (South Village Creek Parkway). Make a left and continue 0.2 miles. Make your first right onto Tram Road. Cross the railroad tracks and make your first left onto Alma Drive. Continue on Alma Drive for 0.5 miles. You will see signs for Village Creek State Park. Turn left into the park.

The width of Village Creek is much greater near Village Creek State Park.

Big Thicket: The Last Texas Bastion
for the Louisiana Black Bear

In the late nineteenth and early twentieth centuries, the Big Thicket region of Southeast Texas was world-renowned for its population of black bears as well as for the area's bear-hunting dogs and houndsmen. The Hooks Bear Camps were locally known as some of the best bear-hunting outfitters. According to a historic opinion piece written by W. T. Block Jr., Old John Kilrain, simply known as Old Kil, was considered to be one of the best bear-hunting guides and houndsmen in the Big Thicket region. Old Kil was born in 1864, prior to Emancipation Day, which technically made him a former slave, although he was probably around one year old when emancipation occurred on June 19, 1865.

So famous was the Big Thicket's bear hunting that President Teddy Roosevelt was scheduled to make a trip to the Big Thicket region to partake in a bear hunt. Unfortunately, Roosevelt never made it to the region because he was called back to Washington to discuss financial matters around the Panama Canal, or so the story goes. Even the famous big-game hunter and last known mountain man of the Southwest, Benjamin Vernon Lilly, spent at least three years in the Big Thicket area hunting black bears.

At the time, Big Thicket boasted a substantial population of a subspecies of black bear known as the Louisiana black bear (*Ursus americanus luteolus*). There has been some debate as to whether the Louisiana black bear should be recognized as a true subspecies. Those biologists who argue for it cite the bear's uniquely elongated face, flat head, and oversized rear molars as distinguishing characteristics of the Louisiana black bear.

The Big Thicket's black bear population dwindled significantly by the mid-twentieth century due to unregulated hunting. Lorraine G. Bonney, in her book, *The Big Thicket Guidebook*, found several sources that suggest the "last" Louisiana black bear in the Big Thicket region was killed in 1955 when it was hit by a car in Woodville, Texas.

Efforts to restore black bears to their historic range have been ongoing. These efforts have mainly been spearheaded by The Louisiana Department of Wildlife and Fisheries. Between 1977 and 2003, several confirmed black bear sightings have occurred in East Texas. It is thought that these bears are likely juvenile or young adult males that have wandered into the Big Thicket area from growing populations of bears in the states of Arkansas and Louisiana. Hunting regulations set forth by the Texas Parks & Wildlife Department (TPWD) make it illegal to hunt black bears in the Lone Star State. Perhaps, with a little luck, future generations of fly rodders might catch a glimpse of an elusive Big Thicket black bear while paddling the waters of Village Creek.

Part 7

The Future of Houston Waterways

SURFACE WATER AND DEMAND

IN 1957, ON THE HEELS OF THE WORST DROUGHT THE STATE HAD experienced in recent memory, the Texas Water Development Board (TWDB) was created. Over the years, the TWDB evolved into a policy-making body that is responsible for providing financial aid to areas in need of water resource development. Additionally, TWDB assists in developing freshwater storage, providing funds to implement wastewater treatment, and studying the effects of agriculture and manufacturing on water resources.

In order to gain a better understanding of local water resources, the TWDB separated the state into sixteen regional water planning zones. Region H includes all of the Houston metropolitan area along with the entire San Jacinto River watershed, parts of the lower Brazos and Trinity Rivers, and all of Galveston Bay. Census data from Region H shows that from the years 2000 to 2015, this area saw a population increase of nearly 2 million people (4.89 million to 6.83 million). Future projections show that by 2070, the region will see a population close to 11.7 million people.

It comes as no surprise that Harris County and Houston have the greatest water demand within Region H. Of all the fifteen counties within the region, Harris County alone is responsible for over half (53 percent) of the annual water usage. Fifty-five percent of all freshwater use is cate-gorized as "municipal" use. "Municipal water" can be defined as the water used for residential, commercial, and institutional purposes. Running the dishwasher, taking a shower, and flushing the toilet are all examples of usage that falls within the municipal use category. Manufacturing makes up about 28 percent of the region's freshwater use.

Approximately three-quarters of the fresh water used annually comes from surface water sources. "Surface water" is categorized as anything that is above ground. Reservoirs are the main contributor to surface water resources. Lake Conroe and Lake Houston (both within the San Jacinto River watershed) and Lake Livingston (northeast of Houston, just beyond the scope of this book) supply most of the fresh water to Region H. These surface water sources are the same waterways that are revered by many in the local angling community.

In the TWDB's annual report, predictions of water availability are made for the next fifty years. The board makes predictions by using many data sources, including census data and water usage data that includes the prolonged drought of the 1950s. The current projections show that the region's current water infrastructure and resources will begin to be strained about fifty years from now. That's when the models show that water usage will start to overtake the available resource. Fortunately, the TWDB recognizes this and is already looking ahead to help supplement the region's water supplies.

Subsidence and the Waning of Groundwater Usage

Several groundwater aquifers exist in close proximity to Region H. The largest is the Gulf Coast Aquifer, which the city of Houston sits atop. Currently, groundwater comprises approximately 23 percent of the fresh water that is used in Region H. However, groundwater usage is expected to be reduced in the future in order to combat the occurrence of subsidence. "Subsidence" is the slow sinking or settling of the ground's surface. This can occur when groundwater is removed from loose soils, like fine-grained sandy aquifers. It is the pressure of the groundwater within the aquifer that helps support the earth's surface. As the water is pulled from the aquifer, the fine-grained sand compacts, resulting in the surface sinking or settling. As an example, a similar geologic phenomenon affects many homeowners along the Gulf Coast. That is, localized subsidence occurs when the ground under a house's foundation shifts, which can result in damages ranging from the cosmetic, like nasty cracks in the drywall, to foundation problems that can cost thousands of dollars to fix. This is an example of subsidence on a small scale, but it can also occur on a citywide scale. This is not a pleasant thought, especially when downtown Houston sits a mere 50 feet above sea level.

In the Houston area, subsidence is monitored by The Harris-Galveston Subsidence District. This local entity has the authority to regulate groundwater withdrawal for the purposes of reducing subsidence. The more groundwater that is removed, the more subsidence will occur. As the city of Houston expands, the Harris-Galveston Subsidence District will work closely with the TWDB in order to monitor subsidence and ease the withdrawal of groundwater from the Gulf Coast Aquifer.

To mitigate the risks of subsidence while still providing fresh water to the growing population of Region H (well, mostly Houston), the TWDB is looking for other strategies to supply water to the region. There will be more focus placed on surface water resources, including an expansion of treatment facilities known as the Northeast Water Purification Plant

Expansion Project. The aim of this facility is to increase the plant's water production by 324 million gallons per day. Lake Houston is the water source that will supply this facility.

The project is expected to be completed by 2024. The hope is that the regional water authorities will meet projected water demands but also reduce the need for groundwater, thus mitigating some of the effects of subsidence. The use of recycled water is also being considered as an option. Recycled water can be used in both potable and nonpotable capacities. Used water may undergo treatment and then be repurposed for nonpotable applications like agriculture or industry. Additionally, it may also undergo specialized treatment and be pumped directly into potable water lines. This latter strategy is fairly new to Texas and not widely adopted at this point, although the TWDB plans to incorporate more recycled water into its plans at a later date.

Chapter 25

AN ANGLER'S ROLE IN PROTECTING WATER RESOURCES

THE DISCUSSION OF WATER RESOURCES IS A VITAL ONE. As anglers, we view our local waterways as both a source of life-giving water and a recreational asset with intrinsic ecological importance. We wade in these waters to catch fish, but we also fill our canteens with these same waters (indirectly, of course, from the spigot) and quench our dry throats on a hot summer day of creek stomping. These waters are important and must be cherished and kept clean.

Respecting the local waterways enough to keep them free of pollution and trash is a cause that should be at the forefront of all Houstonians' minds, even the folks who aren't anglers. The city's drinking water is the same water that the local angling community cherishes. It is the same water that is shared by all citizens in the Houston area. Just knowing that your drinking water comes from the creeks and bayous in our collective "backyards" is enough incentive to keep the waterways clean and trash-free.

The State of Texas has a long history of trying to combat the problem of littering. The "Don't Mess with Texas" campaign is over thirty years old and still going strong. This campaign, along with the Texas Department of Transportation (TxDOT), is responsible for the Adopt-a-Highway program, which boasts roughly 3,800 cleanup groups responsible for picking up litter along Texas roadways. Cleanup programs like Great American Cleanup and Don't Mess with Texas Trash-Off are sponsored by Don't Mess with Texas and other affiliates like Keep Texas Beautiful. In many ways, the Lone Star State is very serious about reducing the amount of litter and keeping communities litter-free and healthy. Sadly, not everyone knows, or cares, how important trash-free environments are.

Despite the state's best efforts, and the efforts of local governments, mass quantities of trash still inundate our local bayous. Everything from tires to shopping carts, refrigerators, and even whole automobiles and boats have been illegally dumped into our local communities. Much of the discarded refuse makes its way into the bayous after flooding events, but it is the careless littering in the first place that is the reason for the trash making its way downstream into the waters.

This sign along Peach Creek is a stern but apt reminder that if you pack it in, then you should pack it out. Let's work together to keep our waterways litter free.

Turtles congregate on abandoned shopping carts to sun themselves. Some animals have adapted to the pollution and litter in the bayous.

Even recently, in 2019 to 2022, with the waves of COVID-19 hitting the country and Texas, more and more trash in the form of latex gloves and discarded masks are finding their way into our natural world. The recent proliferation of litter has even caught the eye of Houston city officials and prompted a call to action. The city called for an anti-litter campaign to address the mass quantities of carelessly discarded masks and gloves as well as the prolific illegal dumping. Many local organizations and private companies have offered assistance to the latest anti-litter campaign.

A local Houston news channel, KPRC 2, ran an article in October 2020 covering the illegal dumpsites throughout the city. In the article, Houston City Councilwoman Martha Castex-Tatum says that over the last several months, the city has cleared multiple dumpsites, sometimes picking up as much as ten tons of trash from the illegal trash piles. She reports that since the start of her cleanup efforts, the amount of trash that has been dumped has decreased about 30 percent, but there is still much more to do.

Other than the obvious eyesore, the environmental effects of pollution and littering can sometimes be difficult to quantify. Looking into the nuances of water chemistry and the effects on aquatic organisms can be a tedious process. However, instances where litter and trash have blatant effects on our waterways can be seen just by taking a stroll along the local bayous. Floating Styrofoam and assortments of plastic bottles (some of which still contain contents like motor oil, antifreeze, and gasoline) have pronounced adverse effects on wildlife. Instances of wildlife entangled and trapped in plastic trash bags and other garbage is not an uncommon sight. Additionally, fish-kills can also be seen from time to time while walking along the bayous.

As if this wasn't enough, garbage that makes its way into the bayous has a tendency to build up at places where the waterway becomes bottlenecked, like culverts and narrow bridges. This can cause flooding issues at these choke points. During periods of heavy rain and flooding, the bottlenecked trash and debris acts as a dam, causing flooding. When polluted waters inundate our roadways, parks, and neighborhoods, it presents a health risk to our communities.

It is an unfortunate fact that illegal dumping is rampant throughout parts of Houston. In a 2017 study, the organization known as Texans for Clean Water looked at the cost of litter removal and illegal dumpsites as well as educational programs focused on the health effects of littering. In total, roughly $21 million were spent on litter removal and prevention. A staggering number. This cost of reducing littering is split among many organizations in the city, but Houston and Harris County pay the brunt. Therefore, for citizens of the Bayou City, this cost is passed down to the residents in the form of taxes. If we want to live in a clean city (while paying less in taxes), we must all do our part to pick up litter when we see it. Even if it's just a couple of extra bottles or cans.

In 2012, the city began placing hidden cameras at known illegal dumpsites in order to stem the pervasive illegal act. Since then, the city has increased its number of cameras to 130 and has reported that the cameras have been successful in finding and prosecuting many perpetrators. The Houston Police Department (HPD) is the entity in charge of enforcing anti-littering and anti-dumping laws within the city. The

Opposite: The Up2U litter campaign advocates that personal responsibility is the key to litter prevention. Their iconic yellow reusable trash bags can be found at several different parks along the Spring Creek Greenway Trail.

HPD has several police officers who are designated environmental crime investigators. Outside of the city limits, but still within Harris County, Precinct One Environmental Division handles the environmental crimes for the entire county.

When it comes down to it, in order to slow the rising tide of trash in our waterways, it is up to local communities to make the difference. Luckily, if any group of people can fight back against littering in our waterways, it would be Texans. Strong state pride and can-do attitude make Texans the perfect folk to spearhead environmental cleanup missions.

The simple efforts of individuals will make a big and lasting difference. Don't Mess with Texas estimates that if every Texan picked up just two pieces of trash a month, the state would be litter-free in one year. There are several well-established and local cleanup events in the Houston area. Texas Conservation Fund sponsors a major event called the River, Lakes, Bays, 'N Bayous Trash Bash (trashbash.org). This event covers cleanup efforts across many of the local Houston bayous, including Brays Bayou, Whiteoak Bayou, Buffalo Bayou, and Cypress Creek. Other cleanup events have occurred recently, including efforts to remove litter from Little White Oak Bayou. This cleanup event was organized by Partners in Litter Prevention and American Bird Conservancy.

Individuals don't have to wait for big, organized trash bash events just to pick up litter along the bayous. Several organizations can help with local grassroots cleanup efforts, including Keep Texas Beautiful (ktb.org) and its local affiliate, Keep Houston Beautiful (houstonbeautiful.org). These organizations can offer assistance in the form of gloves and trash bags in order to supply smaller cleanup crews.

On an individual level, observant and proactive citizens can offer their help by simply picking up litter when walking local trails, bayous, or parks. By simply keeping extra trash bags in your vehicle, you can help with litter prevention. After a day of fishing, before leaving the water, anglers can spend an extra five minutes just picking up some of the trash that might be around the edge of the creek. The Up2U Litter Prevention Campaign, which was started by the Nueces River Authority (nueces-ra.org/CP/UP2U/), does a great job at marketing its iconic yellow mesh trash bags. The Up2U campaign advocates that personal responsibility will ultimately lead to the success of litter prevention. Its reusable trash bags can be seen from time to time in the hands of caring Houstonians, and thanks to an Eagle Scout from Sam Houston Area Council Troop

55, wooden distribution boxes for these trash bags can be found along Buffalo Bayou at Briar Bend and Woodway as well as on Spring Creek at Pundt Park and Jesse H. Jones Park.

If people witness the act of illegal dumping or know of illegal dump-sites that need removed, the best course of action is to call the city municipal number at 311. If you do this, the city will only respond to the illegal dumpsite if it is on a city right-of-way. In addition to that, the Environmental Investigations unit of Harris County Constable Precinct One can be called at (832) 927-1567. For residents of Montgomery County, report illegal dumpsites online at the Montgomery County Environmental Health Services website.

During most months, city officials are inundated with calls from residents reporting illegal dumpsites. Unfortunately, the city isn't always able to follow through in a timely manner with waste-removal crews. Because of this, proactive individuals can help with these efforts by taking matters into their own hands. However, before individuals begin a cleanup effort, there are a couple steps that should be taken.

Wear proper PPE (personal protective equipment) before cleaning a dumpsite. Proper safety attire includes gloves, sturdy footwear, long pants, and long-sleeved shirts. Be cautious when picking up junk. Nails could be sticking out of boards, or broken glass could also be encountered. If the trash has been left for prolonged periods of time, it's possible that snakes and rodents have set up camp in the refuse. Before sticking your fingers under pieces of discarded items like tin or plywood, attempt to flip the item with a stick or with a steel-toed boot, just to be sure there isn't a snake underneath.

Finding the nearest landfill is the next step once all the trash is picked up and thrown into the back of a pickup truck or trailer. Waste Management has an excellent website where drop-off locations can easily be found (wm.com/us/en/drop-off-locations). Just type in the address of the newly cleaned dumpsite, and the website will show you where the nearest landfill is located. Their website also displays hours of operation and what materials are accepted. You'll have to pay a fee based on the weight of the debris, but think of it like a donation to your favorite conservation organization, except the positive impact is more immediate.

Clean water is immensely important to Houston and the surrounding area. Helping to keep this resource clean and trash-free is important to the angling community and to the city as a whole. It can be daunting to think about the challenging obstacles that affect the health of local waters: increasing population density, expanding urbanization, higher demand of surface water supplies, and more litter and pollution. But piece by piece, Texas anglers can make steps toward cleaner waters. It will take time, but the local fishing community is up to the challenge.

Too often we fall into a cyclic trap of negativity and pessimism. We notice additional litter in our favorite bayou, so we throw up our hands in despair and walk away, leaving our local waters to fester. However, when you look at the history of mankind's awareness of environment matters, like awareness in the value of clean waters and an increased interest in wildlife, it seems like we are more conscientious now, and more proactive, than ever before.

We shouldn't despair and stand by idly. In fact, as more and more Houstonians pick up fly rods and head outside to explore the waters of southeastern Texas, interest in the natural world will grow. Our native fishes like spotted bass, bowfin, and gar will see new admiration. People will develop a stronger bond with their surrounding local environment, and our communities will see continued interest in keeping our waterways flowing free of litter and pollution. We just need to keep at it, and keep being responsible anglers.

SHOPS, CLUBS, GUIDES, LIVERIES

LOCAL FLY SHOPS AND GUIDES ARE THE BACKBONE OF HOUSTON'S FLY fishing scene. It is strongly encouraged that anyone interested in the sport should stop in at the local fly shops to learn from the experts, discuss fly patterns and techniques, and swap stories. In addition to the local fly shops, there are other big-box stores in the area, including Cabela's and Bass Pro Shops.

This book caters to the do-it-yourself angler, but if you are new to the sport or just want to learn more about the regional fisheries, contact the local guides found in the following pages. The wealth of knowledge that these anglers have is vast, and you won't be disappointed by any experience you share with them. Bear in mind that many more guides exist in the Houston area that cater to the saltwater scene. Because this book did not address the coastal fisheries, I felt that it was beyond the purview of this work to list saltwater guides. Again, visit your local fly shop if you would like to learn more about fishing the salt and what guides they recommend.

Fly Shops

Bayou City Angler

5750 Woodway Dr., Houston, TX 77057
(832) 831-3104
bayoucityangler.com

Bayou City Angler was established in 2015 and is Houston's only specialty fly shop. The staff at BCA is knowledgeable and can help with anything related to salt water and fresh water. The store is fully stocked with gear and apparel from Sage, Scott, Umpqua, Scientific Anglers, Simms, etc. If you stop in at BCA, you'll feel right at home chatting with the staff while enjoying a frosty beverage.

Below: Gordy & Son's Outfitters

Gordy & Sons, Outfitters

22 Waugh Dr., Houston, TX 77007
(713) 333-3474
gordyandsons.com

Gordy & Sons opened its doors in 2017. It specializes in selling "the very finest guns, fishing equipment, apparel, and accessories from the world's very best brands." A casting pond is located in the front yard, where guests are invited to try out rods before making a purchase. The finely furnished retail shop and gun vault really is something to see. The friendly staff is always willing to help, whether it's finding a new fly rod or picking up fly tying supplies. Gordy & Sons hosts fly tying events and guest lecturers ranging from prominent folks in the hunting industry to nationally recognized fly fishing gurus.

Fishing Tackle Unlimited

10303 Katy Freeway, Houston, TX 77024
(888) 943-1861
fishingtackleunlimited.com

Fishing Tackle Unlimited (FTU) was started by two Houston brothers in 1979. There are three locations in the Houston area. In addition to the store off Katy Freeway (I-10), there is a location in Sugar Land (13831 Southwest Freeway) and another southeast of downtown at 12800 Gulf Freeway. At two locations (Katy Freeway and Gulf Freeway), Fishing Tackle Unlimited sells both conventional tackle and fly fishing tackle. The store in Sugarland only sells conventional gear. FTU also carries a wide array of boat accessories and several fishing-oriented paddlecraft.

Orvis Woodlands

9595 Six Pines Dr., The Woodlands,
TX 77380
(281) 203-6150
**stores.orvis.com/us/texas
/the-woodlands**

The Woodlands Orvis store is conveniently located near I-45 and is the closest fly shop to Lake Conroe. Much of the staff are true fly anglers and are happy to swap information and tips about fishing north of the city. Check the store's online calendar or give it a call, as it frequently hosts free casting classes and intro to fly tying events.

Orvis Houston

5727 Westheimer Rd., Houston, TX 77057
(713) 783-2111
stores.orvis.com/us/texas/houston

This Orvis shop is located just west of the I-610 Loop. The staff are friendly and happy to chat about fresh water and salt water alike. It has a large showroom equipped with apparel and most anything else you'd need to hit the water.

Orvis Houston

Wandering Star Adventure Emporium

1504-B Yale St., Houston, TX 77008
(832) 618-1148
shopwanderingstar.com

Wandering Star isn't a fly shop; it's more of a local outdoor store. However, it does carry gear oriented toward fly anglers. Wandering Star is stocked with Free Fly Apparel, Smith Optics, Benchmade Knives, and a bunch of camping gear. You won't find a more welcoming and friendly staff. They are always excited to hear about local adventures as well as adventures abroad. If you are down in the Houston Heights, definitely check out Wandering Star.

Cabela's

2421 Gulf Freeway. S., League City, TX 77573
(346) 231-0200

This Cabela's store is located southeast of Houston in League City. They carry a selection of fly fishing rods, reels, and other tackle. This store mainly caters to saltwater anglers, but it also carries bass rods.

Bass Pro Shops

5000 Katy Mills Circle #415, Katy, TX 77494
(281) 688-1296

Two Bass Pro Shops exist in the Houston area. Aside from the Katy location, another store is located in Pearland (1000 Bass Pro Dr., Pearland, TX 77047). At the Katy location, you can find fly tying supplies as well as fly tackle and accessories.

Guides

As mentioned previously, the following guides are specific to the freshwater fisheries in the Houston area. There are many fly fishing guides that service the coastal fisheries, but that is beyond the scope of this book. To learn about the saltwater guides, visit Bayou City Angler, Gordy & Sons, or Fishing Tackle Unlimited to discuss the guides they recommend.

Houston Fly Fishing Guide Services

houstonflyfishing@gmail.com

@houstonflyfishing

houstonflyfishing.com

Outdoorsman and Houston native Danny Scarborough is well known as one of Houston's premier freshwater fly guides. Danny has intimate knowledge of local fisheries ranging from the vast waters of Lake Conroe to the concrete ditches of downtown. Danny was a regional pioneer for pursuing bowfin on the fly, and he offers this experience to his clients. Danny holds several waterbody records for fly fishing and holds a wealth of knowledge about black bass, temperate bass, carp, bowfin, and just about any other freshwater fish that swims in the Houston area. If you book a trip with Danny, you won't be disappointed.

Metro Anglers

markmarmon@gmail.com

(713) 666-8868

metroanglers.com

Mark Marmon is the original freshwater fly fishing guide in the Houston metropolitan area. Marmon has been chasing carp, bass, catfish, gar, mullet, and tilapia in the urban waterways for over forty years. He is a certified casting instructor and offers private and group casting instructions. Marmon was one of the first fly anglers in the country to pursue grass carp on the fly, and he was instrumental in showcasing Houston's concrete flats. In addition to guiding the Houston area, Marmon also offers guided trips on private bass waters and trout fishing on the Guadalupe River in Central Texas. Marmon's willingness to teach younger generations of fly anglers speaks volumes of his devotion to the sport of fly fishing.

Danny Scarborough

Alex Sosa

Buffalo Bayou Fishing Champs

@buffalo.bayou.fishing.champs
instagram.com/buffalo.bayou.fishing.champs/

Although he isn't a fly fishing guide, Alex Sosa deserves mention in this section of the book for his efforts in promoting urban fishing in Buffalo Bayou. Sosa offers guided fishing trips on the Buffalo Bayou, where anglers use conventional gear and fish from his fully stocked Alumacraft. Many trips occur at night with the lights of downtown glittering in the background. Anglers will have opportunities to land alligator gar and monster catfish, all on conventional gear. Book a trip with Alex by sending him a message through Instagram.

Clubs

Texas Flyfishers of Houston
texasflyfishers.org

Texas Flyfishers of Houston is a 501(c)(3) nonprofit organization associated with the International Federation of Fly Fishers. This club is a wealth of knowledge and expertise. Meetings are held monthly (either in person or digitally) and include many guest lecturers. This club also organizes and hosts fishing trips all over the state, from the Gulf Coast to the freshwater lakes. The club also holds annual expos and auctions for gear, flies, and fly fishing art. Texas Flyfishers of Houston is a fantastic club.

Paddlecraft Rentals and Shuttles

North Lake Conroe Paddling Company

13988 Calvary Rd., Willis, TX 77318
(936) 203-2697
northlakeconroepaddlingco.com

This kayak rental company is located behind Stow-Away-Marina on the banks of Lake Conroe. Touring kayaks and fishing kayaks can be rented. Shuttle services are also offered for paddlers who want to get out and see more of Lake Conroe.

North Lake Conroe Paddling Company

Bayou City Adventures

1520 Silver St., Houston, TX 77007

(713) 538-7433

bayoucityadventures.org

Bayou City Adventures offers canoe and kayak rentals for folks who want to paddle the famous Buffalo Bayou. In addition to Buffalo Bayou, offsite rentals are also available by reservation only. Give Bayou City Adventures a call to discuss its rental policy.

Southwest PaddleSports

26322 I-45, Spring, TX 77386

(281) 292-5600

paddlesports.com

Southwest PaddleSports has been around for thirty years. Its warehouse is conveniently located near I-45 in Spring. It offers sit-on-top kayaks and stand-up paddleboard rentals. Its hours of operation are irregular, so it is best to give the store a call before heading up to their shop.

Riva Row & Lakes Edge Boat House

1970 Hughes Landing Blvd., The Woodlands, TX 77380

2101 Riva Row, The Woodlands, TX 77380

(281) 222-4433

lakesedgeboathouse.com

The city of The Woodlands runs two kayak rentals in the vicinity of Lake Woodlands. Riva Row Boat House services the Woodlands Waterway in the Town Center, and the Lakes Edge Boat House is located at Hughes Landing on the northeastern shore of Lake Woodlands.

EasTex Canoe Trails

1698 US 96, Silsbee, TX 77656

(409) 385-4700

eastexcanoes.com

EasTex Canoe Trails has been around since 1978. It offers canoe rentals and shuttle services for people interested in paddling the waterways of Big Thicket, specifically Village Creek and the Neches River. Additionally, it also offers guided tours.

Big Thicket Outfitters

115 Connolly Rd., Vidor, TX 77662

(409) 786-1884

bigthicketoutfitters.com

Big Thicket Outfitters specializes in canoe and kayak rentals as well as camping gear rentals. It also offers swamp tours and pontoon boat tours of the Big Thicket National Preserve.

STREAM ACCESS

Chapter 5: West Fork San Jacinto River and Lake Conroe
  Stubblefield Lake Recreational Area, Huntsville (30.56391, -95.63570)
  Forest Service Road 204A, Montgomery (30.51585, -95.61146)
  Cagle Recreation Area, New Waverly (30.51884, -95.59153)
  Forest Service Road 204, Montgomery (30.46030, -95.62826)
  Scott's Ridge Boat Ramp, Montgomery (30.45310, -95.63028)
  Stow-A-Way Marina, Willis (30.47342, -95.56746)
  I-45 South, Conroe (30.24518, -95.45663)
  West Essex Drive, Conroe (30.23232, -95.42738)
  North Woodloch Street, Conroe (30.21795, -95.41098)
  East River Road, Conroe (30.18609, -95.37957)
  TX 99 bridge, Spring (30.14083, -95.33883)
  Eastex Freeway Service Road bridge, Kingwood (30.02821, -95.25759)
  Lake View Park, Atascocita (30.02245, -95.16823)

Chapter 6: East Fork San Jacinto River
  Sam Houston National Forest, Intersection of Shaw Rd and FM 945
      (30.422650, -95.136753)
  Lone Star Hiking Trail bridge, Sam Houston National Forest, Cleveland
      (30.42960, -95.13481)
  FM 945 bridge, Cleveland (30.42518, -95.12482)
  Low Water Bridge, Cleveland (30.35538, -95.10852)
  TX 105 Business bridge, Cleveland (30.33639, -95.10374)
  TX 105 bridge, Cleveland (30.31420, -95.11342)
  FM 2090 bridge (30.21433, -95.10254)
  River Trail, Lake Houston Wilderness Park, (30.13278, -95.12969)
  BJ's Marina, Huffman (30.05918, -95.13176)

Chapter 7: Peach Creek and Caney Creek

Woodbranch Dr. bridge, New Caney (30.18245, -95.18428)

Roman Forest Park, New Caney (30.17288, -95.17702)

FM 1485 bridge over Peach Creek (30.14688 -95.17150)

FM 1485 bridge over Caney Creek (30.14896, -95.19268)

Peach Creek Ln. bridge, Lake Houston Wilderness Park (30.13748, -95.16904)

Canoe Launch Rd., Lake Houston Wilderness Park, New Caney (30.11978, -95.17304)

Chapter 8: Spring Creek

Montgomery County Preserve (30.11155, -95.45204)

Old Riley Fuzzel Road Preserve, Spring (30.09333, -95.40567)

Pundt Park (30.08389, -95.37542)

Carter Park, Spring (30.05281, -95.32654)

Jesse H. Jones Park (30.02961, -95.29436)

Chapter 12: Cypress Creek

Little Cypress Creek Preserve (29.98994, -95.65378)

Mercer Arboretum, Humble (30.03825, -95.38296)

Treaschwig Rd. bridge (30.03350, -95.36773)

Cypresswood Dr. bridge (30.02986, -95.33019)

Chapter 13: Sheldon Lake

Garrett Rd., Houston (29.88295, -95.18592)

Pineland Rd., Houston (29.85105, -95.17444)

Chapter 14: White Oak Bayou and Little White Oak Bayou

Clark Henry Park (29.88523, -95.55184)

North Parking for White Oak Bayou Greenway Trail (29.86981, -95.48010)

Victory Disc Golf Course, Houston (29.86379, -95.46756)

West Tidwell Park, Houston (29.84738, -95.46175)

White Oak Bayou Greenway Trail near T.C. Jester Blvd. (29.79104, -95.41939)

Stude Park, Houston (29.77989, -95.38241)

Woodland Park, Houston (29.78350, -95.37064)

Hogg Park (29.77802, -95.36720)

Chapter 15: Buffalo Bayou and its Tributaries
Fun Fair Positive Soccer Complex, George Bush Park (29.73610, -95.72268)
Prince Creek Drive bridge, Katy (29.76681, -95.72870)
Terry Hershey Park at Memorial Mews St. (29.77367, -95.62328)
Terry Hershey Park at Dairy Ashford Rd. (29.76151, -95.60565)
Briarbend Park, Houston (29.74586, -95.50685)
Memorial Park at Woodway Dr. (29.76448, -95.45801)
Hogg Bird Sanctuary (29.75856, -95.42186)
Bayou City Adventure at Sabine St. bridge (29.76250, -95.37582)
Allen's Landing Park (29.76418, -95.35970)

Chapter 16: Brays Bayou
Arthur Storey Park (29.69630, -95.55771)
Brays Bayou Greenway Trail at I-610 West, Houston (29.68034, -95.45869)
Brays Bayou Greenway Trail at Greenwillow Street, Houston (29.68412, -95.44920)
Brays Bayou Greenway Trail at Bevlyn St., Houston (29.69032, -95.43047)
Brays Bayou Greenway Trail at Brompton Rd., Houston (29.69762, -95.42344)
Bayou Parkland, Houston (29.70766, -95.38430)
MacGregor Park (29.71092, -95.34086)

Chapter 17: Park Ponds
Burroughs Park, Tomball (30.13521, -95.57724)
Northshore Park, The Woodlands (30.16896, -95.47574)
Mary Jo Peckham Park, Katy (29.80474, -95.82035)
Lake Friendswood Park, Friendswood (29.47975, -95.18087)
Kickerillo-Mischer Preserve, Houston (29.98790, -95.56340)
Tom Bass Regional Park, Houston (29.59053, -95.35373)

Chapter 24: Village Creek
McNeely Rd. bridge (30.46621, -94.32315)
FM 418 Rd. bridge (30.39777, -94.26484)
TX 327 bridge, Kountze (30.34690, -94.23949)
Baby Galvez Rd. (30.33455, -94.20396)
US 96 bridge, Lumberton (30.28568, -94.19146)
Village Creek State Park, Lumberton (30.25496, -94.17120)

ACKNOWLEDGMENTS

WHILE WRITING THIS BOOK, I RELIED HEAVILY ON THE EXPERTISE OF MANY extraordinary fly anglers from the Houston area. Within these pages is a culmination of knowledge from this community of hardcore, dirty ditchin' creek stompers. This book was a group effort; I merely put the words on a piece of paper. Thank you all so much for your devotion and support of this book. Without you, this work would have never come to fruition.

A sincere thank you to all those who went fishing with me or contributed to this book in some way: Zach Wallace, Robert Scruggs, Didi Ooi, Paul Robinson, Angel Rodriguez, Adam Samale, Drew Fletcher, Will Baxter, Nick Rizopoulos, Hiro Yamamoto, Alex Brekke, Matus Sobolic, Chris Hunt, Emily Fojtik, Kyle Hampton, Liam Smith, Dan Sheehan, Eric Ostrum, and Wes Ferguson. Thank you to Terry and Roxanne Wilson for their support and for answering all of my e-mails. Thank you to CJ De Ochoa, Xavier Jaime, and Jose Mata for not only going fishing with me and introducing me to different waters but also being genuinely eager to see this book hit the press. Thank you to Stephen Lonon and Roberto Martinez for being happy, fun-loving dudes who were excited to explore the creeks of the Pineywoods and then go home to their wives riddled with mosquito bites and covered in mud. You guys are awesome.

A very special thank you to the following people:

Danny Scarborough is one of the best fly anglers in the Houston area. Without his expertise and generosity, I'd likely still be on the water trying to land my first bowfin. Danny was always available to answer questions and was never shy about giving me a straightforward answer. Danny was a wealth of knowledge for nearly all of the Houston-area waterways. Danny's familiarity with Peach Creek, Caney Creek, Lake Conroe, and Brays Bayou contributed immensely to this work. I can't thank you enough, Danny.

The godfather of urban fly fishing, Mark Marmon, has been instrumental in showcasing the recreational importance of Houston's urban waterways. Who knows where urban anglers would be without Marmon's pioneering efforts? Mr. Marmon was incredibly gracious with his time and knowledge. Danny Scarborough said it best when he told me, "Mark Marmon is the 'Original Gangster' of urban carping."

Joe Mills was another angler who helped immensely with the chapters on Houston's urban waterways. Joe has been fishing White Oak Bayou for many years and is considered a local expert when it comes to chasing urban carp. Joe contributed fantastic photos of carp and the urban environments and was kind enough to review the chapter on White Oak Bayou. Appreciate it so much, Joe.

Jack Boyd is one of the best fly anglers in the Houston area. Even as a young man, he is an expert in angling for urban fishes, especially carp, koi, and bass. Thank you, Jack, for spending time with me, showing me the ropes, and contributing to this work. Your knowledge of the urban waterways was immensely important to this book.

Stavros Cotsoradis is another young man I consider to be one of the finest in the area. Stavros was willing to hit the water at the drop of a dime. The memories I made with Stavros exploring Houston's hidden waters won't soon be forgotten. Thanks for all of your time, Stavros.

Trey Alvarez has become one of my go-to fishing partners in the Houston area. By sheer happenstance, we ran into each other at Sheldon Lake, and since then we have gone on many fishing adventures. Trey is a sucker for chasing gar, and he almost always has a G Funk fly (designed by his uncle, Joey Ramirez) tied onto his line. Trey, I can't tell you how appreciative I am of your willingness to go fishing with me. Thank you, my friend.

Joey Ramirez is no longer a full-time resident of Houston, but that doesn't mean that his contributions to this book were anything less than significant. For his entire youth, Joey explored the waters of Houston and Lake Conroe. Joey's decades of angling experience provided valuable information for this book. We had some unforgettable times on Lake Conroe, pursuing bass and bowfin.

College professor and marine biologist Travis Richards was an integral part of this book. Travis is just as happy blue lining hidden streams in the Pineywoods as he is trudging through the saltwater marshes on the Texas coast. Because of Travis' professional background as a biologist, many fishing excursions morphed into fascinating discussions on ecology and often included sporadic scavenger hunts for snakes, turtles, and lizards. Thanks for being a stalwart companion, Travis.

Nick Heaverlo is not only a coworker and friend but has also become one of my go-to fishing buddies. Nick is always ready to stomp through a local creek, and he never shies away from adventure, no matter if the weather is a blistering 100 degrees or below freezing. The fishing adventures we have shared are ingrained in my memory. I can't wait to see where we go exploring next. Thanks for always being there, Nick.

Tanya Xu, Nick's fiancée, has also been an integral part of this book. Tanya joined us on numerous outings, especially to Peach Creek and Lake Conroe. Tanya, thank you for your willingness to explore local creeks and for being a proponent of Houston's vast waterways. You're the best.

I'd like to thank the staff at Gordy & Sons, especially Andy Packmore, Marcos Enriquez, and Baron Boyette for their support and kindness. All of the resources and information you provided helped with the creation of this work. Also, the staff at Bayou City Angler, especially Alan Antonson, have been very generous with providing information, expertise, and pictures. Thank you all for your help and guidance.

The members of Texas Flyfishers of Houston, especially Don Puckett, Ron Mayfield, and John Eldred, have supported this work wholeheartedly. I sincerely thank each of you for your contributions.

Aaron Reed, whether he knows it or not, has been a mentor to me. Not only did Aaron help with the editing and review process for this book, but he has also been an ardent supporter of Houston-area creeks and streams. Aaron saw the importance of highlighting smaller waterways and encouraged me to push forward even when I was second-guessing the subject matter. Aaron is an advocate for all Texas waters, big and small. Without him, this work would never have seen the light of day. Thank you, my friend.

A big thank you to Mark Sedenquist and Megan Edwards of Imbrifex Books. I am grateful for the opportunity to work with Imbrifex Books and to have the backing of this wonderful company.

Lastly, I'd like to thank my wife, Ellen. Without her unwavering support, this book would have never come into existence. Ellen was right beside me through this whole process, from the first meeting with Mark and Megan all the way until the end. Ellen encouraged me to write, even when I didn't want to. She was patient with me and generously contributed her time to the completion of this work. I mean it when I say I couldn't have done this without you. You're an incredible partner.

Photo Credits

INTERIOR PHOTOS BY THE AUTHOR EXCEPT ON THESE PAGES:
Alan Antonson (283, 299); Chris Barclay (27); Jack Boyd (292, 293, 294); Ty Cleeb (221); Stavros Cotsoradis (258, 312); Ellen Dortenzo (115 – angler photo, 295); Nick Heaverlo (Part 1 – page 9, 52, 298, 223); Mark Marmon (241); Jose Mata (25); Joey Ramirez (196); Travis Richards (217 – inset of tilapia, 288, 292, 309); Danny Scarborough (174, 181, 244, 284, 290, 291, 301); Liam Smith (252 – inset of grass carp); Alex Sosa, (222)

SOURCES AND FURTHER READING

THE ART OF FLY FISHING IS RICH IN LITERATURE. IT'S DOUBTFUL THAT FLY anglers will ever be left wanting for reading material. Many books, publications, and online resources helped shape this book. Specifically, Aaron Reed's *Fly Fishing Austin & Central Texas*, Phil Shook's *Fly Fisher's Guide to Texas*, Page and Burr's *Peterson Field Guide to Freshwater Fishes*, Terry and Roxanne Wilson's *The Bluegill Diaries*, Jack Ellis' *The Sunfishes*, and Natalie H. Wiest's *Canoeing and Kayaking Houston Waterways*. Also, the Texas Parks & Wildlife Department is awash in fantastic information on Texas river law, fish species, and paddling trails. The Texas State Historical Association was another invaluable resource, and its digital *Handbook of Texas* was used frequently throughout the writing process. For further reading, check out the list of books below:

Books

Bonney, Lorraine G. *The Big Thicket Guidebook*. Denton: Big Thicket Association and the University of North Texas Press, 2011.

Ellis, Jack. *The Sunfishes*. New York: Lyons & Burford Publishers, 1995.

Graves, John. *Goodbye to a River*. New York: The Curtis Publishing Company, 1959.

Hicks, Danny. *Texas Blue-Ribbon Fly-Fishing*. Portland, OR: Frank Amato Publications, Inc., 2008.

Hutchison, Kevin. *Fly-Fishing the Texas Hill Country*. Smithville, TX: Fishhead Press, 2008.

Kirkley, Gene. *A Guide to Texas Rivers and Streams*. Houston: Gulf Publishing Company, 1983.

Page, Lawrence M., and Brooks M. Burr. *Peterson Field Guide to Freshwater Fishes* of *North America and North of Mexico*. New York: Houghton Mifflin Harcourt Publishing Company, 2011

Leavell, Lorraine. *Family Fishing Holes*. Houston: Baylake Publications, 1999.

Livingston, A. D. *Bass on the Fly*. Camden, ME: Ragged Mountain Press, 1994.

McConnell, Robert H. *Fly Fishing the Sam*. Independently published, IngramSpark, 2020.

Reed, Aaron. *Fly Fishing Austin & Central Texas*. Las Vegas: Imbrifex Books, 2020.

Scates, Chuck, and Phil H. Shook. *Fly Fishing the Texas Coast*. Boulder, CO: Pruett Publishing Company, 1999.

Shook, Phil H. *Flyfisher's Guide to Texas*. Belgrade, MT: Wilderness Adventures Press, Inc., 2001.

Watson, Geraldine Ellis. *Reflections on the Neches*. Denton: University of North Texas Press, 2003.

Wiest, Natalie H. *Canoeing and Kayaking Houston Waterways*. College Station: Texas A&M University Press, 2012.

Wilson, Terry, and Roxanne Wilson. *The Bluegill Diaries*. Independently published, CreateSpace, 2017.

Wilson, Terry, and Roxanne Wilson. *Largemouth Bass Fly Fishing: Beyond the Basics*. Independently published, 2019.

Other Sources

"Baby Galvez Resort Brought Visitors from All Over Texas." *The Silsbee Bee,* November 12, 2008. https://issuu.com/gdickert/docs/silsbee_bee_sesquicentennial/8.

Bayou Preservation Association. "Trash-Free Bayous Program." Accessed March 2020. https://www.bayoupreservation.org/Programs/Trash-Free-Bayous-Program.

Block, William T. "The Big Thicket Bear Hunters Club of Kountze." Accessed September 1, 2021. http://wtblock.com/WtblockJr/BearHunters.htm.

Burns & McDonnell. "The Cost of Litter & Illegal Dumping in Texas." February 20, 2017.

Churchill, Timothy N., and Phillip W. Bettoli. "Spotted Bass *Micropterus punctulatus* (Rafinesque, 1819)." American Fisheries Society, 2015. http://usgs-cru-individual-data.s3.amazonaws.com/pbettoli/intellcont/Churchill%20and%20Bettoli_2015-1.pdf.

Daugherty, et al. "Otolith Based Age Estimates of Alligator Gar Assessed Using Bomb Radiocarbon Dating to Greater than 60 Years." *North American Journal of Fisheries Management* 40, no. 3 (2020): 613–621.

Diaz, Mario. "Illegal dumping in Houston: The challenge and who is investigating" *Click 2 Houston.com*, March 16, 2021.

Godbout, et al. "Morphological Models for Identifying Largemouth Bass, Spotted Bass, and Largemouth Bass X Spotted Bass Hybrids." *North American Journal of Fisheries Management* 29, no. 5 (2009): 1425–1437.

Fishes of Texas Project Database (version 2.0); accessed 2020, http://www.fishesoftexas.org/.

Lodhia, Pooja. "Man Attacked by 8-foot Alligator at East Houston Park." *ABC 13*, July 2, 2014.

Miesen, Paniz. "BIG's Top Five Most and Top Five Least Impaired Water Bodies Project." Bacteria Source Identification Report, 2017.

Region H Water Planning Group. "2021 Regional Water Plan: Volume 1," October 2020. https://www.twdb.texas.gov/waterplanning/rwp/plans/2021/H/RegionH_2021RWP_V1.pdf?d=7670.62500002794.

Texas Parks & Wildlife Department. "East Texas Black Bear Conservation and Management Plan 2005–2015," July 2005. https://tpwd.texas.gov/publications/pwdpubs/media/pwd_pl_w7000_1046.pdf.

Texas Parks & Wildlife Department. "Freshwater Fishes Found in Texas." Accessed September 24, 2021. https://tpwd.texas.gov/landwater/water/aquaticspecies/inland.

Texas Parks & Wildlife Department. "Texas Paddling Trails." Accessed September 20, 2021. https://tpwd.texas.gov/fishboat/boat/paddlingtrails/.

Texas State Historical Association, multiple authors. "Handbook of Texas Online." Accessed December 21, 2020. https://www.tshaonline.org/handbook.

USGS. "Texas Water Dashboard." Accessed September 24, 2021. https://txpub.usgs.gov/txwaterdashboard/index

INDEX